Fulfilling

Your

Highest

Spiritual

Potential

Kim Michaels

The Avatar Revelations, vol 4

Fulfilling Your Highest Spiritual Potential

Kim Michaels
More to Life

Fulfilling Your Highest Spiritual Potential

Copyright © 2018 Kim Michaels. All rights reserved. No part of this book may be used, reproduced, translated, electronically stored or transmitted by any means except by written permission from the publisher. A reviewer may quote brief passages in a review.

MORE TO LIFE PUBLISHING

www.morepublish.com

For foreign and translation rights,

contact: info@ morepublish.com

ISBN: 978-87-93297-55-5

The information and insights in this book should not be considered as a form of therapy, advice, direction, diagnosis, and/or treatment of any kind. This information is not a substitute for medical, psychological, or other professional advice, counseling and care. All matters pertaining to your individual health should be supervised by a physician or appropriate health-care practitioner. No guarantee is made by the author or the publisher that the practices described in this book will yield successful results for anyone at any time. They are presented for informational purposes only, as the practice and proof rests with the individual.

Content

Introduction   7
1 | The selves that followed the primal self   9
2 | Invoking freedom from having to compensate   21
3 | Overcoming the control aspect of the primal self 37
4 | Invoking freedom from the control self   53
5 | Accepting that Christ accepts you   69
6 | Invoking the acceptance of Christ 87
7 | Grasping the progressiveness of revelation   103
8 | Invoking the closing of the gap   127
9 | It is time to express your Christhood   147
10 | Invoking the vision to express my Christhood   163
11 | The dilemma of being on earth   183
12 | Invoking All-Pervading Wisdom 193
13 | The hidden anger of spiritual people   207
14 | Invoking Mirror-Like Wisdom   217
15 | Equality vanishes superiority and inferiority   233
16 | Invoking the Wisdom of Equality   243
17 | Discernment shows you when enough is enough 255
18 | Invoking Discerning Wisdom   261
19 | Overcoming envy be accomplishing all things   269
20 | Invoking All-Accomplishing Wisdom   279
21 | The will of your I AM Presence is your will   293
22 | Invoking the Diamond Will   305
23 | Being the Christ in Saint Germain's Golden Age 321
24 | Invoking Christhood in Saint Germain's Golden Age   337
25 | Being ready for the teaching   357
26 | Invoking readiness for the teaching   373

INTRODUCTION

This book is one of the workbooks building on the novel *My Lives with Lucifer, Satan, Hitler and Jesus*. The novel introduces the idea that many spiritual people have come to earth as volunteers or "avatars." We have then received deep spiritual traumas as a result of what we have experienced here. Many of us still carry these traumas with us, and it can explain why we sometimes can feel as if we are not making progress on the spiritual path or why there are certain issues we cannot overcome. How to overcome these traumas is explained (along with practical exercises) in the book *Healing Your Spiritual Traumas*.

This book contains further teachings on these concepts, but it also explains how to fulfill your potential for manifesting the higher states of consciousness called Christhood and Buddhahood.

Please note that it is recommended that you read the novel and work through *Healing Your Spiritual Traumas* before using this book. The reason is that these books contain many important teachings that can help you make use of this book

This book contains a number of invocations that you are meant to give aloud. If you are not familiar with giving such invocations, you can find further teachings and instructions on the website *www.transcendencetoolbox.com*. You can also give the invocations along with a recording and you can purchase recordings of the invocations in this book on the website *www.morepublish.com*.

1 | THE SELVES THAT FOLLOWED THE PRIMAL SELF

I AM the Buddha Kuan Yin, known to many people in this part of the world as the Bodhisattva of Compassion, yet I am far more than what people see me as in this part of the world. Naturally, I acknowledge and I take joy in the devotion that many people have for me and the love they pour into the beautiful chants, as you have done yourselves during this hour where you have truly accomplished a great work in terms of calming the emotional body of the earth.

The maelstrom of fear

My beloved hearts, what have the fallen beings done to the emotional body on earth? They have done many things but the primary thing I wish to bring to your attention is that they have inserted a whirlpool, a maelstrom of fear. This maelstrom is incredibly strong. If you look at people all over the world, you will see that many, many people have lived this entire lifetime having their emotional bodies being tied into, driven by and sometimes overwhelmed by this collective planetary maelstrom of fear in the emotional body of the planet or the collective consciousness.

Many, many people have lived in such fear, some of them for many lifetimes, that they have not in this lifetime been able to actually feel without having their emotional body dominated by fear. My beloved, you cannot *become,* you cannot *be,* the Christ in action if you have fear in your emotional body, certainly not if your fear is tied into this planetary maelstrom of fear. It goes without saying that you cannot be the Buddha if you have fear, but some of you have not actually realized that you cannot be the Christ if you have fear in your emotional body.

Therefore, I speak not just to you who are here but I speak to the student body worldwide. I speak to all who would call themselves ascended master students, whether they will recognize this messenger or not, and I speak to all people who are spiritual and open to the spiritual side of life and I speak into the collective consciousness: "You cannot be the Christ if your emotional body has a tie to this planetary momentum of fear."

My beloved, why would your emotional body have a tie to this planetary momentum of fear? Well, it goes back to the teachings we have given you on the birth trauma. Some of you (not all of you but some of you), when you first took embodiment on earth, when you were exposed to a traumatic event perpetrated by the fallen beings, you were so shocked by this that there was a rift in your emotional body. This opened your emotional body to a rushing-in of these energy waves that rolled with the chaotic, disharmonious vibrations of fear.

We have, of course, given the teachings in the book about *My Lives* that many of you are avatars. Of course, not all of you are avatars. Some of you are the original inhabitants of the earth. You will also (after the fallen beings started embodying here) have been exposed to some kind of trauma that was so shocking to you that you could have opened your emotional body to an influx of this fear-based energy.

Keeping you tied to fear

What the fallen beings have been very clever, very aggressive, very persistent in maintaining is that you have a tie between your emotional body and this planetary momentum of fear. My beloved, fear is an emotion. Fear exists, primarily at least, in the emotional body. It is an energy, it is a vibration, it is a momentum. It is rolling, it is moving, often in chaotic and disharmonious ways. Once you are in it and you are overwhelmed by it, what can you do? Well, as some of you will know, once you are in it, it is not easy to get out of it. Because once you are truly in a vibration of fear, your emotional body is in such chaos that your mental body cannot fulfill its rightful position of having command over the emotional body. We have given you the teaching that the energy flows from your I AM Presence into your identity body, into your mental body, into your emotional body and then into the physical.

We have also given the teaching in the new book that on planet earth, you can be exposed to such trauma that you have the reverse energy flow where energy can flow, through the pain of the physical body, into the emotional body, up into the mental, up into the identity body, at least the lower part of the identity body. Once you are exposed to this trauma, you lose that original energy flow and it can be difficult for you to establish it until you have overcome this original birth trauma.

The original inhabitants of the earth

The teaching I give you here is that even though we have given you the teaching on the birth trauma for avatars, it also applies to those of you who are the original inhabitants of the earth because you were also exposed to a trauma. It was not a birth trauma in a sense that it happened in your first embodiment on earth. It happened after you had embodied on earth for a long time and the fallen beings were allowed to embody here. It is not, as such, a birth trauma but it is still a trauma. Whether you want to call it your birth trauma or just your trauma is a play of words but it applies to all of you who are spiritual people.

We know very well that when we give a teaching, we cannot give a teaching that applies to all people. The new book has been given in the context of an avatar coming here from a natural planet and therefore carrying a subconscious memory of what life is like on a natural planet. Naturally, there are teachings in the book that also apply to the original inhabitants of the earth, primarily the birth trauma but also, in a sense, the teachings about a natural planet. Those of you who are the original inhabitants of the earth, you will have experienced the earth in a higher state than it has been in since the fallen beings came here, and even before that. If the earth had not descended below that state of a natural planet, the fallen beings could not have embodied here, would not have been allowed to embody here.

What I submit to you is that those of you who are the original inhabitants of the earth, it is easier for you to have this rift in your emotional body than it is for an avatar. Those of you who are the original inhabitants, for you the earth is your primary frame of reference whereas for the avatars, the natural planet is often their primary frame of reference. Those of you who are among the original inhabitants, you are more tied to the earth. Therefore, you can more easily go into a vibration of fearing what happens on the earth, what happens in the physical octave. It is more likely that those of you who are among the original inhabitants have this tie to the planetary spiral of fear. If you do, it is very important, it is *critically* important, that you cut this tie before you can put on your Christhood.

Getting out of fear

What do you do when you recognize you are in this vibration, this maelstrom of fear? Well, as I said, you cannot do what some people can do and use their mental bodies to start reasoning about the fear, why it is irrational to have this fear and why it is based on an illusion and why they should not be having it. Some people are able to override their fears this way, but many people cannot do this, especially if you have the tie to this planetary momentum.

What can you do? Well, you cannot use your identity body or your mental body to override your emotional body. You cannot use your emotional body to override your emotional body. What can you do? Well, does it not stand to reason, my beloved, that if you have a reverse energy flow, you can use your physical body to override your emotional body, to take command over your emotional body?

This can be done in various ways, but what you have done with this hour of chanting is an example of how you can use the capacity of the physical body. You can give an invocation, give a decree or in many cases it is more efficient to give a chant like you have done here. You can use the recording of this chant to take command over your emotional body whenever you feel it is in upheaval. When you use the capacity of the physical body to give this chant, to use the power of the spoken word, the power of your voice, then you can calm the emotional body. When you have achieved some kind of calmness of the emotional body, then you can call for the help of the ascended masters, Archangel Michael, Astrea, Mother Mary and others to help you cut the tie to that planetary momentum.

Doubt is the open door for fear

Be aware here that even though we have talked about the reverse energy flow, an emotion never exists alone. An emotion is based on some belief in the mental body, and any belief in the mental body is based on a sense of identity in the identity body. Before you can really cut that momentum, you need to realize that fear never arises on its own. It always springs from doubt. Doubt is the open door for fear to enter your emotional body and doubt begins in the mental body but it also reaches into the identity body.

Now, my beloved, we have talked in recent dictations about the limitations of the linear, analytical, logical, rational mind. What have you done during this hour of chanting? If you were centered in your hearts and really allowed yourself to flow with the chant, flow with the sound waves, flow with the rhythm, then you have neutralized your logical, rational, linear, analytical mind. This can then open you up to looking at what is the doubt behind your fear.

It may be easy for you to acknowledge and recognize that you have the fear and what you fear, what the condition is that you fear. But what is the doubt in your mental body that opened you up to the fear? It may have been, as just one among many examples, that you were exposed to a situation where the fallen beings either killed you or killed many people in your family or society. Therefore, in your mental body there was this doubt that you could protect yourself from this, that you could not avoid this, that God could not protect you from this, that there was no force on the earth that could protect you from this.

Once you begin to identify the doubt, well, where does the doubt come from? Doubt is a condition of the mental body and it springs from the fact that the analytical mind can look at any issue and it can come up with arguments *for* the issue or *against* the issue and it can keep doing this indefinitely.

It is like a Ping-Pong match between two internal selves, internal spirits, in your identity body. One is throwing an argument at the other. The other is either refuting the first argument or throwing another argument and you can see it ping, ping, ping, ping—how these two spirits are ping-ponging arguments back and forth. You are standing there, not knowing which one is the ultimate argument, which one is right, which one is not right.

Who is the "you" that is standing there? It is the "you" you see yourself as in the identity body. When was that "you" created? When you received that trauma! Whether it was your birth trauma or your earth trauma, when you received that trauma, you created a certain identity. This identity carries within it the belief that your abilities here on earth are limited. There is something that is limiting your abilities and therefore there is some condition on earth, perpetrated by the fallen beings, that you cannot overcome, protect yourself from or avoid. You are a limited being, you are an *inherently* limited being—that is what this self believes.

Breaking the spell

Now, how do you get out of this catch-22? My beloved, why have we not given this teaching a year or two ago when it applies to many people? Well, because we prefer not to give a teaching until we have given you the tools to deal with the issue we are bringing to your attention. Until we had given the teachings about the birth trauma, which we can also call the earth trauma now, you did not have the tools to overcome this. Whether you are an original inhabitant or an avatar, you now have the tools in the book, *Healing Your Spiritual Traumas*, on how to start identifying and eventually overcoming the birth trauma.

When you overcome the birth trauma, you will feel – *literally* – (as many of you can already attest) that the weight of the world has fallen from your shoulders. It is the weight of the world that you have been carrying on your shoulders since you received that trauma. It opened you up to tying in to the energies of the earth, whether that was a planetary maelstrom of fear or some planetary momentum in the mental body or in the identity body. You have been tied into this momentum and therefore you have carried the weight of those energies, the weight of the world's energies. When you use these tools and teachings to overcome this birth trauma, then you can overcome the fear or any other momentum you have in the identity, mental and emotional bodies and that will give you a new sense of freedom.

Overcoming doubt

My beloved, I said that fear springs from doubt but doubt springs from a limited sense of identity. The only way to truly overcome fear is to overcome doubt but how do you overcome doubt? Only by realizing that you are more than this identity, the self you have in your identity body. Who is

1 | *The selves that followed the primal self*

the "you" that is more? Well, I said, who is the "you" that is experiencing fear? Who is the "you" that is having doubt? That is the "you" you have created in the mental body as a reaction to the trauma you were exposed to by the fallen beings. The "you" that can realize you are more than this "you" is what we have called the Conscious You. The Conscious You cannot step outside the "mortal you" as long as you have the birth trauma because it pulls the Conscious You into identifying yourself as the mortal self, the earth self.

When you resolve the birth trauma, then you have the opportunity to use what we have called intuition (we have also called it pure awareness) where you can experience that you step outside of the self, the lower self. Then, you will have an *experience*, my beloved, and the experience that you can have through pure awareness is, of course, beyond anything that you see or experience in the physical octave. It is also beyond any emotion you can have in your emotional body. It is beyond any mental reasoning, logic or argumentation that you have in your mental body. It is beyond any sense of identity you have in your identity body. Once you experience pure awareness or experience that connection, that flow, to your I AM Presence, you will have a different perspective on everything that is happening in your four lower bodies. You cannot truly attain this until you have dealt with the birth trauma.

Now, my beloved, we have never said that once you overcome the birth trauma, you have overcome all aspects of your psychology. You know how there can be a situation where, for example, pieces of ice can have been jammed up and they are all packed together very tightly, but there is one piece of ice that is holding all the others and if you pull that out, the rest will start flowing. You know how in the old days they would build these stone arches and they would have to support all of the stones on the side until they put in the keystone at the top. Well, your birth trauma and the self that was created, which we have called the *primal* self, this is the keystone in the arch of your human construct, your human structure, the structure in your four lower bodies.

Once you pull it out, it becomes so much easier to start moving the other stones and overriding them. That is when you can begin to identify whether you have a certain momentum in one of the four lower bodies, or perhaps eventually you will identify it in all of the four lower bodies. Some of you, and some of you to your surprise, have been on the spiritual path for years or decades but you have discovered that you still have some physical addiction or some tie to some physical activity that you feel you *have* to do. Some of you will discover that you have that tie to the emotional maelstrom of the collective consciousness or you have other emotional patterns. Some of you will discover that you have a mental pattern of wanting to argue, wanting to reason, wanting to evaluate and analyze everything. Some of you realize that you have a desire to understand everything and some of you will discover that in your identity body, you have a momentum, an addiction in a certain way, that is based on your primal self.

Trying to understand everything

It is not really the primal self, it is an offshoot of your primal self. After you created the primal self, you started creating other selves in a reaction to conditions on earth and this can take various forms. The two main ones are that you are seeking to evaluate everything that is going on here on earth and trying to put it in some larger context where you can understand it. All of you, including this messenger, have in your early stages of studying ascended master teachings used the teachings of the ascended masters to create this world view, this view of the universe in your identity body where you could make sense of what is happening and what you have experienced on earth.

You still think that in your identity body there should be an ultimate understanding so that everything on earth can be explained and understood. My beloved, it can never, ever happen. First of all, because any self you have in the identity body is not capable of understanding, but second of all, because there is no understanding for certain phenomena. This is one of the important points made in the *My Lives* book. There are certain things that the fallen beings do that cannot be explained or understood based on the rational, analytical, linear mind. They sometimes do things deliberately to confuse you and other times they have no reason for what they are doing other than their desire to do evil, or as it says in the book: "to be an artist that paints with the blood of humanity." You cannot ever explain this.

You can, of course, come to some understanding, which is what we have given in the book and in other teachings about fallen beings, about what they do, why they are here. My beloved, you cannot truly grasp that understanding unless you step outside of that self in the identity body and connect directly to your I AM Presence and to your ascended teachers. You receive that, not understanding but total experience from us, from your I AM Presence. There is a difference, my beloved, between *understanding* and *experiencing*. Many of you are at the point where now that you have started working on your birth trauma, overcome your birth trauma, you are ready to experience.

All of you have experienced in some way the reality of the teachings we are giving or you would not be here. When you overcome the birth trauma, you can go into a process of consciously expanding your ability to experience the reality, a higher reality, my beloved. What is this higher reality? Well my beloved, it is not based on anything that your identity body can grasp, anything your mental body can grasp, anything your emotional body can deal with or, of course, anything your physical brain can handle. It is beyond your four lower bodies. It is a sense of reality that is beyond your four lower bodies and only this will allow you to know what is real and what is unreal on this planet, where the fallen beings have muddied everything up with the duality consciousness to an extreme degree.

Compensation for loss

Now, I said there were two tendencies in your identity body. One is trying to understand and put into context. The other is trying to compensate for what you felt you lost when you received that birth trauma or earth trauma. When you were shocked by the fallen beings, the self you created in the identity body is based on a sense of loss. It may be that you lost certain things in the outer but what did you truly lose? You lost your child-like innocence, your inner sense of reality. *That* was what you lost. Ever since then, this self that you created in the identity body has been attempting to compensate for this loss, which can be done in many different ways.

In your identity body is a self that somehow wants to find some kind of identity. You see an extreme outcome of this where there are people in the world who will feel that because they belong to a spiritual lineage, because they belong to a genetic lineage, because they have some kind of special ability or quality, because they are old souls or whatever, then they feel they are someone special. This fills the need of this self that wants to compensate.

There are other ways of doing it and, again, all of you have at the early stages used the teachings of the ascended masters to compensate for the loss you felt in the beginning. Now, that you have found the teachings of the ascended masters (that you believe have a higher reality), you suddenly feel that you are not so inadequate, not so incomplete, not so un-whole as you feel in that self in the identity body. Some of you have gotten into creating selves in the mental body that are constantly seeking to compensate by being very intelligent, very knowledgeable, very logical, rational, very good at arguing or reasoning. You think this compensates for this loss where you felt that you had lost your ability to know what is real and unreal because the fallen beings had put you in such doubt.

Others have created a compensatory mechanism in your emotional body where you somehow are seeking to use your emotional body to compensate for the fear, to overcome the fear, to deny the fear, to suppress the fear so you do not feel it. You will see that there are people in spiritual movements who have taken on this aura of speaking softly, walking slowly, appearing to be in complete control but they have achieved this by suppressing their emotions. Some of you have noticed that sometimes you have emotions come up. This can be because some of you have such a strong momentum in the mental body of suppressing emotions, but it is not healthy and it will not lead you to be free to suppress emotions. At some point, you need to acknowledge that it is not that *you* have an emotion, it is that there is a self in the emotional body that has an emotion and you are not that self. Therefore, you can let the self die and you can call to the ascended masters to consume it and the momentum of energy behind it.

Others of you have a compensatory mechanism in the physical, at the physical level. For some of you this comes through as a desire to work with the physical body. Many, many bodybuilders that you see in the world are trying to make the physical body so big and strong that they somehow feel invincible in the physical. This is a compensatory mechanism for the fact that in the higher bodies they have selves that feel very vulnerable in the physical body. For others it is martial arts. Martial arts have been used in previous ages to provide genuine spiritual growth for some people. If you are living in a very violent time, in a very violent culture, it can actually be a stepping stone to spiritual growth that you learn a certain martial arts technique so you can defend yourself against being attacked. My beloved, once you are on the path of the ascended masters and you aim at manifesting Christhood, you can go beyond the martial arts, you no longer need this.

Others have used other things, other indulgences of the physical octave. It can be physical addictions that give you a sense of relief so that you do not even have to feel how inadequate you normally feel or how vulnerable you normally feel. For others it can be other things: doing things in the physical, becoming very capable of doing things in the physical, whether in your career, in your job, by travelling, by knowing everything, by having a physical skill. You will see people on the Internet in videos who have some bizarre physical skill and ability with the physical body and it is, again, the compensatory mechanism.

There are so many of these that I will not attempt to name all of them. The important point is that once you have dealt with the birth trauma or the earth trauma, you can start looking for these in your four lower bodies. You can start unravelling them so that you can overcome this sense and you can learn to identify this sense of feeling a compulsion to go into a certain activity. Whenever you feel this compulsion, which is also what the Buddha called an "attachment," then you know there is a self there that is limiting you on the spiritual path and that will prevent you from being the Christ in action.

My beloved, this actually completes the release I wanted to give you. I realize that it is a big mouthful on the first day of this conference. On the other hand, you have prepared yourselves so well by the activities you have done today and by this hour of chanting that I felt it appropriate to give you this gift of joy from my heart. You realize, I hope, that I am not putting a burden upon you that now you need to look at yourself and feel bad because you have this or that momentum.

I am giving you an opportunity to be free and in freedom there is joy. In fact, we might say that on a planet like earth with the density you find here, only in freedom can you experience joy, true joy, peaceful joy. Many people on earth consider that when they have some kind of achievement, some kind of victory, then they feel joyful, they feel the joy of victory but this is not peaceful joy, it is not inner joy and it is not Divine joy.

Well, I AM Divine joy and I will give my Divine joy to you, if you will only ask.

2 | INVOKING FREEDOM FROM HAVING TO COMPENSATE

In the name I AM THAT I AM, Jesus Christ, I call to all representatives of the Divine Mother, especially Kuan Yin, to help me see the selves that build on my primal self, including…

[Make personal calls.]

Part 1

1. Kuan Yin, help me see that I cannot *become*, I cannot *be*, the Christ in action if I have fear in my emotional body, especially not if my fear is tied into the planetary maelstrom of fear.

> O Kuan Yin, what sacred name,
> fill me now with Mercy's Flame.
> In giving mercy I am free,
> forgiving all is magic key.

> In Kuan Yin's sweet melody,
> I am set free my Self to be.
> In Kuan Yin's vitality,
> I claim my immortality.

2. Kuan Yin, help me see if a previous embodiment on earth exposed me to a traumatic event that generated a rift in my emotional body, opening it to the chaotic, disharmonious vibrations of fear.

> O Kuan Yin, I now let go,
> of all attachments here below.
> All pent-up feelings I release,
> free from emotional disease.

> **In Kuan Yin's sweet melody,**
> **I am set free my Self to be.**
> **In Kuan Yin's vitality,**
> **I claim my immortality.**

3. Kuan Yin, help me recognize if I am in this vibration, this maelstrom of fear. Help me see that I can use my physical body to override my emotional body by giving invocations and chants.

> O Kuan Yin, why must I feel,
> that life falls short of my ideal?
> All expectations I give up,
> my mind is now an empty cup.

> **In Kuan Yin's sweet melody,**
> **I am set free my Self to be.**
> **In Kuan Yin's vitality,**
> **I claim my immortality.**

4. Kuan Yin, I call forth the help of the ascended masters, Archangel Michael, Astrea and Mother Mary to help me cut all ties to the planetary momentum of fear.

> O Kuan Yin, transcend the past,
> as all resentment gone at last.

From future nothing I expect,
eternal now I won't reject.

**In Kuan Yin's sweet melody,
I am set free my Self to be.
In Kuan Yin's vitality,
I claim my immortality.**

5. Kuan Yin, help me see that an emotion never exists alone. An emotion is based on some belief in the mental body, and any belief in the mental body is based on a sense of identity in the identity body.

O Kuan Yin, uplifting me,
beyond Samsara's raging sea.
All safe inside your Prajna boat,
the farther shore no more remote.

**In Kuan Yin's sweet melody,
I am set free my Self to be.
In Kuan Yin's vitality,
I claim my immortality.**

6. Kuan Yin, help me realize that fear never arises on its own. It always springs from doubt. Doubt is the open door for fear to enter my emotional body. Doubt begins in the mental body but it also reaches into the identity body.

O Kuan Yin, your alchemy,
with miracles you set me free.
As I forgive, I am forgiven,
by guilt I am no longer driven.

**In Kuan Yin's sweet melody,
I am set free my Self to be.
In Kuan Yin's vitality,
I claim my immortality.**

7. Kuan Yin, help me see the doubt in my mental body that opened me up to the fear. Help me see if I doubt that I could protect myself from evil, that God could protect me, that any force on earth can protect me from the fallen beings.

> O Kuan Yin, all worries gone,
> with nothing done, no thing undone.
> Through separate self I will not do,
> and thus I rest, all one with you.

> **In Kuan Yin's sweet melody,**
> **I am set free my Self to be.**
> **In Kuan Yin's vitality,**
> **I claim my immortality.**

8. Kuan Yin, help me see that doubt is a condition of the mental body and it springs from the fact that the analytical mind can look at any issue and it can come up with arguments *for* the issue or *against* the issue and it can keep doing this indefinitely.

> O Kuan Yin, your sanity,
> now sets me free from vanity.
> For truly, what is that to me;
> I just let go and follow thee.

> **In Kuan Yin's sweet melody,**
> **I am set free my Self to be.**
> **In Kuan Yin's vitality,**
> **I claim my immortality.**

9. Kuan Yin, help me see if there is something like a Ping-Pong match between two internal selves in my identity body, throwing arguments back and forth, leaving me not knowing which one is the ultimate argument.

> O Kuan Yin, so sweet the sound,
> that emanates from holy ground.
> As I let go of ego's chore,
> I find myself on farther shore.

**In Kuan Yin's sweet melody,
I am set free my Self to be.
In Kuan Yin's vitality,
I claim my immortality.**

Part 2

1. Kuan Yin, help me see that the "you" that is paralyzed by the selves is the "you" I see myself as in the identity body. This "you" was created when I received my birth trauma or earth trauma.

> O Kuan Yin, what sacred name,
> fill me now with Mercy's Flame.
> In giving mercy I am free,
> forgiving all is magic key.

**In Kuan Yin's sweet melody,
I am set free my Self to be.
In Kuan Yin's vitality,
I claim my immortality.**

2. Kuan Yin, help me see that this identity carries within it the belief that my abilities here on earth are limited. There is something that is limiting my abilities. There is some condition on earth, perpetrated by the fallen beings, that I cannot overcome, protect myself from or avoid. This self believes I am an inherently limited being.

> O Kuan Yin, I now let go,
> of all attachments here below.
> All pent-up feelings I release,
> free from emotional disease.

**In Kuan Yin's sweet melody,
I am set free my Self to be.
In Kuan Yin's vitality,
I claim my immortality.**

3. Kuan Yin, help me use all of the tools I have to overcome my birth trauma or earth trauma until I feel that the weight of the world has fallen from my shoulders. This is the weight of the world that I have been carrying on my shoulders since I received that trauma.

> O Kuan Yin, why must I feel,
> that life falls short of my ideal?
> All expectations I give up,
> my mind is now an empty cup.
>
> **In Kuan Yin's sweet melody,**
> **I am set free my Self to be.**
> **In Kuan Yin's vitality,**
> **I claim my immortality.**

4. Kuan Yin, help me see that my trauma opened me up to tying in to the energies of the earth. I have been tied into this momentum and therefore I have carried the weight of those energies, the weight of the world's energies. Help me overcome the fear or any other momentum I have in the identity, mental and emotional bodies and attain a new sense of freedom.

> O Kuan Yin, transcend the past,
> as all resentment gone at last.
> From future nothing I expect,
> eternal now I won't reject.
>
> **In Kuan Yin's sweet melody,**
> **I am set free my Self to be.**
> **In Kuan Yin's vitality,**
> **I claim my immortality.**

5. Kuan Yin, help me see that fear springs from doubt but doubt springs from a limited sense of identity. Help me realize that I am more than this identity, the self I have in my identity body.

> O Kuan Yin, uplifting me,
> beyond Samsara's raging sea.
> All safe inside your Prajna boat,
> the farther shore no more remote.

> In Kuan Yin's sweet melody,
> I am set free my Self to be.
> In Kuan Yin's vitality,
> I claim my immortality.

6. Kuan Yin, help me see that the "you" that can realize I am more is the Conscious You. The Conscious You cannot step outside the "mortal you" as long as I have the birth trauma because it pulls the Conscious You into identifying myself as the mortal self, the earth self.

> O Kuan Yin, your alchemy,
> with miracles you set me free.
> As I forgive, I am forgiven,
> by guilt I am no longer driven.

> In Kuan Yin's sweet melody,
> I am set free my Self to be.
> In Kuan Yin's vitality,
> I claim my immortality.

7. Kuan Yin, help me resolve the birth trauma and then step outside of the lower self and experience pure awareness.

> O Kuan Yin, all worries gone,
> with nothing done, no thing undone.
> Through separate self I will not do,
> and thus I rest, all one with you.

> In Kuan Yin's sweet melody,
> I am set free my Self to be.
> In Kuan Yin's vitality,
> I claim my immortality.

8. Kuan Yin, help me experience that pure awareness is beyond anything that I see or experience in the physical octave. It is also beyond any emotion, any mental reasoning, logic or argumentation and any sense of identity.

> O Kuan Yin, your sanity,
> now sets me free from vanity.
> For truly, what is that to me;
> I just let go and follow thee.
>
> **In Kuan Yin's sweet melody,**
> **I am set free my Self to be.**
> **In Kuan Yin's vitality,**
> **I claim my immortality.**

9. Kuan Yin, help me experience pure awareness and experience the flow from my I AM Presence, so I gain a different perspective on everything that is happening in my four lower bodies.

> O Kuan Yin, so sweet the sound,
> that emanates from holy ground.
> As I let go of ego's chore,
> I find myself on farther shore.
>
> **In Kuan Yin's sweet melody,**
> **I am set free my Self to be.**
> **In Kuan Yin's vitality,**
> **I claim my immortality.**

Part 3

1. Kuan Yin, help me see that having overcome the birth trauma does not mean I have overcome all aspects of my psychology. My primal self is the keystone in the arch of the structure in my four lower bodies, but it is not the only self.

> O Kuan Yin, what sacred name,
> fill me now with Mercy's Flame.
> In giving mercy I am free,
> forgiving all is magic key.

**In Kuan Yin's sweet melody,
I am set free my Self to be.
In Kuan Yin's vitality,
I claim my immortality.**

2. Kuan Yin, help me overcome any physical addiction or tie to a physical activity that I feel I *have* to do. Help me overcome any tie to the emotional maelstrom of the collective consciousness or other emotional patterns.

O Kuan Yin, I now let go,
of all attachments here below.
All pent-up feelings I release,
free from emotional disease.

**In Kuan Yin's sweet melody,
I am set free my Self to be.
In Kuan Yin's vitality,
I claim my immortality.**

3. Kuan Yin, help me overcome any mental pattern of wanting to argue, wanting to reason, wanting to evaluate and analyze everything. Help me realize if I have a desire to understand everything.

O Kuan Yin, why must I feel,
that life falls short of my ideal?
All expectations I give up,
my mind is now an empty cup.

**In Kuan Yin's sweet melody,
I am set free my Self to be.
In Kuan Yin's vitality,
I claim my immortality.**

4. Kuan Yin, help me discover if, in my identity body, I have a pattern of seeking to evaluate everything and trying to put it in some larger context where I can understand it. Help me see if I have used the teachings of the ascended masters to create a world view where I can make sense of what I have experienced on earth.

O Kuan Yin, transcend the past,
as all resentment gone at last.
From future nothing I expect,
eternal now I won't reject.

**In Kuan Yin's sweet melody,
I am set free my Self to be.
In Kuan Yin's vitality,
I claim my immortality.**

5. Kuan Yin, help me overcome the illusion in my identity body that there should be an ultimate understanding so that everything on earth can be explained and understood.

O Kuan Yin, uplifting me,
beyond Samsara's raging sea.
All safe inside your Prajna boat,
the farther shore no more remote.

**In Kuan Yin's sweet melody,
I am set free my Self to be.
In Kuan Yin's vitality,
I claim my immortality.**

6. Kuan Yin, help me accept that there is no understanding for certain phenomena. There are certain things that the fallen beings do that cannot be explained or understood based on the rational, analytical, linear mind.

O Kuan Yin, your alchemy,
with miracles you set me free.
As I forgive, I am forgiven,
by guilt I am no longer driven.

**In Kuan Yin's sweet melody,
I am set free my Self to be.
In Kuan Yin's vitality,
I claim my immortality.**

7. Kuan Yin, help me step outside of the self in the identity body and connect directly to my I AM Presence and to my ascended teachers. Help me receive the total experience from you and my I AM Presence that is beyond understanding.

> O Kuan Yin, all worries gone,
> with nothing done, no thing undone.
> Through separate self I will not do,
> and thus I rest, all one with you.

> **In Kuan Yin's sweet melody,**
> **I am set free my Self to be.**
> **In Kuan Yin's vitality,**
> **I claim my immortality.**

8. Kuan Yin, help me overcome the birth trauma and go into a process of consciously expanding my ability to experience the higher reality that is beyond what my identity body, mental body, emotional body and physical brain can handle.

> O Kuan Yin, your sanity,
> now sets me free from vanity.
> For truly, what is that to me;
> I just let go and follow thee.

> **In Kuan Yin's sweet melody,**
> **I am set free my Self to be.**
> **In Kuan Yin's vitality,**
> **I claim my immortality.**

9. Kuan Yin, help me attain the sense of reality that is beyond my four lower bodies and is the only way to know what is real and what is unreal on this planet.

> O Kuan Yin, so sweet the sound,
> that emanates from holy ground.
> As I let go of ego's chore,
> I find myself on farther shore.

> In Kuan Yin's sweet melody,
> I am set free my Self to be.
> In Kuan Yin's vitality,
> I claim my immortality.

Part 4

1. Kuan Yin, help me see the tendency in my identity body of trying to compensate for what I felt I lost when I received the birth trauma or earth trauma. I lost my child-like innocence, my inner sense of reality. Ever since then, a self has been attempting to compensate for this loss.

> O Kuan Yin, what sacred name,
> fill me now with Mercy's Flame.
> In giving mercy I am free,
> forgiving all is magic key.

> **In Kuan Yin's sweet melody,**
> **I am set free my Self to be.**
> **In Kuan Yin's vitality,**
> **I claim my immortality.**

2. Kuan Yin, help me overcome the desire to compensate that is expressed as a compulsion to find some way in which I am special compared to other people.

> O Kuan Yin, I now let go,
> of all attachments here below.
> All pent-up feelings I release,
> free from emotional disease.

> **In Kuan Yin's sweet melody,**
> **I am set free my Self to be.**
> **In Kuan Yin's vitality,**
> **I claim my immortality.**

3. Kuan Yin, help me see if I have used the teachings of the ascended masters to compensate for the loss by thinking I am so special because I am in these teachings.

> O Kuan Yin, why must I feel,
> that life falls short of my ideal?
> All expectations I give up,
> my mind is now an empty cup.

> **In Kuan Yin's sweet melody,**
> **I am set free my Self to be.**
> **In Kuan Yin's vitality,**
> **I claim my immortality.**

4. Kuan Yin, help me see if I have selves in the mental body that are constantly seeking to compensate by being very intelligent, knowledgeable, logical, rational, very good at arguing or reasoning.

> O Kuan Yin, transcend the past,
> as all resentment gone at last.
> From future nothing I expect,
> eternal now I won't reject.

> **In Kuan Yin's sweet melody,**
> **I am set free my Self to be.**
> **In Kuan Yin's vitality,**
> **I claim my immortality.**

5. Kuan Yin, help me see if I have created a compensatory mechanism in my emotional body where I am seeking to use my emotional body to compensate for the fear, overcome the fear, deny the fear, suppress the fear so I do not feel it.

> O Kuan Yin, uplifting me,
> beyond Samsara's raging sea.
> All safe inside your Prajna boat,
> the farther shore no more remote.

> In Kuan Yin's sweet melody,
> I am set free my Self to be.
> In Kuan Yin's vitality,
> I claim my immortality.

6. Kuan Yin, help me acknowledge that it is not that *I* have an emotion, it is that there is a self in the emotional body that has an emotion and I am not that self. I am letting the self die and I am calling to Archangel Michael and Astrea to consume it and the momentum of energy behind it.

> O Kuan Yin, your alchemy,
> with miracles you set me free.
> As I forgive, I am forgiven,
> by guilt I am no longer driven.

> In Kuan Yin's sweet melody,
> I am set free my Self to be.
> In Kuan Yin's vitality,
> I claim my immortality.

7. Kuan Yin, help me see if I have a compensatory mechanism at the physical level expressed as a desire to make the physical body invincible. Help me see if I have physical addictions or if I am trying to compensate by becoming very capable of doing things in the physical, whether in my career, my job or by having a physical skill.

> O Kuan Yin, all worries gone,
> with nothing done, no thing undone.
> Through separate self I will not do,
> and thus I rest, all one with you.

> In Kuan Yin's sweet melody,
> I am set free my Self to be.
> In Kuan Yin's vitality,
> I claim my immortality.

8. Kuan Yin, help me see these compensatory mechanisms in my four lower bodies so I can start unravelling them and overcome any compulsion to go into a certain activity. Whenever I feel a compulsion, there is a self that is preventing me from being the Christ in action.

O Kuan Yin, your sanity,
now sets me free from vanity.
For truly, what is that to me;
I just let go and follow thee.

**In Kuan Yin's sweet melody,
I am set free my Self to be.
In Kuan Yin's vitality,
I claim my immortality.**

9. Kuan Yin, help me overcome the primal self and unravel all the other selves so I can experience the freedom that is the source of true joy, peaceful joy, Divine joy.

O Kuan Yin, so sweet the sound,
that emanates from holy ground.
As I let go of ego's chore,
I find myself on farther shore.

**In Kuan Yin's sweet melody,
I am set free my Self to be.
In Kuan Yin's vitality,
I claim my immortality.**

Sealing

In the name of the Divine Mother, I call to Mother Mary for the sealing of myself and all people in my circle of influence in the creative flow of the Divine Mother, the River of Life. I call for the multiplication of my calls by all representatives of the Divine Mother, so that we form the perfect figure-eight flow of "As Above, so below." Thus, I accept that this is fully manifest, because the mouth of the Lord, the Divine Mother that I AM, has spoken it. Amen.

3 | OVERCOMING THE CONTROL ASPECT OF THE PRIMAL SELF

I AM the Ascended Master Jesus, or as I sometimes say, I AM the Ascended Master Jesus Christ. Why do I sometimes say Jesus and sometimes say Jesus Christ? For no reason, my beloved, other than that is how I feel like expressing myself at that moment.

Why is it that some of you have put your attention on trying to understand why I sometimes do this and sometimes say that? It is, that as a result of the shock of encountering the fallen beings, you have created this self in the identity body that needs to feel that it has a certain grasp, a certain understanding, of the world and how it works because then you can feel safe.

How many have manifested Christhood?

My beloved, the question I want to put before you in this release is this. For now quite a number of decades, we of the ascended masters have given teachings through sponsored messengers who could receive a direct dictation from us. Even from the very beginning of this dispensation of the Living Word, we have given teachings about the fact that I was not the idol and the exception that mainstream Christianity has made me out to be. Instead, I was meant to be the example of the potential that all people have. Now, if you look back at these many decades of giving teachings, of how we have attracted over that time millions of people who have (at least at some level) studied the teachings we have given. When you look back at this, the question then arises: "How many people have been able to take the teachings we have given and manifest and express a certain level of Christhood? How many have been able to overcome the programming of denying yourself as having a Christ potential and actually begin to exercise that Christ potential?" This is the question that I wish you to contemplate and even also discuss during this conference and, of course, beyond.

It is not just a general question of why more people have not done this. Of course, as you who are here know, it is about looking at yourself. The question also is: "Why haven't *I* manifested a higher degree of Christhood?" Now, my beloved, I wish to make you aware, for some of you have not quite locked in to this, that we have (actually since the beginning but especially over the last several years) attempted to actually bring about a shift in you.

Freedom from the judging mind

You see, my beloved, what the fallen beings have done for ages, but especially what they have done through mainstream Christianity, is to create the idea of sin. You are somehow imperfect and God is the angry being in the sky who judges you and either sends you to hell or takes you to heaven. They have even attempted to project that I, as the Living Christ or as the Planetary Christ, I am judging you and either raising my thumb and sending you to heaven or lowering my thumb and sending you to hell. We have attempted to help you see that this is *not* the case.

Over the last couple of years, especially the Lady Masters, primarily Mother Mary, have attempted to help you see that we do not judge you at all but we certainly do not judge you the way the fallen beings judge you and the way the fallen beings have managed to make you judge yourselves. I wish you to be very, very, very clear in your minds that I am not giving you this teaching and presenting you with this question because I want you to judge yourselves and feel bad because you have not manifested a higher degree of Christhood. What is the goal of the Living Christ? What is the goal of me as the Ascended Christ? What is the goal of all ascended masters? My beloved, we have only one goal. Will you please fixate in your mind that the ascended masters have only one goal. It is to set you free. Immediately, your mind says: "From what! From what do the masters want to set me free?" We want to set you free from the mind that asks this question because it is *that* mind that is keeping you trapped.

How to bring out teachings

Do you understand, my beloved, that we here in the ascended realm are constantly monitoring the planet? We take a very long view and for a very long time, it was limited what we could do, what we could bring out. Do you understand that if you look back at the teachings we have now given, not quite for a century but coming towards that landmark, you can ask yourself: "Why weren't these teachings given earlier?" Well, actually they *were* given earlier but in a more private, often secret, setting.

There was no way to give them in a public setting. This has partly to do with the fact that the fallen beings managed to pervert Christianity and make sure that Christianity became the primary tool for actually suppressing the true teachings of Christ, namely the teachings that are meant to set you free. For centuries, in Europe and elsewhere, it was not possible to publicly give the teachings we have been giving. Of course, there is also the purely practical, pragmatic aspect of how do you distribute teachings.

You might know that in the 1930s we sponsored an organization called the I AM Movement. When you go back to that time, which those of you who have grown up in the Internet age can hardly envision, you see that the primary means of communication back then was the mail system. What did the fallen beings manage to do? They managed to actually make the United States government prevent the I AM Movement, at least for a time, from using the mail system. You see that it was really only after the advent of the Internet that there has been a much better opportunity for us to bring forth teachings and spread them out to a larger audience.

What blocks Christhood

Now, at the same time we, of course, constantly monitor the collective consciousness and the growth in the collective consciousness. There has in almost every age been some people, a few individuals, who were open to these teachings of how you free yourself. It is only within the last decade or two that the collective consciousness has reached a level where we have been able to bring forth the, actually quite advanced and sophisticated, teachings we have brought forth through this messenger, beginning with the duality consciousness, the epic mindset and going all the way up to our latest releases on the birth trauma.

Now my beloved, Kuan Yin gave you important keys in her dictation, which I recommend that you study many times, but I will build upon the foundation she has set. Again, the question: You have people who have an outer teaching that Jesus Christ was not an exception but an example that all can follow if they are willing to apply themselves. Many of these people also had practical tools: invoking the violet flame, decrees and other tools that they could use. Why is it that so many people have not been able to internalize and apply this to the point where they could express their Christhood? Now again, there is no blame here, my beloved. There is no blame, there is not even a saying that you *should* have manifested a higher decree of Christhood. We are simply having a conversation where we are calmly and neutrally considering what is the mechanism that prevents people from expressing their Christhood.

Of course, the reason we have very carefully, gradually given you the teachings we have given you is that it all leads up to what we have now called the birth trauma or the earth trauma. In other words, whether you are one of the original inhabitants of the earth or whether you are one who has come here from another world, another planet, potentially a natural planet, this all applies to you. The simple fact is this (and we have said this several times but I will say it again): When you first take embodiment on a planet like earth or (even if you have embodied here many times) when you for the first time encounter the fallen beings and their unlimited willingness to do evil and to hurt you and other people, it will be a shock, it will be a trauma. It has been that way for all of us who have embodied on earth.

Blaming yourself for reacting

Again, there is no blame, there is no reason to look at this with regret but some of you, *many* of you, still do this. You still think, my beloved, as this messenger certainly thought even up until he received these teachings back in December on the primal self, you should somehow have been able to come here as an avatar and remain untouched by what is going on, on earth, you should not have gotten your hands dirty.

My beloved, it is only a self that feels this way, and I need you to come to consciously see this self, see that it is a self, that is existing in your identity body but even reaches into the mental and emotional. I need you to step back and separate yourself from this self that thinks you should have been able to do things differently. It is the very same self that will take the teaching I am giving you and say: "I should have been able to manifest my Christhood sooner and why wasn't I?"

Well, my beloved, why have you not been able to manifest your Christhood sooner? You have not been able because you have not had the knowledge and the teachings to deal with the primal self. What is the one thing, the absolutely one thing, that prevents sincere spiritual seekers from manifesting Christhood? Take note! I am not saying all people because when you look at the people on earth, they have many different selves at many different levels. I am talking about the sincere spiritual seekers who have studied our teachings, who have applied our teachings, sometimes for many years. What is the one thing that is preventing you from being the Living Christ in action? Well, that one thing is your primal self.

Kuan Yin gave you teachings on this and I will take them a step further. When you first encounter the fallen beings (or at least when you first realize that their capacity for evil is unlimited, they have no limitations, they have no boundaries for what they will do to others and what kind of havoc and suffering they will cause), it is a shock. It is such a shock that you literally cannot live with it, you cannot deal with it.

How you created the primal self

Here you are, you are in a physical body, you cannot withdraw from the physical body, you cannot just step back and say: "Oh, I don't want to be on this planet anymore, I'm putting down this physical body and going back to where I came from." You cannot do that! You are here, you are in the physical body, you realize there are these beings (we have called them fallen beings, you probably saw them as something else) who will do absolutely anything they can to hurt and destroy you or to hurt and destroy other people. You cannot get away from them but you cannot live with the knowledge that they are here, with the fear of what they will do next.

With observing all the suffering they create, you are suddenly faced with this dilemma. You are here on earth, you cannot get out of here so you have to find a way to exist here while knowing that the fallen beings also exist here. How do you deal with this? Well, you deal with it by creating the primal self. The primal self, as Kuan Yin said, has this need to create an overall view of the earth, how it works, why God allows evil to exist, why there is evil on earth. You also need to recognize that there is an aspect of the primal self that has as its primary task to make you feel somewhat safe, to give you some sense of equilibrium here on earth.

What I am saying is: Before you encountered the fallen beings, you felt relatively safe. You had a sense of equilibrium, a sense of constancy, a sense of confidence in life, in the future. You encounter the fallen beings, you realize they have an unlimited willingness to perpetrate evil, and suddenly you lose that, as you might say, childhood innocence. You lose the inner sense of safety, of security, of equilibrium. The primary task of the primal self is to restore in you some sense of equilibrium, some sense of safety and how does it do this? It does this in various ways. In order to do it, it creates more than one self, depending on your individual psychological makeup, depending on what you experience, not only in the first lifetime where you encountered the fallen beings but in the lifetimes that come after. You have a somewhat complex apparatus, but nevertheless the idea I wish to give you here is that there is an aspect of your primal self that wants to create this sense of security, of equilibrium, of having life and your life on earth somewhat under control.

My beloved, again we are not blaming you. We are not saying there is something wrong with this. We are not saying you should not have done this—we all did the same thing. What else can you do when you first encounter the shock of these beings who will do anything to destroy you? What you are capable of doing and you have the teachings to do, is to start looking at this primal self, this aspect of the primal self, this security self, this control self.

Controlling the world to feel safe

In a very straightforward manner, we can say that this aspect of the primal self has been attempting to control the world in order to make itself feel safe. The mechanism is simple: If you feel you are in control, then you can feel safe. If you look at this honestly, this is what is driving a lot of the fallen beings. They feel fundamentally unsafe and because they can never get back into oneness (unless they turn around, which they are not willing to do), they cannot overcome that sense of not being safe and that is why they have to have this ultimate control.

Why was Stalin willing to kill millions of people? Because of this need for control that he had. It really only shows you how great was his fear, and therefore how low was his spiritual attainment. If you are needing to kill other people in order to make yourself feel safe, then obviously you have a tremendous fear, you are driven by that fear. Therefore, in a sense, regardless of how you may appear to the world, you are a powerless being. You may exercise physical power but in an inner sense, you are powerless. He was one of the most powerless beings you have seen in recent history. Hitler, of course, being equally powerless, Mao Tse Tung being even more powerless than either of the two.

You see this, and therefore you need to recognize here that you have this tendency, and it is understandable and it is inevitable, but it is not inevitable that you carry this self with you for the rest of this lifetime. That is why we have given you these teachings so that you can throw off this heavy yoke of this security addict, this control-freak self that you have in your identity body. You can come to look at it, you can come to see it, see it for what it is, step back from it and realize: "This is not who I am. This is not who I am."

Now my beloved, what we are very well aware of as ascended masters, is that we are walking a very delicate balance. In order to set you free, as is our goal, we have to do two things. We have to, first of all, make you aware that you are not free. This can be very, very disturbing to you. Do you understand why it is disturbing to you? Well, it is disturbing because the control self that you have created in order to gain a sense of security and equilibrium, needs to feel that it has a basic grasp of how this planet works.

Of course, you are trapped by that self. It is that self that imprisons you more than anything else. When we start exposing that such a self exists, how will the self react? It will react as if it is a matter of life and death to refute what we are saying, to make you *not* accept what we are saying, not lock in to what we are saying, not apply what we are saying. You can look at yourself and a very good test for this is to take the book *My Lives* and see how you reacted to this book. The more you are disturbed by the book, the more it shows you that you have this self that has felt, perhaps over many lifetimes, that it had a certain grip of how the world works. It had things under control, it had worked out a system in itself that if only you did certain things and did not do other things, then you would be safe.

Overcoming the control-freak self

Now my beloved, this self is, in a certain sense, right. What is the primary condition that makes you unsafe on earth? It is the fallen beings. Why would they attack you? Why would they attempt to destroy you? Because their primary, their greatest, fear is that someone becomes the Living Christ in embodiment, someone dares to express their Christhood. That is their primary fear. Therefore, they will, when someone comes into the planet or rises to a certain level of Christhood, do everything they can to destroy that person and prevent them from expressing their Christhood.

What happened when you first encountered the fallen beings and experienced that they were willing to do anything in their power to destroy you personally? You received a shock, the trauma, and as a result of that, you created this aspect of the primal self, this control self. Again, it is all understandable. You are in physical embodiment, you experience there is someone who is willing to kill you, torture you, put you down, humiliate you, do anything they can to destroy you. You cannot get out of the body. You may not be able to get away from them physically. What can you do so that you can actually survive mentally, emotionally not only in that lifetime but in succeeding embodiments? Well, the control self is very quick to realize that according to its perception, the only way to feel safe on earth is to *not* be the Christ on earth, to not challenge the fallen beings. If you do not challenge the fallen beings by being the Christ, then they will leave you alone and this is correct. If you do not challenge them, they *will* leave you alone. You recognize here that the control self has managed to create a sense that it is safe, it is secure, as long as it stays within certain boundaries and does not do anything that challenges the fallen beings.

Some of you have lived in this sense of security for many, many, many lifetimes. In fact, all of you have some sense of security. Not all of you have lived in it for lifetimes because some of you have in your recent lifetimes been exposed to wars and other traumatic events. You have not had that sense of security for quite as long. Some of you have had this sense of security for a very long time. What happens when we give you the teachings we have given you on the primal self and on Christhood? What happens is, as Kuan Yin said, that you actually go through a period where you use the teachings of the ascended masters to reinforce the control self's sense that it has the world under control.

You can even take the teachings we have been giving and you can use them to reinforce a certain world view. Again, we go back to the question: Why is it that we have given these teachings for decades and so few people have been able to manifest Christhood? It is because the majority of the people who followed an ascended master teachings, they never challenged the control aspect of the primal self, the control self. They never challenged it. Partly because they did not have the teaching because, again, we had to go very gradually and build this up. Again, there is no blame here. There is no sense that: "Oh, they should have been able to do this." I am simply describing what is happening so that you who are open to this can understand it and go higher.

Postponing your Christhood

My beloved, what have people done with ascended master teachings? They have built the sense that: "Yes, I see that Jesus Christ was meant to be an example and I see that I have the potential to manifest Christhood." In previous dispensations people were more focused on qualifying for their ascension, just as you see many people in the Christian movements focusing on their salvation. In other words, we have said before that what the Catholic church did from the beginning was to define the goal that life on earth is suffering, you are just a sinner, you do not have a Christ potential here on earth, what you should worry about is what happens after the life on earth so you can be saved and go to heaven. Many ascended master students simply took our teachings and built this sense that the primary goal of an ascended master student is to qualify for your ascension. Of course, that happens at the end of this life or after this life.

Again, using the teachings to postpone being the Christ, postponing going through a decisive change. You are sort of saying: "Oh, I just need to give enough violet flame for the rest of my life that I balance at least 51% of my karma, and then I'll ascend after this lifetime and I don't have to be the Christ, I don't have to challenge the fallen beings." Again, no blame here but a straightforward, very direct, simple discussion about what has been happening.

Of course, we started giving some teachings through this messenger, actually from the very beginning, that were challenging, that went beyond what was given in previous dispensations: the duality consciousness, the epic mindset. You will see, if you look at the history of our releases through this messenger, that there have been these periods, even in his messengership, where we have stepped up the teachings to a higher level. Some of the students who were there for the previous teachings could not handle the new teachings. What have they done? Well, they had to construct some kind of scenario where they had an excuse for withdrawing, perhaps even saying that the messenger had now become a false messenger, had lost his mantle and this and that.

This all goes back to the fact that these teachings challenged the sense of security of these peoples' control selves. They had used the previous teaching to reinforce their sense of being in control. Now, we gave a new teaching that for some people disturbed their sense of being in control. They came to a point where, at least subconsciously, they realized that they could not actually embrace this teaching and at the same time maintain their sense of being in control. The teaching was challenging one of the illusions they had used to build that sense of being in control.

They came to a point where they had to choose: Are you hot or cold? Will you follow the Living Christ or will you not? They chose not to and they had to come up with an excuse, and a convenient excuse was (as has been done in previous dispensations): "Oh, the messenger has lost his mantle, he is giving false teachings, she is giving false teachings, the masters are no longer sponsoring this organization, the masters would never say this, the masters would never be so direct about not eating sugar." And so forth and so on. We have seen these excuses from ascended master students over the decades. Again, no blame, no sense of what should or should not have been done, but we must say that from an ascended perspective, there comes a point where you have seen this human self, this control self, do its thing so many times that it is time we simply talk about this in an open and straightforward manner that is very difficult to explain away.

What is your goal in this lifetime?

The simple thing is this: When I walked the earth in a physical body, I many times would challenge people. Again, you realize I had only three years and I had to challenge people: Would they follow me and come up higher or would they stay where they felt secure, where they felt safe.

Again, I have to do the same thing here. Now again, there is no blame, there is no saying what you *should* or *should not* do. You need to recognize here, you need to decide, what is your goal in this lifetime. You can decide that you are comfortable at the level of being a student of the ascended masters and their teachings. You can continue practicing them at that level, but you need to ask yourself whether it is actually your goal to fulfill, what we earlier this summer called, the highest potential of your Divine plan? "Is it my goal to express Christhood at a higher level than I have done so far?" If this is your goal, and again I am not blaming you, I am not even saying that if it is not your goal, you should withdraw from the teachings. You can still study the teachings in whatever way you want.

What I am needing to set before you is this: You cannot be the Living Christ and at the same time maintain your sense of security and being in control. It cannot be done, you cannot serve two masters, you cannot serve God and mammon. The mammon being a symbol for this aspect of the primal self that wants to feel it is always in control so it can always feel safe.

You have the popular saying in the United States: "Better safe than sorry," but this is created by the fallen beings because the Christ is neither safe nor sorry. That is a state of consciousness you can only get to by looking at this aspect of your primal self, by being willing to see it and by separating yourself from it and letting it die, as we have given you the teachings and the tools to do. Again, we are not setting a goal before you that you cannot reach because we have been very careful, very methodical, in giving you the teachings and the tools so that this is possible for you.

What people have done to feel safe

My beloved, if you look back over history, you will see that there were some people who had gotten so good at controlling their outer situation in order to feel safe that they had created this momentum of isolating and insulating themselves from the world. You can see, for example, if you look back at medieval times, how many of the kings and the queens and the noble people, they had managed to set themselves up, living a very privileged, comfortable lifestyle. They had surrounded themselves with big stone walls or even armies and they could live there in their ivory towers and they could feel safe because in a sense they were isolated, they were insulated from what was going on in the world. They did not really realize the suffering of their own people, the people who supported their lifestyle, so they felt safe.

You have seen people who have used some spiritual teaching to set themselves up in a monastery or a spiritual retreat and in some kind of spiritual retreat setting where they were, again, isolated and insulated from the world. Some of you have done this in past lifetimes. Now again, it can be constructive to do this for a while but if it gets to a point where this is just your control self that is wanting to feel safe, then it no longer leads to growth.

I ask you to simply consider this. If you read the *Gospel of Thomas*, you will see that it says in there that there comes a point where you have a certain knowledge and then you will be disturbed, but when you go beyond being disturbed, then you will be the ruler of all, meaning in your own psyche. You will be a master, you will have self-mastery.

What I am giving you is this knowledge that you have an aspect of the primal self that wants to stay in control. When I give you this knowledge, you *will* be disturbed because this self will react by feeling it is threatened on its life—and it *is* threatened on its life. When you see that you no longer need that self, then you can let it die and it *will* die. It does not want to die and so it is willing to keep you trapped in the sense of being unsafe in order to maintain its own existence. You will be disturbed but when you use the tools and teachings to free yourself from this aspect of the primal self and let it die, then you will have peace. Then, you will feel freedom and you will feel such a new sense of freedom that you cannot even imagine it right now.

You are safe as a formless being

How can you actually get to that point? Well, we have given you now so many teachings on the Conscious You. The importance of this teaching is: Who you really are as a being in embodiment is a formless being that has come down into a world of form. We have told you that in order to express yourself in this world of form, you have to create these structures in your four lower bodies but you are not your own creation. What happened as a result of this trauma was that you created the primal self and you started thinking that this was who you were, or at least who you had to be in order to be safe on earth. If you really use these teachings on the Conscious You, you can realize you are still a formless being, and as a formless being you cannot be hurt by whatever happens on earth. You see what I am offering you here? I am setting before you life and death. I am setting before you two choices. You have the death consciousness, which is represented by the control self that thinks you are safe only if you have the world under control. It actually thinks that the only way to be safe in this world (ultimately) is to be able to control the world completely. This is death because, of course, you can never control the world. No individual can ever do so.

The alternative is life. It is to realize you do not need to control the world in order to feel safe. You need to reconnect. You need to re-awaken. You need to become conscious of who you are as a formless being. Then, you realize that you can be safe in this world even in the state it is in. You can be safe without having to control the world and it is only, my beloved, when you feel safe without having to control the world that you can start expressing your Christhood. It is only *then* that you will dare to challenge the fallen beings.

My beloved, without wanting to point the finger at anyone in particular, you have seen that in the past there have been people who have been so concerned about being attacked or destroyed by the fallen beings that they felt they constantly had to protect themselves from this. How can you function that way in the long run? It again becomes such a strain to have to defend yourself, and in this day and age, hopefully you will not be killed or tortured by the fallen beings because we have moved beyond this. In a way, it is safer to express your Christhood today than it has been in the past. Still, you need to get to that point where you have overcome the fear of the fallen beings. They are not running your life, they are not your frame of reference. The ascended masters, your I AM Presence, the world beyond form is your frame of reference. That is when you can feel safe in expressing Christhood.

How can you be the Christ in action? Well, you cannot be the Christ in action if there is a control self in your identity body that feels that expressing your Christhood makes you unsafe and fears what will happen if you express your Christhood.

Overcoming the need for safety

My beloved, you have to find a way to overcome that need for safety in this world by controlling the world. This is what I have now made you aware of. As I said, we have given you the teachings on the primal self, on how to overcome it. If you use these teachings, if you are willing to let go of this, if you are willing to be temporarily disturbed until you have applied the teachings, then there will come that point where you will be free.

As we have said before, an internal self was always created to deal with a certain problem on earth. In its very programming, in its very make-up, it is designed to deal with that problem. The internal self will keep projecting at you that the problem is real, that the problem exists, that the problem affects you and that you have to do something about it. This control self will project at you that: "Evil is real, there is a real danger, you could be persecuted, you have to feel safe, you have to continue doing something to feel safe." My beloved, there is that point (even described in the Bible) where I said to one person who wanted to bury his dead father: "What is that to thee, follow thou me, let the dead bury their dead."

Are you willing to walk with me into a higher level of consciousness? Then, take the hand that I offer you and let me walk with you until you are so anchored in Christ that you can look at this control self and say: "I no longer need you because now I have the hand of the ascended Jesus Christ and *there* is my safety. It is in Christ that I am safe, that I am saved, that I am secure, that I have my connection to oneness, that I know I am a formless being and therefore cannot be destroyed or threatened by anything in this world. It is in Christ I find my refuge, not in the outer self that wants to control the world."

My beloved, what do you want, life or death? It is not an all-or-nothing choice, as I said. I recognize that some people are not ready to embrace this teaching. It may take you time before you are ready. If so, then continue to study the teachings and apply them as you can. But some of you are ready to step up to that higher level.

You cannot, you *cannot* manifest your Christhood, you cannot walk with me, you cannot take my hand until you start separating yourself from this primal self, this control self that absolutely must feel it has control over the world. Therefore, it cannot leave its nets and walk with the Living Christ, leaving everything behind. It is not that you need to leave everything behind in an outer sense, but you need to leave that self behind. That is the one thing that prevents you from manifesting Christhood.

The delicate balance of the masters

My beloved, we are always walking a delicate balance. What can you handle? What can you not handle? What are you ready for? What are you not ready for? Many times when I walked the earth, I would confront people in a very direct manner. We have told the story that I walked up to some of my disciples and said: "Leave your nets and follow me." I turned around and walked away and if they did not follow me, they had lost the opportunity. This is not the way we work now where we give these teachings. We recognize that it may take time for you to embody the teaching, to be ready to embrace a certain teaching. We are not trying to create this image that all of you should be ready for Christhood today. We recognize that some of you still have to go through some steps.

I hope you also recognize that you yourself are walking a delicate balance. You must realize, that you are in these teachings because you want to grow on the path, but there is an aspect of this outer self, this primal self, that does not want you to grow. Yes, there are times where you can say: "I am not ready for that teaching, I need more time, I need to go through several steps before I can embrace it." There also comes a point where you need to say: "Is it just my control self that wants me to think I am not ready? In reality, I am ready and then the question is: 'Am I willing?'" You need to sometimes push yourself, you need to sometimes step back, look at yourself in the mirror and say: "Where am I at on my path? Have I perhaps allowed my control self to use the teachings to create the sense that I am comfortable if I stay at this level and I don't go beyond it? Am I perhaps ready to take a decisive step forward, to leave something behind and embrace a new day? Am I ready for a more direct encounter with the ascended masters?" For some of you, you need to still follow an outer teaching but there are others of you that are ready to say: "Should I forever sit here passively and listen to a messenger who has a connection to the ascended masters or am I ready to establish a more direct connection for myself with the ascended masters?"

A teaching is always given at different levels. In a sense, it always gives your control self an excuse for not applying the teaching. It is up to you, it is *your* responsibility to evaluate: "When am I ready and when is it just an excuse of my control self that says I am not ready."

With this, I have given you what I want to give you for now. I am grateful for your attention, for your willingness to even endure a teaching that, of course, will be disturbing. My beloved, did you really expect that you could come to a conference and the theme is "Being the Living Christ" and you would not be disturbed? Because if you did expect this, you might look at the self that expects this and say: "Ah, now I see you. I am not you."

This can be the beginning of you separating yourself from that self and realizing that the self, of course, has an unrealistic expectation of what it means to be the Christ. It thinks you can be the Christ without challenging the fallen beings or rather without challenging the control self's sense of being in control. This, my beloved, cannot be done. I have said it before. I will probably say it again because I need to keep saying it until it clicks and you get it: "You cannot serve two masters." "Which master do I want to serve from now on?"

4 | INVOKING FREEDOM FROM THE CONTROL SELF

In the name I AM THAT I AM, Jesus Christ, I call to all representatives of the Divine Mother, especially Jesus, to help me overcome all compulsory tendency to want to control the world, other people or myself, including…

[Make personal calls.]

Part 1

1. Jesus, help me overcome the programming of denying myself as having a Christ potential and actually begin to exercise that Christ potential. Help me see why I have not manifested a higher degree of Christhood.

> O Jesus, blessed brother mine,
> I walk the path that you outline,
> a great example to us all,
> I follow now your inner call.

> O Jesus, let the Fire of Joy,
> consume the devil's subtle ploy,
> transfigured is our planet earth,
> the golden age is given birth.

2. Jesus, help me accept that the ascended masters do not judge me the way the fallen beings judge me and the way the fallen beings have managed to make me judge myself.

> O Jesus, open inner sight,
> the ego wants to prove it's right,
> but this I will no longer do,
> I want to be all one with you.

> **O Jesus, let the Fire of Joy,
> consume the devil's subtle ploy,
> transfigured is our planet earth,
> the golden age is given birth.**

3. Jesus, help me see that the goal of all ascended masters is to set me free. Help me see that a part of my mind says: "From what! From what do the masters want to set me free?" You want to set me free from the mind that asks this question because it is *that* mind that is keeping me trapped.

> O Jesus, I now clearly see,
> the Key of Knowledge given me,
> my Christ self I hereby embrace,
> as you fill up my inner space.

> **O Jesus, let the Fire of Joy,
> consume the devil's subtle ploy,
> transfigured is our planet earth,
> the golden age is given birth.**

4. Jesus, help me see that the mechanism that prevents me from expressing my Christhood is my birth trauma or earth trauma. When I first encountered the fallen beings and their unlimited willingness to do evil, it was a shock, it gave me a trauma.

O Jesus, show me serpent's lie,
expose the beam in my own eye,
as Christ discernment you me give,
in oneness I forever live.

**O Jesus, let the Fire of Joy,
consume the devil's subtle ploy,
transfigured is our planet earth,
the golden age is given birth.**

5. Jesus, help me see if I blame myself for reacting and think I should have been able to remain untouched by what is happening on earth, I should not have gotten my hands dirty.

O Jesus, I am truly meek,
and thus I turn the other cheek,
when the accuser attacks me,
I go within and merge with thee.

**O Jesus, let the Fire of Joy,
consume the devil's subtle ploy,
transfigured is our planet earth,
the golden age is given birth.**

6. Jesus, help me see that it is only a self that feels this way. Help me see that it is a self that is existing in my identity body but even reaches into the mental and emotional. Help me step back and separate myself from this self that thinks I should have been able to do things differently.

O Jesus, ego I let die,
surrender ev'ry earthly tie,
the dead can bury what is dead,
I choose to walk with you instead.

**O Jesus, let the Fire of Joy,
consume the devil's subtle ploy,
transfigured is our planet earth,
the golden age is given birth.**

7. Jesus, help me see that the one thing that prevents me from manifesting Christhood is my primal self. When I first encounter the fallen beings, it is a shock. It is such a shock that I literally cannot live with it, I cannot deal with it.

> O Jesus, help me rise above,
> the devil's test through higher love,
> show me separate self unreal,
> my formless self you do reveal.

> **O Jesus, let the Fire of Joy,**
> **consume the devil's subtle ploy,**
> **transfigured is our planet earth,**
> **the golden age is given birth.**

8. Jesus, help me see that I was in the physical body, I realized there are these beings who will do absolutely anything to hurt me and other people. I cannot get away from them but I cannot live with the knowledge that they are here, with the fear of what they will do next.

> O Jesus, what is that to me,
> I just let go and follow thee,
> with this I do pass ev'ry test,
> to find with you eternal rest.

> **O Jesus, let the Fire of Joy,**
> **consume the devil's subtle ploy,**
> **transfigured is our planet earth,**
> **the golden age is given birth.**

9. Jesus, help me see that by observing all the suffering they created, I was faced with a dilemma. I was here on earth, I could not get out of here so I had to find a way to exist here while knowing that the fallen beings also exist here. I dealt with this by creating the primal self.

> O Jesus, fiery master mine,
> my heart now melting into thine,
> I love with heart and mind and soul,
> the God who is my highest goal.

4 | Invoking freedom from the control self

**O Jesus, let the Fire of Joy,
consume the devil's subtle ploy,
transfigured is our planet earth,
the golden age is given birth.**

Part 2

1. Jesus, help me see that the primal self has this need to create an overall view of the earth, how it works, why God allows evil to exist, why there is evil on earth. Help me recognize that there is an aspect of the primal self that has as its primary task to make me feel somewhat safe, to give me some sense of equilibrium here on earth.

O Jesus, blessed brother mine,
I walk the path that you outline,
a great example to us all,
I follow now your inner call.

**O Jesus, let the Fire of Joy,
consume the devil's subtle ploy,
transfigured is our planet earth,
the golden age is given birth.**

2. Jesus, help me see that the primary task of the primal self is to restore in me some sense of equilibrium. It does this by creating a complex apparatus of selves to give me the sense of having my life on earth somewhat under control.

O Jesus, open inner sight,
the ego wants to prove it's right,
but this I will no longer do,
I want to be all one with you.

**O Jesus, let the Fire of Joy,
consume the devil's subtle ploy,
transfigured is our planet earth,
the golden age is given birth.**

3. Jesus, help me start looking at this aspect of the primal self, this self that has been attempting to control the world in order to make itself feel safe. The mechanism is simple: If I feel I am in control, then I can feel safe.

> O Jesus, I now clearly see,
> the Key of Knowledge given me,
> my Christ self I hereby embrace,
> as you fill up my inner space.
>
> **O Jesus, let the Fire of Joy,**
> **consume the devil's subtle ploy,**
> **transfigured is our planet earth,**
> **the golden age is given birth.**

4. Jesus, help me recognize that I have this tendency, and it is understandable and it is inevitable, but it is not inevitable that I carry this self with me for the rest of this lifetime.

> O Jesus, show me serpent's lie,
> expose the beam in my own eye,
> as Christ discernment you me give,
> in oneness I forever live.
>
> **O Jesus, let the Fire of Joy,**
> **consume the devil's subtle ploy,**
> **transfigured is our planet earth,**
> **the golden age is given birth.**

5. Jesus, help me throw off the heavy yoke of this security addict, this control-freak self that I have in my identity body. Help me come to look at it, see it for what it is, step back from it and realize: "This is not who I am. This is not who I am."

> O Jesus, I am truly meek,
> and thus I turn the other cheek,
> when the accuser attacks me,
> I go within and merge with thee.

**O Jesus, let the Fire of Joy,
consume the devil's subtle ploy,
transfigured is our planet earth,
the golden age is given birth.**

6. Jesus, help me see that this self represents a catch-22. I am trapped by that self, but when I start seeing that such a self exists, the self will react as if it is a matter of life and death to make me *not* accept this knowledge.

O Jesus, ego I let die,
surrender ev'ry earthly tie,
the dead can bury what is dead,
I choose to walk with you instead.

**O Jesus, let the Fire of Joy,
consume the devil's subtle ploy,
transfigured is our planet earth,
the golden age is given birth.**

7. Jesus, help me see the self that feels it has a certain grip of how the world works. It has things under control, it has worked out a system in itself that if only I do certain things and do not do other things, then I will be safe.

O Jesus, help me rise above,
the devil's test through higher love,
show me separate self unreal,
my formless self you do reveal.

**O Jesus, let the Fire of Joy,
consume the devil's subtle ploy,
transfigured is our planet earth,
the golden age is given birth.**

8. Jesus, help me see that the control self thinks the only way to feel safe on earth is to *not* be the Christ on earth, to not challenge the fallen beings. If I do not challenge the fallen beings by being the Christ, then they will leave me alone. The control self has a sense that it is safe as long as it stays within certain boundaries and does not do anything that challenges the fallen beings.

O Jesus, what is that to me,
I just let go and follow thee,
with this I do pass ev'ry test,
to find with you eternal rest.

**O Jesus, let the Fire of Joy,
consume the devil's subtle ploy,
transfigured is our planet earth,
the golden age is given birth.**

9. Jesus, help me see how I have used the teachings of the ascended masters to reinforce the control self's sense that it has the world under control. I have used the teachings to reinforce the world view of the control self.

O Jesus, fiery master mine,
my heart now melting into thine,
I love with heart and mind and soul,
the God who is my highest goal.

**O Jesus, let the Fire of Joy,
consume the devil's subtle ploy,
transfigured is our planet earth,
the golden age is given birth.**

Part 3

1. Jesus, I recognize that my goal in this lifetime is *not* to be comfortable at the level of being a student of the ascended masters and their teachings. My goal is to fulfill the highest potential of my Divine plan. My goal is to express Christhood at a higher level than I have done so far.

O Jesus, blessed brother mine,
I walk the path that you outline,
a great example to us all,
I follow now your inner call.

4 | Invoking freedom from the control self

> O Jesus, let the Fire of Joy,
> consume the devil's subtle ploy,
> transfigured is our planet earth,
> the golden age is given birth.

2. Jesus, help me see that I cannot be the Living Christ and at the same time maintain my sense of security and being in control. I cannot serve two masters, I cannot serve God and mammon, the mammon being a symbol for this aspect of the primal self that wants to feel it is always in control so it can feel safe.

> O Jesus, open inner sight,
> the ego wants to prove it's right,
> but this I will no longer do,
> I want to be all one with you.

> O Jesus, let the Fire of Joy,
> consume the devil's subtle ploy,
> transfigured is our planet earth,
> the golden age is given birth.

3. Jesus, help me look at this aspect of my primal self, separate myself from it and let it die.

> O Jesus, I now clearly see,
> the Key of Knowledge given me,
> my Christ self I hereby embrace,
> as you fill up my inner space.

> O Jesus, let the Fire of Joy,
> consume the devil's subtle ploy,
> transfigured is our planet earth,
> the golden age is given birth.

4. Jesus, help me see if I have created this momentum of isolating and insulating myself from the world, even using a spiritual teaching to set myself up in situations where I am isolated and insulated from the world.

O Jesus, show me serpent's lie,
expose the beam in my own eye,
as Christ discernment you me give,
in oneness I forever live.

O Jesus, let the Fire of Joy,
consume the devil's subtle ploy,
transfigured is our planet earth,
the golden age is given birth.

5. Jesus, help me see that when I acknowledge that I have an aspect of the primal self that wants to stay in control, I *will* be disturbed because this self will react by feeling it is threatened on its life.

O Jesus, I am truly meek,
and thus I turn the other cheek,
when the accuser attacks me,
I go within and merge with thee.

O Jesus, let the Fire of Joy,
consume the devil's subtle ploy,
transfigured is our planet earth,
the golden age is given birth.

6. Jesus, help me see that I no longer need that self so I can let it die. I see that the self does not want to die and it is willing to keep me trapped in the sense of being unsafe in order to maintain its own existence.

O Jesus, ego I let die,
surrender ev'ry earthly tie,
the dead can bury what is dead,
I choose to walk with you instead.

O Jesus, let the Fire of Joy,
consume the devil's subtle ploy,
transfigured is our planet earth,
the golden age is given birth.

7. Jesus, help me free myself from this aspect of the primal self and let it die, so I will have peace and feel such a new sense of freedom that I cannot even imagine it right now.

> O Jesus, help me rise above,
> the devil's test through higher love,
> show me separate self unreal,
> my formless self you do reveal.

> **O Jesus, let the Fire of Joy,**
> **consume the devil's subtle ploy,**
> **transfigured is our planet earth,**
> **the golden age is given birth.**

8. Jesus, help me experience that who I really am as a being in embodiment is a formless being that has come down into a world of form. In order to express myself in this world of form, I have to create these structures in my four lower bodies but I am not my own creation.

> O Jesus, what is that to me,
> I just let go and follow thee,
> with this I do pass ev'ry test,
> to find with you eternal rest.

> **O Jesus, let the Fire of Joy,**
> **consume the devil's subtle ploy,**
> **transfigured is our planet earth,**
> **the golden age is given birth.**

9. Jesus, help me see that when I created the primal self, I started thinking that this was who I am, or at least who I had to be in order to be safe on earth. Help me realize I am still a formless being, and as a formless being I cannot be hurt by whatever happens on earth.

> O Jesus, fiery master mine,
> my heart now melting into thine,
> I love with heart and mind and soul,
> the God who is my highest goal.

O Jesus, let the Fire of Joy,
consume the devil's subtle ploy,
transfigured is our planet earth,
the golden age is given birth.

Part 4

1. Jesus, I choose to rise above the death consciousness, the control self that thinks I am safe only if I have the world under control. I choose life by realizing I do not need to control the world in order to feel safe. I need to reconnect, re-awaken and become conscious of who I am as a formless being.

O Jesus, blessed brother mine,
I walk the path that you outline,
a great example to us all,
I follow now your inner call.

**O Jesus, let the Fire of Joy,
consume the devil's subtle ploy,
transfigured is our planet earth,
the golden age is given birth.**

2. Jesus, help me realize that I can be safe in this world even in the state it is in. I can be safe without having to control the world, and it is only when I feel safe without having to control the world that I can start expressing my Christhood. It is only *then* that I will dare to challenge the fallen beings.

O Jesus, open inner sight,
the ego wants to prove it's right,
but this I will no longer do,
I want to be all one with you.

**O Jesus, let the Fire of Joy,
consume the devil's subtle ploy,
transfigured is our planet earth,
the golden age is given birth.**

3. Jesus, help me get to the point where I have overcome the fear of the fallen beings. They are not running my life, they are not my frame of reference. The ascended masters, my I AM Presence, the world beyond form is my frame of reference and I feel safe in expressing Christhood.

> O Jesus, I now clearly see,
> the Key of Knowledge given me,
> my Christ self I hereby embrace,
> as you fill up my inner space.
>
> **O Jesus, let the Fire of Joy,
> consume the devil's subtle ploy,
> transfigured is our planet earth,
> the golden age is given birth.**

4. Jesus, help me see that an internal self is always created to deal with a certain problem on earth. The internal self will keep projecting that the problem is real, that the problem affects me and that I have to do something about it.

> O Jesus, show me serpent's lie,
> expose the beam in my own eye,
> as Christ discernment you me give,
> in oneness I forever live.
>
> **O Jesus, let the Fire of Joy,
> consume the devil's subtle ploy,
> transfigured is our planet earth,
> the golden age is given birth.**

5. Jesus, help me see this self for the unreality it is and say: "What is that to me, I will follow you, and let the dead bury their dead." I am willing to walk with you into a higher level of consciousness.

> O Jesus, I am truly meek,
> and thus I turn the other cheek,
> when the accuser attacks me,
> I go within and merge with thee.

**O Jesus, let the Fire of Joy,
consume the devil's subtle ploy,
transfigured is our planet earth,
the golden age is given birth.**

6. Jesus, I take the hand that you offer me and I walk with you until I am so anchored in Christ that I can look at this control self and say: "I no longer need you because now I have the hand of the ascended Jesus Christ and there is my safety. It is in Christ that I am safe, that I am saved, that I am secure, that I have my connection to oneness, that I know I am a formless being and therefore cannot be destroyed or threatened by anything in this world. It is in Christ I find my refuge, not in the outer self that wants to control the world."

O Jesus, ego I let die,
surrender ev'ry earthly tie,
the dead can bury what is dead,
I choose to walk with you instead.

**O Jesus, let the Fire of Joy,
consume the devil's subtle ploy,
transfigured is our planet earth,
the golden age is given birth.**

7. Jesus, I want life not death. I am ready to embrace this teaching. I want to separate myself from this primal self, leave its nets and walk with the Living Christ, leaving that self behind.

O Jesus, help me rise above,
the devil's test through higher love,
show me separate self unreal,
my formless self you do reveal.

**O Jesus, let the Fire of Joy,
consume the devil's subtle ploy,
transfigured is our planet earth,
the golden age is given birth.**

8. Jesus, help me see that I am ready and say: "It is just my control self that wants me to think I am not ready. In reality, I am ready and I am also willing."

> O Jesus, what is that to me,
> I just let go and follow thee,
> with this I do pass ev'ry test,
> to find with you eternal rest.
>
> **O Jesus, let the Fire of Joy,**
> **consume the devil's subtle ploy,**
> **transfigured is our planet earth,**
> **the golden age is given birth.**

9. Jesus, I am ready to take a decisive step forward, to leave something behind and embrace a new day. I am ready for a more direct encounter with the ascended masters. I will not forever sit here passively and listen to a messenger who has a connection to the ascended masters, for I am ready to establish a more direct connection for myself with the ascended masters.

> O Jesus, fiery master mine,
> my heart now melting into thine,
> I love with heart and mind and soul,
> the God who is my highest goal.
>
> **O Jesus, let the Fire of Joy,**
> **consume the devil's subtle ploy,**
> **transfigured is our planet earth,**
> **the golden age is given birth.**

Sealing

In the name of the Divine Mother, I call to Mother Mary for the sealing of myself and all people in my circle of influence in the creative flow of the Divine Mother, the River of Life. I call for the multiplication of my calls by all representatives of the Divine Mother, so that we form the perfect figure-eight flow of "As Above, so below." Thus, I accept that this is fully manifest, because the mouth of the Lord, the Divine Mother that I AM, has spoken it. Amen.

5 | ACCEPTING THAT CHRIST ACCEPTS YOU

I AM the Ascended Master Jesus Christ. I come to give you another installment in what I have planned to give you for this conference on how to be the Living Christ in action. Now my beloved, when I originally gave the *Master Keys to Personal Christhood,* I was facing the situation that I talked about this morning, that we have to look at where people are at in consciousness—where the collective consciousness is at, where the spiritual people are at, what we have released before, what we can release now. I gave a course that was meant to take people (even some people who have come from a Christian background and therefore had been brought up with a traditional view of Christ and Christianity) and reach out to them and give them something that could help them come closer to Christhood.

This has helped some people who were ready for it but, of course, it was not possible to really give a course at the time that could get people (who were not ready for it) over the hump and start expressing their Christhood. The reason for this was, as I explained this morning, that until you have confronted, seen through and let die this primal self, you really cannot begin to dare to express your Christhood because you are not free to express it.

What it means to be the Christ

Now that we have this teaching, we can, of course, give you more on what it means to be the Living Christ. Basically, what it means to be the Living Christ is to be a being who is not reacting to conditions on earth, who is not caught in a spiral of reacting to what you have experienced on earth. This means you do not react to earth through the filter of your primal self that sprang from your birth trauma. Truly, as long as you have the primal self, it will (as I explained last year) color the way you approach life on earth. In a sense, we could say that as long as you have that primal self, you cannot really be free to be the Christ because the primal self is created in reaction to what you experienced on earth.

As long as you are seeking to feel safe, feel secure, seeking to compensate for something you did in the past, then everything you do will spring from this need: the need to understand and put into a context, the need to be in control, the need to feel secure, the need to compensate. You will even use a spiritual teaching to try to fulfill this need. Therefore, you cannot really be the Christ because the Christ is the mediator between Spirit and the matter realm. You cannot be the mediator between Spirit and the matter realm until you have established a stronger connection to the spiritual realm and you dare to be free to express in the matter realm what comes through that connection.

If you are not connected to the spiritual realm, you cannot be the mediator. On the other hand, if you are not free to express whatever impulse comes through that connection, you cannot be the mediator either, at least not in the full capacity. You may say: "How then, have people achieved some degree of Christhood without having the teaching on the primal self?"

Well, it is, of course, not absolutely necessary to have a teaching on the primal self in order to overcome the primal self. What have we given you as a tool for overcoming the primal self? It is based on the key ingredient on the spiritual path: self-observation.

Throughout the ages, there have been people, a few people, who have been able to use that ability of the Conscious You to step outside of its current sense of self and observe yourself, your outer self, from without. Therefore, you can begin to separate yourself from it and so you can, of course, manifest a degree of Christhood. Some of you have done this even before you have received this teaching. Nevertheless, we give you the teaching because a critical mass of people are ready for it and can use it to accelerate their growth and get to this point where, instead of just having Christhood in glimpses, you can have it on a more ongoing basis. Many of you, who have a certain spiritual attainment from past lives, you have established some inner connection. Therefore, you have been able to express Christhood in certain moments. In many cases, you have not been able to do this to the full capacity that is in your Divine plan for this lifetime.

The hidden gift of Christ

What I will give you now is a teaching about how you can go further with expressing that Christhood. Again, I am assuming, of course, that if you are serious about this, you will make use of the teachings we have given in the *My Lives* book and in the book *Healing Your Spiritual Traumas* so you can begin to overcome that primal self. Once you begin to overcome the primal self, then it can help you to understand what I will give you here.

Now my beloved, I would like you to step back from the entire overlay that has been produced by official Christianity, especially in these past 17 centuries since the formation of the Roman Catholic church. I would like you to try and step back from all this—all the modern-day interpretations of Jesus and what it means to be the Christ. Step back and look at what you know about my actual life, what actually happened. What was I seeking to accomplish? What was it I really wanted to give people? Although this is not portrayed very well in the scriptures, there is at least some hints of it. I always attempted to give people an experience that there is more than their current level of consciousness, there is a higher level of consciousness than their current level of consciousness. Now, this is a very difficult task, or at least not a task that can be done in an absolute way because, as we have given you the teaching, there are 144 levels of consciousness on earth.

During that lifetime, during my three-year ministry, I met people at all 144 levels of consciousness, or I should say at least the lower levels of consciousness because I met few people at the 144th level. I had met some of them before the last three years of my ministry but during my ministry where I was in Palestine, I did not actually meet any at the higher levels of consciousness. Nevertheless, you meet a person who is at a very low level of consciousness, you cannot give that person the same that you give a person at a higher level of consciousness. There is no point in trying to give to people below the 48th level of consciousness what you can give to people above the 48th level, as they would not be able to grasp it. You have the story that I meet a man who is thirsty and I do not attempt to give him a spiritual teaching, I give him a cup of cold water in Christ's name. You see that I adapted my gift to where people were at in consciousness. However, what I want to tell you and teach you is that there is something that is not portrayed in the scriptures and that has not been understood by the majority of Christians or, for that matter, the majority of spiritual, New Age, mystical people. It is that whatever I could give people according to their level of consciousness, I gave them something else. Even when I gave someone a cup of cold water, there was something more conveyed from me to that person than the water itself. What was that something? Well, I will approach it in two ways.

You cannot understand Christ

Many of you, who are spiritual people, are very used to studying a teaching and seeking to understand that teaching. If you look at the spectrum of religious and spiritual people, you will see that there are many people who think (especially in this modern day where people are so affected by the logical, rational, linear thinking) that it is a matter of *understanding* a teaching. Grant you, you have the saying that: "The truth shall make you free" and people today interpret this to mean that the truth is an understanding. You are trapped by an illusion and once you have the understanding that dispels the illusion, you are free from the illusion. This, of course, is to a large degree correct. You *can* overcome illusions by coming to see that they are illusions and therefore you are free from them.

There is the old parable given in India that if you are holding something that you think is a snake, you are afraid, but when you see that it is just a rope, then the fear is gone. There is some validity to this but even though I also gave teachings and sought to give people understanding, that was not primarily what I attempted to give people. In fact, when I gave teachings, they were just a vehicle, just like the cup of cold water was a vehicle. The cup of cold water was a vehicle to give my greater gift to one person at a certain level of consciousness. The teachings were my vehicle to give to other people at another level of consciousness and so on and so forth. Whatever I gave, it was just a vehicle for giving what was the greater gift that I wanted to give. What was that greater gift? Well, here is the question to ask yourself: "Can I understand Christ with my linear, analytical mind? Can I fully *understand* Christ?" The answer is a very, very clear and very definitive "NO!" You cannot fully *understand* Christ. You can understand some aspects and some characteristics of Christ. You can understand the contrast between what is clearly antichrist and what is the higher understanding of Christ. There are things you can understand, but you cannot grasp the totality of Christ through understanding. "Wisdom is the principal thing and with all thy getting, get understanding." This is valid at a certain level but it will not take you beyond a certain level.

Understanding versus grasping

Given that we are in an intellectual age, I wish to introduce that there is a difference between *understanding* and *grasping*. You can understand something in a linear, analytical way without grasping it. You have the old saying that: "You cannot see the forest for the trees." You are so focused on the details that you cannot step back and look at the big picture. This is what the linear, analytical mind often does to people.

They are so focused on details that can be expressed in words that the linear mind can deal with, that it can analyze, categorize, label and put into nice little file folders and boxes in its database. Because they are so focused on these details, they cannot step back and look at the big picture. You cannot grasp Christ by looking at details, aspects. You can only grasp Christ fully when you step back and *experience* Christ. In other words, grasping Christ is not a matter of understanding, it is a matter of experiencing, it is an experiential matter, an experiential process, you might say. Whatever I gave to people when I was in embodiment, I always attempted to give them that greater gift so that they could experience that there is something beyond their present level of consciousness.

At least they could experience that *I* was beyond their present level of consciousness. I was at a higher level of consciousness and therefore it was possible to be at a higher level of consciousness. Of course, this was adapted to their level of consciousness. A person at the 3rd level of consciousness cannot grasp or experience Christ in the same fullness as one who is at the 96th level. No matter what level of consciousness you are at, you can experience that there is a step that is above yours because you can always grasp and experience the step that is right above the level you are at. What was it I attempted to give to people?

The Christ and free will

This is where you need to make use of all of the teachings we have given you because it is too much for me to give this in one dictation. I can only give you the highlights, then you will have to go and find the teaching that talks more about it, if there is a certain aspect of it you have not fully grasped. What we have given you is that free will is absolute, it is totally free.

When God gave extensions of itself free will, the Creator did not sit and create a standard for what was the right choices and the wrong choices. The Creator did not in its mind have a judgment of how people should exercise their free will. Therefore, the Creator gave free will and it was and it is completely *free*. The Creator's purpose for doing this is, of course, to create extensions of itself that can start with what we have called a point-like sense of self and gradually expand it until you reach the fullness of the Creator consciousness. The Creator is ultimately seeking to create other Creators. In order to grow to the level of Creator consciousness, you start out as a co-creator with a limited sense of self that you can gradually expand.

The only way to expand your sense of self is to have free will, to make choices. You create something, you experience that creation and then you evaluate based on your experience: "Do I want more of the same experience or do I want a higher experience. Do I want more *of* or do I want more *than?*"

In order for this process to unfold, the co-creators have to have completely free will because you have to have the option to do anything you can think of doing, anything you can imagine, anything you can envision. You have to be allowed to create it, experience the results of it and therefore gradually choose that you want a higher and higher experience. This is how the process works, this is how the process of the growth in consciousness works. You understand that we have given you these very profound, very elaborate, teachings on how the spheres were created. When a sphere is created, it is not permanent, the beings in it are not permanent and this is to give them the opportunity to do anything they want with free will.

Now of course, how can you have free will? This is a point that has often been misunderstood by human beings who have been misled by the fallen beings, who are always seeking to create doubt about everything. The fallen beings will want you to believe that having free will means you can do anything you want. Now, in a sense it is correct. When you have free will, you can do anything you want but how are you going to do anything? Well, you do something by formulating a matrix in your mind, projecting it on the Ma-ter light and the Ma-ter light then takes on the form of that. You now experience what you have created, or rather co-created.

If you did not experience the consequences of your choices, you would not have made any choices, you would not actually have exercised free will. If a choice does not have a consequence, it is not a choice and there is nothing you can learn from it. You can only learn by creating a consequence and experiencing the consequence. What the fallen beings want you to think is that if you create a consequence that limits you or that is unpleasant, then you should not have to experience that consequence. If you have really free will, you should be able to avoid the consequences.

My beloved, here is what the fallen beings do not grasp and what most people, quite frankly, do not grasp either because this planet has been so influenced by the fallen beings. You always have the option to escape the consequences of your previous choices. We have said it before: Anything you can co-create, you can also un-create. The trick, my beloved, is: "How do you project a matrix on the Ma-ter light?"

You create a self in your four lower bodies and you project through that self onto the Ma-ter light. When you are in a particular sense of self and projecting on the Ma-ter light, you create a particular consequence that is an out-picturing of that self. What the fallen beings want you to believe is that you should be able to escape the consequences without dissolving that self. The reality is that you *can* escape the consequences of your previous choices, but only by transcending the self through which you created those consequences. If you continue to project through that self, you will continue to re-create and re-create the same consequences. It is that simple, my beloved. *It is that simple.*

Growth through consequences

How do you learn? How do you grow? You grow by formulating a self based on your current sense of identity, maybe a very narrow point-like, self-centered sense of identity. You project through that self, you experience the consequence. If you want more of that consequence, you continue to project through that self until you have had enough of that experience. When you have had enough of the experience, you can step outside of that self or you can at least expand and refine that self and create a higher experience through the new self. This is how co-creation works. The fallen beings, of course, have managed to cause people to forget this. Nevertheless, the simple fact is this: Whatever you have co-created through one self, you can transcend by creating a new self and co-creating through that. Then, given the cycles of the material world, you will experience a new consequence.

What have I also said? God has no judgment of how you exercise your free will in an unascended sphere. In other words, God says you are allowed to come into embodiment with a point-like sense of self where you are naturally very focused on yourself. You are not able at that point to consider how your choices affect other people, how they affect the whole of the planet or the whole of the universe. You do not have that awareness. You are only focused on "me, myself and I." How does what I do affect myself? As you gradually expand your sense of self, you become able to become more and more aware of how your choices affect the whole. You become more and more aware that you are actually part of that whole. Therefore, you affect the whole and the whole affects you.

The way you grow in consciousness, when you come to that level, is that you refine your sense of self to become more and more one with the whole, more and more One. You come into oneness, rather than being focused on a separate self. Then, you can eventually come to the point where you are so in Oneness, you have actually let go of that separate self and then you can ascend. Then, you become a permanent being and eventually when a critical mass of the lifestreams, the co-creators, in a sphere have reached that point, then the whole sphere becomes permanent.

Building Christ consciousness

What does it take for you to come to the point where you have no desire to exercise your free will in a selfish manner? Well, it basically takes that you have to experience having done, not necessarily everything that can be done in a selfish manner but at least a critical mass of what can be done in a selfish manner to where you have personally had enough of it. God has no judgment as to how you go through that process. You have been given free will, you have been given a very, very long time span for you to explore all of the avenues of selfishness, of self-centeredness. When you have had enough of exploring those avenues, then you begin to transcend them. That is why we have given you the concept that you descend, and as you descend, you are in the immersion phase. You immerse yourself in life on earth or wherever you start your sojourn as a co-creator. You are immersing yourself in that environment, you are building a self based on that environment. Then, as you begin to awaken, you begin to expand your sense of self to being aware of the whole rather than being aware of a very small portion of it. You do this by going through this being immersed, identifying yourself as a separate self, projecting onto the Ma-ter light, experiencing the consequences. Then, when you have had enough of that, you begin to awaken. You begin to become aware of how your consequences affect, first, other people, then, the greater environment that you are in, then, the whole of the entire sphere. This is, in a sense, the Christ consciousness.

The Christ consciousness is the mediator between the Creator and his creation, between Spirit and matter, between the spiritual realm and the unascended sphere. The Christ consciousness is aware that there is a spiritual realm beyond this sphere. It is also aware that the sphere is a whole, that everything is connected, everything is One. Even science has now realized and proven through myriads of experiments that the entire universe is an interconnected whole. Nobody has begun to draw the philosophical consequences of this, but nevertheless they have proven it.

This is what you see through the Christ consciousness—you become aware of the whole. Now, as you rise in Christ consciousness, you, of course, also begin to have that outer understanding where you see the contrast between the illusions of duality, the lies of the fallen beings and the higher awareness of Christ that is based on an awareness of the whole, namely that everything is connected.

Making peace with free will

As you become aware of this, you begin to see through the illusions that the fallen beings have given about free will. You will, as part of this process (and this is what we have given you the tools to do with the primal self) come to a point where you can make peace with free will. You can accept free will, you can also make peace with being on earth, you can accept the earth as it is right now.

How can you accept the earth in its current highly imperfect state? Well, you can only do that when you accept free will and accept that the conditions you see on earth are an out-picturing in matter of what is found in the four lower bodies of a majority of human beings in embodiment. It is an out-picturing of the collective consciousness. It is necessary, because these people need to *experience*. As I have said, you need to experience certain things in order to grow. When you step into duality, which is what happens on an unnatural planet, then you need to see it out-pictured by physical matter because you are not able to learn it just in the mind.

We have said before that all of you are *experiential* beings. That is why we have given the perspective in the *My Lives* book that some of you have been embodied for a very long time on earth. You might consider, as I talked about earlier this year, that why does it take so long? Because there are a certain amount of experiences you need to have. When you begin to understand free will, you realize that there are people on earth who have not yet had enough of the kind of experiences that you see them having. You can come to a point where you accept this, you make peace with this. Therefore, you can free yourself from this judgment, this collective consciousness, this demon of judgment that the fallen beings have created that some things are wrong and some things should not be happening.

You can, as this messenger himself realized, even come to a point where you realize that even when people are suffering, their suffering is a result of choices they have made. They are not consciously aware of those choices, but nevertheless they still have the option to raise their awareness and begin to look at themselves instead of looking at the outer conditions.

You realize, my beloved, that as long as people are projecting that: "I am suffering because of outer conditions," then they are not teachable for a spiritual teacher. They become teachable only when they begin to consider whether there is something in their minds that is at least part of their suffering. My beloved, those people who are not teachable to a spiritual teacher, they need to see conditions out-pictured in matter—even if they do not realize and acknowledge that it is their own consciousness that is creating them. It is the only way they can eventually have enough of that experience and cry out for help.

My beloved, you can come to that point where you look at the equation on earth and you make peace with the way things are on earth. You make peace with you being on earth. However, you can only come to that point when you have at least begun to overcome the primal self because before that, your primal self will pull you into reacting to the way conditions are on earth. Therefore, you will judge those conditions through the primal self. The primal self, of course, can only see that since it caused your trauma and made you suffer, this is wrong and this should not be happening. You see, you cannot be a peace with free will and with conditions on earth through the primal self, only when you begin to separate yourself from it.

The acceptance of Christ

My beloved, when you come to that point where you have made peace with free will, you can come to another point that is the gift that I really wanted to give to all people. That is, you can understand that Christ accepts you for who you are no matter where you are at in consciousness. It will require quite some contemplation for all of you before you can fully grasp this because you have seventeen centuries of programming by official Christianity that wants you to believe that Christ will only accept you when you live up to certain conditions.

I will say this again. You have seventeen centuries of programming by the fallen beings that Christ will only accept you when you live up to certain conditions and those are conditions that can be defined here on earth—meaning, they are conditions that can be grasped by the dualistic, linear, even by the fallen, mind. Of course, Christ is beyond that mind and therefore these conditions could never be the conditions of the Christ mind. The fallen beings cannot grasp that the Christ mind has no conditions because the Creator has no conditions and the Christ mind knows how free will needs to outplay itself and how it needs to be done on an unnatural planet.

It knows that this is not the only type of planet, that there are billions of other planets. It has that greater perspective that it is not a disaster for the entire universe what is going on, on this little planet, called earth. When you are on earth, you want to think (because the fallen beings want you to think that earth is so important) that it is perhaps even the only planet in the entire universe and that God is so concerned about what is happening on earth.

In reality, when you have the Christ mind, you have the greater perspective where you can see that whatever is going on, on earth is not affecting the entire universe because this planet is so small that it cannot pull the rest of the universe down, given the billions of planets that are in an upward spiral. This is simply being allowed because the lifestreams who are in embodiment on earth have not had enough of that experience.

Now, when you have that perspective, when you yourself begin to experience this, you can come to a point where you can consciously ask yourself the question: "Does Christ or does Jesus (if you prefer to make it personal) accept me as I am right now?" When you ask yourself this question, and when you have started to separate yourself from the primal self, you can come to *experience* that yes I, Jesus Christ, accept you for who you are right now.

There are no conditions you have to fulfill in order to earn my acceptance. I have always accepted you for who you are right now. Even when some of you met me 2,000 years ago where you were in a much lower consciousness than you are today, I still accepted you for who you were back then. In these 2,000 years, some of you have carried with you this outer self based on the fallen judgment where you think that because you have not yet managed to live up to this standard of perfection, I still do not accept you today. As long as you are seeing the world through the filter of the primal self, you cannot overcome that. You will think (because the primal self can only think this way) that there must be *some* condition that you have to live up to in order for Christ to accept you—but it is a lie of the fallen beings.

When you begin to separate yourself from the primal self, you can come to the point where you can consciously ask yourself the question. Then, if you open your heart to me, I will give you (as you are able to receive it) the direct experience that I accept you for who you are right now. That is the experience that I wanted to give to all people 2,000 years ago and I want to give to them today.

Giving Jesus' acceptance to others

I am not in embodiment today, how can I give people that experience? I can only give it to other people through you, but you cannot be the instrument for me giving that experience to other people until you have had the experience yourself and you have accepted that I accept you.

What does it mean to be the Living Christ in action? Well, it means many things, of course, but what I want to put before you in this discourse, is that it means that you become an instrument for giving to all people you meet (regardless of their level of consciousness) the experience that you accept them for who they are and you have no judgment of them.

Now, I know that even after you have started separating yourself from your primal self, you still have other selves, as we have said before, that you have created in succeeding lifetimes after your first embodiment. This means that many of you will have to go through some clean-up where you start looking at these selves and see where you have built a self that has a standard that says: "Things have to be judged according to whether they are right or wrong, that there are some things that must be wrong and there are some things that must be right, there must be a truth and there must be a lie, there must be error." There must be this and there must be that. You can begin to separate yourself from these selves because you need to fix in your mind this one idea: Dualistic judgment has nothing to do with Christ discernment. Dualistic judgment has nothing to do with Christ discernment.

The fallen beings cannot have Christ discernment. They want you to think that you can actually refine dualistic judgment to the point where it gives you entry into the kingdom of heaven. Some of them believe this themselves. It cannot be done! With all the teachings we have given you on the fallen beings and the fall, you are able to see that it cannot be done.

Christ discernment—yes, there is an absolute truth that Christ discernment knows. Therefore, Christ discernment can see the errors and the lies. When you meet a person and you have Christ discernment, you can see that that person may be at a very selfish level of consciousness. They may believe in a lot of illusions, they may be doing actions that are clearly violating the free will of other human beings. My beloved, here is the essential realization: Even though you see a person's level of consciousness, even though you see their actions, you can still (when you are in the Christ mind) radiate to that person acceptance. Not acceptance of what they are doing, not acceptance of what they are believing but acceptance that behind all of these outer selves, there is a Conscious You that is an extension of the Creator's being.

God only wants to set people free

In some cases, when the Conscious You in that person experiences that unconditional acceptance from you, the Conscious You may snap out of the lower selves and reconnect and, at least in a brief glimpse, experience that it is an unconditional being, it is a formless being that is not bound by the conditions in form. My beloved, regardless of what you might think, the consequence of truly making peace with free will is that you realize that God has no desire to punish anyone no matter what they have done. God only has one desire: it is to set people free.

This means that you can meet a person in a lower state of consciousness but that person still deserves the opportunity to be free. Therefore, that person still deserves to receive that unconditional acceptance through you from the Living Christ, from the universal Christ, from the ascended Christ that I am. I am not asking you even to accept people with your outer mind. I am asking you to set aside the outer mind so you can be an open door for them being given an impulse of acceptance from me. Will you let *me* judge who is worthy to receive acceptance rather than letting *your outer mind* judge this? Then, you can take a momentous step, a decisive step, forward on your path to Christhood, a decisive step closer to being able to express Christhood to the full potential that you defined in your Divine plan.

Again, this does not mean that you accept everything people are doing. It does not mean that you do not challenge people. It does not mean that you do not in a calm and straightforward manner expose to them what they are doing. Beyond all of this, is that acceptance.

Now, if you take the book about *My Lives,* you will see that it is described in there how the protagonist encountered Lucifer when he was going through that final judgment and how the protagonist finally was able to express unconditional love towards Lucifer. This was the only thing that really brought forth a shift in Lucifer's mind. Now of course, you realize – I trust – that we used the name Lucifer in the book because it is the name that most people associate with fallen angels or dark beings. It does not mean that there has not been, in the long history of this planet, several fallen beings who have used the name Lucifer and who have then been brought to a judgment at another time than was described in the book. Again, do not be fixated on these outer things. Look beyond the outer things and realize that the important thing in the *My Lives* book is the story that is being told and what it symbolizes. My beloved, if Lucifer deserved unconditional acceptance, then surely any being you can meet for the rest of this lifetime deserves the same.

Suspending judgment

Again, will you suspend the judgment of your outer selves and let *me* be the judge of who deserves an impulse of acceptance through me? Of course, to do this you have to first experience that I accept you for who you are, even with the outer selves that you have, even with the tendency to judge that you might have. I accept you for who you are right now. I accept that God gave you the free will that has allowed you to create the sense of identity you have right now. I have no desire to scold you, to punish you, to make you feel bad. I only have a desire to offer you the unconditional acceptance that regardless of what you have done on earth, of what you have experienced in past lives, I only have one desire: to help you be free when you are willing to be free. That is the only desire of Christ.

There are many people who will not be able to accept what I say because they are still so trapped in the judgmental mind and the thinking that when you have done something really bad, such as kill millions of people, you deserve to be punished. My beloved, you do not need to be punished by God because you have already punished yourself. In order to kill millions of people, you have to put yourself in a state of consciousness that causes you intense suffering. Therefore, as long as you are in this state of consciousness, as many fallen beings have been for a very, very long time span, you are punishing yourself. Why would God need to add to that punishment when God sees that it is created through an unreal self?

You realize again: Free will is free in the sense that you can always rise above your previous creation. You can never make a choice that suspends your ability to make new choices. This will contradict what many of you have experienced. You have experienced making a choice at an early point in your life to do something and created consequences that might still be affecting you decades later. Yet, you understand, my beloved, you still have the option to separate yourself from the self through which you created those choices.

My beloved, here is an absolute truth: If you could fully separate yourself from that consciousness, you could actually undo the physical consequence. Many of you will not be able to fully overcome the previous self but you will be able to rise so much higher that you look at the consequences in a different way. Therefore, you are not suffering from them in the same way as you did.

You see, my beloved, as I said, the fallen beings want you to think that if you make a choice that you do not like, then if you really had free will, if free will was really free, you should not have to suffer the consequences. As I said, you still have free will even though you have made many, many, choices in past lives and you have created the sense of self you currently have. You may say: "But that sense of self has very few options, has very limited choices." And that is correct. You have created a limited self and it has limited options because, my beloved, for every time you create a self in the four lower bodies, you are limiting the options you can see, the choices you can see. You are seeing through the filter of that self and it is filtering out the other options.

You still, no matter how complex of a self you have created, you still have the option to start the awakening process, to start awakening from identification with those selves and, therefore, one-by-one letting them die—getting rid of those internal spirits. That option you always have and you can never lose it. Those of you who have been willing to go through this process, as some of you have, you will know that you have grown in freedom and that you look at life in a different way today than you did a few years ago.

I encourage you to look at how you react to this teaching. If you still feel that you do not fully grasp it, that you cannot fully accept it, if you still feel the pain of being limited and you are not sure that what I am telling you is really true, then seek out those who have gone further in the process than you have yourself. Talk to these people, listen to them, ask them to explain what were the insights that helped them. Then, you might find that they will inspire you to take the next step on your path so that you can also come to the point where you are now free. You have made peace with being on earth but, first of all, more than anything else, you can come to the point where you can accept yourself for who you are right now. Not that you think you are perfect and you do not need to grow, but you accept yourself because you have experienced my acceptance of you.

Again, my beloved, will you please consider suspending your judgment of yourself and stop projecting upon me that I am judging you the way you judge yourself—and because you judge yourself as being imperfect, I could not possibly accept you. Will you please allow me to be the judge of whether I will accept you? Therefore, you put yourself in a state of mind where you say: "Oh, I'm not the judge of whether Jesus accepts me. It is up to Jesus to judge and so I have to be completely open to experiencing whatever Jesus wants to give me. I cannot be judging that Jesus couldn't accept me because then I'm not open to him, I'm not letting him be the judge."

You can work on this, coming to a point where you put yourself in a neutral state of mind. If you can be neutral, you will experience my acceptance of you. Why? Because right now I am standing next to each and every one of you and I am holding out my hands and saying: "Will you please accept my total unconditional acceptance of you?" I am offering, my beloved. If you do not experience my offering, it can only be because you are consciously or subconsciously rejecting it. The gift is given. Will you accept it?" Then, with gratitude for that acceptance, I thank you for your attention and for being the instruments for radiating this into the collective consciousness.

6 | INVOKING THE ACCEPTANCE OF CHRIST

In the name I AM THAT I AM, Jesus Christ, I call to all representatives of the Divine Mother, especially Jesus, to help me overcome all illusions and selves that prevent me from accepting that Christ accepts me, including…

[Make personal calls.]

Part 1

1. Jesus, help me see that what it means to be the Living Christ is to be a being who is not reacting to conditions on earth, who is not caught in a spiral of reacting to what I have experienced on earth. I do not react to earth through the filter of my primal self that sprang from my birth trauma.

> O Jesus, blessed brother mine,
> I walk the path that you outline,
> a great example to us all,
> I follow now your inner call.

**O Jesus, let the Fire of Joy,
consume the devil's subtle ploy,
transfigured is our planet earth,
the golden age is given birth.**

2. Jesus, help me see that as long as I have the primal self, it will color the way I approach life on earth. I am not free to be the Christ because the primal self is created in reaction to what I experienced on earth.

O Jesus, open inner sight,
the ego wants to prove it's right,
but this I will no longer do,
I want to be all one with you.

**O Jesus, let the Fire of Joy,
consume the devil's subtle ploy,
transfigured is our planet earth,
the golden age is given birth.**

3. Jesus, help me see that as long as I am seeking to feel safe, feel secure, seeking to compensate for something I did in the past, then everything I do will spring from this need: the need to understand and put into a context, the need to be in control, the need to feel secure, the need to compensate.

O Jesus, I now clearly see,
the Key of Knowledge given me,
my Christ self I hereby embrace,
as you fill up my inner space.

**O Jesus, let the Fire of Joy,
consume the devil's subtle ploy,
transfigured is our planet earth,
the golden age is given birth.**

4. Jesus, help me see that the Christ is the mediator between Spirit and the matter realm. I cannot be the mediator between Spirit and matter until I have established a stronger connection to the spiritual realm and I dare to be free to express in the matter realm what comes through that connection.

> O Jesus, show me serpent's lie,
> expose the beam in my own eye,
> as Christ discernment you me give,
> in oneness I forever live.
>
> **O Jesus, let the Fire of Joy,
> consume the devil's subtle ploy,
> transfigured is our planet earth,
> the golden age is given birth.**

5. Jesus, help me step back from the overlay that has been produced by official Christianity and see that what you really wanted to give people was an experience that there is more than their current level of consciousness, there is a higher level of consciousness.

> O Jesus, I am truly meek,
> and thus I turn the other cheek,
> when the accuser attacks me,
> I go within and merge with thee.
>
> **O Jesus, let the Fire of Joy,
> consume the devil's subtle ploy,
> transfigured is our planet earth,
> the golden age is given birth.**

6. Jesus, help me see that I cannot understand Christ with my linear, analytical mind, I cannot fully *understand* Christ because there is a difference between *understanding* and *grasping*. I cannot grasp Christ by looking at details, only when I step back and *experience* Christ.

> O Jesus, ego I let die,
> surrender ev'ry earthly tie,
> the dead can bury what is dead,
> I choose to walk with you instead.
>
> **O Jesus, let the Fire of Joy,
> consume the devil's subtle ploy,
> transfigured is our planet earth,
> the golden age is given birth.**

7. Jesus, help me see that the only way to expand my sense of self is to have free will, to make choices. I create something, I experience that creation and then I evaluate based on my experience: "Do I want more of the same experience or do I want a higher experience. Do I want more *of* or do I want more *than?*"

> O Jesus, help me rise above,
> the devil's test through higher love,
> show me separate self unreal,
> my formless self you do reveal.
>
> **O Jesus, let the Fire of Joy,**
> **consume the devil's subtle ploy,**
> **transfigured is our planet earth,**
> **the golden age is given birth.**

8. Jesus, help me see that in order for this process to unfold, I must have a completely free will, so I can do anything I can imagine and then experience the consequences. I co-create by creating a self in my four lower bodies and I project through that self onto the Ma-ter light.

> O Jesus, what is that to me,
> I just let go and follow thee,
> with this I do pass ev'ry test,
> to find with you eternal rest.
>
> **O Jesus, let the Fire of Joy,**
> **consume the devil's subtle ploy,**
> **transfigured is our planet earth,**
> **the golden age is given birth.**

9. Jesus, help me see that I can escape the consequences of my previous choices by transcending the self through which I created those consequences. If I continue to project through that self, I will continue to re-create the same consequences.

> O Jesus, fiery master mine,
> my heart now melting into thine,

I love with heart and mind and soul,
the God who is my highest goal.

**O Jesus, let the Fire of Joy,
consume the devil's subtle ploy,
transfigured is our planet earth,
the golden age is given birth.**

Part 2

1. Jesus, help me see that in order to come to the point where I have no desire to exercise my free will in a selfish manner, I have to experience having done a critical mass of what can be done in a selfish manner so that I have personally had enough of it.

O Jesus, blessed brother mine,
I walk the path that you outline,
a great example to us all,
I follow now your inner call.

**O Jesus, let the Fire of Joy,
consume the devil's subtle ploy,
transfigured is our planet earth,
the golden age is given birth.**

2. Jesus, help me see that God has no judgment of how I go through that process. When I have had enough of co-creating through a separate self, the Christ consciousness is the mediator that allows me to rise above being self-focused.

O Jesus, open inner sight,
the ego wants to prove it's right,
but this I will no longer do,
I want to be all one with you.

> **O Jesus, let the Fire of Joy,**
> **consume the devil's subtle ploy,**
> **transfigured is our planet earth,**
> **the golden age is given birth.**

3. Jesus, help me make peace with free will so I can accept that the conditions I see on earth are an out-picturing in matter of what is found in the four lower bodies of a majority of human beings. This is necessary, because people need to *experience* in order to grow.

> O Jesus, I now clearly see,
> the Key of Knowledge given me,
> my Christ self I hereby embrace,
> as you fill up my inner space.

> **O Jesus, let the Fire of Joy,**
> **consume the devil's subtle ploy,**
> **transfigured is our planet earth,**
> **the golden age is given birth.**

4. Jesus, help me accept that there are people on earth who have not yet had enough of the kind of experiences they are having. Help me make peace with this so I am free from this judgment, this collective consciousness, this demon of judgment that the fallen beings have created, saying that some things are wrong and some things should not be happening.

> O Jesus, show me serpent's lie,
> expose the beam in my own eye,
> as Christ discernment you me give,
> in oneness I forever live.

> **O Jesus, let the Fire of Joy,**
> **consume the devil's subtle ploy,**
> **transfigured is our planet earth,**
> **the golden age is given birth.**

5. Jesus, help me realize that even when people are suffering, their suffering is a result of choices they have made. They are not consciously aware of those choices, but nevertheless they still have the option to raise their awareness and begin to look at themselves instead of looking at the outer conditions.

> O Jesus, I am truly meek,
> and thus I turn the other cheek,
> when the accuser attacks me,
> I go within and merge with thee.
>
> **O Jesus, let the Fire of Joy,**
> **consume the devil's subtle ploy,**
> **transfigured is our planet earth,**
> **the golden age is given birth.**

6. Jesus, help me look at the equation on earth and make peace with the way things are on earth. Help me make peace with me being on earth.

> O Jesus, ego I let die,
> surrender ev'ry earthly tie,
> the dead can bury what is dead,
> I choose to walk with you instead.
>
> **O Jesus, let the Fire of Joy,**
> **consume the devil's subtle ploy,**
> **transfigured is our planet earth,**
> **the golden age is given birth.**

7. Jesus, help me see that the gift you really wanted to give to all people is the awareness that Christ accepts us for who we are no matter where we are at in consciousness. Help me overcome the programming by official Christianity that wants me to believe that Christ will only accept me when I live up to certain conditions.

> O Jesus, help me rise above,
> the devil's test through higher love,
> show me separate self unreal,
> my formless self you do reveal.

> **O Jesus, let the Fire of Joy,**
> **consume the devil's subtle ploy,**
> **transfigured is our planet earth,**
> **the golden age is given birth.**

8. Jesus, help me see that Christ is beyond the fallen beings and therefore their conditions could never be the conditions of the Christ mind. The fallen beings cannot grasp that the Christ mind has no conditions because the Creator has no conditions. The Christ mind knows how free will needs to outplay itself and how it needs to be done on an unnatural planet.

> O Jesus, what is that to me,
> I just let go and follow thee,
> with this I do pass ev'ry test,
> to find with you eternal rest.

> **O Jesus, let the Fire of Joy,**
> **consume the devil's subtle ploy,**
> **transfigured is our planet earth,**
> **the golden age is given birth.**

9. Jesus, help me see the Christ perspective that it is not a disaster for the entire universe what is happening on this little planet. Help me overcome the illusion of the fallen beings that earth is so important and that God is so concerned about what is happening on earth.

> O Jesus, fiery master mine,
> my heart now melting into thine,
> I love with heart and mind and soul,
> the God who is my highest goal.

> **O Jesus, let the Fire of Joy,**
> **consume the devil's subtle ploy,**
> **transfigured is our planet earth,**
> **the golden age is given birth.**

Part 3

1. Jesus, help me come to the point where I can consciously ask myself the question: "Does Jesus accept me as I am right now?" Help me *experience* that you do accept me for who I am right now.

> O Jesus, blessed brother mine,
> I walk the path that you outline,
> a great example to us all,
> I follow now your inner call.
>
> **O Jesus, let the Fire of Joy,**
> **consume the devil's subtle ploy,**
> **transfigured is our planet earth,**
> **the golden age is given birth.**

2. Jesus, help me accept that there are no conditions I have to fulfill in order to earn your acceptance. You have always accepted me for who I am in that moment.

> O Jesus, open inner sight,
> the ego wants to prove it's right,
> but this I will no longer do,
> I want to be all one with you.
>
> **O Jesus, let the Fire of Joy,**
> **consume the devil's subtle ploy,**
> **transfigured is our planet earth,**
> **the golden age is given birth.**

3. Jesus, help me overcome the outer self, based on the fallen judgment, that thinks that because I have not yet managed to live up to this standard of perfection, you do not accept me.

> O Jesus, I now clearly see,
> the Key of Knowledge given me,
> my Christ self I hereby embrace,
> as you fill up my inner space.

> O Jesus, let the Fire of Joy,
> consume the devil's subtle ploy,
> transfigured is our planet earth,
> the golden age is given birth.

4. Jesus, help me see that the primal self can only think that there must be *some* condition that I have to live up to in order for Christ to accept me. Help me see that this is a lie of the fallen beings.

> O Jesus, show me serpent's lie,
> expose the beam in my own eye,
> as Christ discernment you me give,
> in oneness I forever live.

> O Jesus, let the Fire of Joy,
> consume the devil's subtle ploy,
> transfigured is our planet earth,
> the golden age is given birth.

5. Jesus, I open my heart to you and I am willing to receive the direct experience that you accept me for who I am right now.

> O Jesus, I am truly meek,
> and thus I turn the other cheek,
> when the accuser attacks me,
> I go within and merge with thee.

> O Jesus, let the Fire of Joy,
> consume the devil's subtle ploy,
> transfigured is our planet earth,
> the golden age is given birth.

6. Jesus, help me see that this is the experience you want to give to all people. You can give it to other people through me, but I cannot be the instrument for you giving that experience to other people until I have had the experience myself and I have accepted that you accept me.

> O Jesus, ego I let die,
> surrender ev'ry earthly tie,

the dead can bury what is dead,
I choose to walk with you instead.

**O Jesus, let the Fire of Joy,
consume the devil's subtle ploy,
transfigured is our planet earth,
the golden age is given birth.**

7. Jesus, help me become an instrument for giving to all people I meet the experience that you, Jesus, accept them for who they are and you have no judgment of them.

O Jesus, help me rise above,
the devil's test through higher love,
show me separate self unreal,
my formless self you do reveal.

**O Jesus, let the Fire of Joy,
consume the devil's subtle ploy,
transfigured is our planet earth,
the golden age is given birth.**

8. Jesus, help me go through the clean-up where I start seeing any other selves and see where I have built a self that has a standard that says: "Things have to be judged according to whether they are right or wrong." Help me separate myself from these selves.

O Jesus, what is that to me,
I just let go and follow thee,
with this I do pass ev'ry test,
to find with you eternal rest.

**O Jesus, let the Fire of Joy,
consume the devil's subtle ploy,
transfigured is our planet earth,
the golden age is given birth.**

9. Jesus, help me fix in my mind the idea that dualistic judgment has nothing to do with Christ discernment. Dualistic judgment has nothing to do with Christ discernment.

> O Jesus, fiery master mine,
> my heart now melting into thine,
> I love with heart and mind and soul,
> the God who is my highest goal.
>
> **O Jesus, let the Fire of Joy,**
> **consume the devil's subtle ploy,**
> **transfigured is our planet earth,**
> **the golden age is given birth.**

Part 4

1. Jesus, help me realize that even though I see a person's level of consciousness, when I am in the Christ mind, I can still radiate to that person acceptance. Not acceptance of what they are doing, not acceptance of what they are believing but acceptance that behind all of these outer selves there is a Conscious You that is an extension of the Creator's Being.

> O Jesus, blessed brother mine,
> I walk the path that you outline,
> a great example to us all,
> I follow now your inner call.
>
> **O Jesus, let the Fire of Joy,**
> **consume the devil's subtle ploy,**
> **transfigured is our planet earth,**
> **the golden age is given birth.**

2. Jesus, help me see that I can meet a person in a lower state of consciousness but that person still deserves the opportunity to be free. The person still deserves to receive that unconditional acceptance through me from the Living Christ, from the universal Christ, from the ascended Christ that you are.

> O Jesus, open inner sight,
> the ego wants to prove it's right,
> but this I will no longer do,
> I want to be all one with you.
>
> **O Jesus, let the Fire of Joy,**
> **consume the devil's subtle ploy,**
> **transfigured is our planet earth,**
> **the golden age is given birth.**

3. Jesus, I will let *you* judge who is worthy to receive acceptance rather than letting *my outer mind* judge this. Help me take that decisive step closer to being able to express Christhood to the full potential that I defined in my Divine plan.

> O Jesus, I now clearly see,
> the Key of Knowledge given me,
> my Christ self I hereby embrace,
> as you fill up my inner space.
>
> **O Jesus, let the Fire of Joy,**
> **consume the devil's subtle ploy,**
> **transfigured is our planet earth,**
> **the golden age is given birth.**

4. Jesus, I will suspend the judgment of my outer selves and let you be the judge of who deserves an impulse of acceptance through me. Help me experience that you accept me for who I am, even with the outer selves that I have. You accept that God gave me the free will that has allowed me to create the sense of identity I have right now.

> O Jesus, show me serpent's lie,
> expose the beam in my own eye,

as Christ discernment you me give,
in oneness I forever live.

**O Jesus, let the Fire of Joy,
consume the devil's subtle ploy,
transfigured is our planet earth,
the golden age is given birth.**

5. Jesus, help me experience your unconditional acceptance and accept that regardless of what I have done on earth, of what I have experienced in past lives, you only have one desire: to help me be free when I am willing to be free. And I am indeed willing to be free.

O Jesus, I am truly meek,
and thus I turn the other cheek,
when the accuser attacks me,
I go within and merge with thee.

**O Jesus, let the Fire of Joy,
consume the devil's subtle ploy,
transfigured is our planet earth,
the golden age is given birth.**

6. Jesus, help me accept the absolute truth that if I could fully separate myself from a dualistic self, I could actually undo the physical consequence created through that self. Help me see that no matter how complex of a set of selves I have created, I still have the option to start the awakening process and let them die.

O Jesus, ego I let die,
surrender ev'ry earthly tie,
the dead can bury what is dead,
I choose to walk with you instead.

**O Jesus, let the Fire of Joy,
consume the devil's subtle ploy,
transfigured is our planet earth,
the golden age is given birth.**

7. Jesus, help me come to the point where I can accept myself for who I am right now and experience your acceptance of me. Jesus, I am suspending my judgment of myself. I stop projecting upon you that you are judging me the way I judge myself. I will allow *you* to be the judge of whether you will accept me.

> O Jesus, help me rise above,
> the devil's test through higher love,
> show me separate self unreal,
> my formless self you do reveal.

> **O Jesus, let the Fire of Joy,**
> **consume the devil's subtle ploy,**
> **transfigured is our planet earth,**
> **the golden age is given birth.**

8. Jesus, I hereby say: "I am not the judge of whether Jesus accepts me. It is up to Jesus to judge. I am completely open to experiencing whatever Jesus wants to give me. I cannot be judging that Jesus couldn't accept me because then I'm not open to him, I'm not letting him be the judge." Help me be in a neutral state of mind and experience your acceptance of me.

> O Jesus, what is that to me,
> I just let go and follow thee,
> with this I do pass ev'ry test,
> to find with you eternal rest.

> **O Jesus, let the Fire of Joy,**
> **consume the devil's subtle ploy,**
> **transfigured is our planet earth,**
> **the golden age is given birth.**

9. Jesus, I know that right now you are standing next to me and you are holding out your hands and saying: "Will you please accept my total unconditional acceptance of you?" Jesus, I will indeed accept your gift.

> O Jesus, fiery master mine,
> my heart now melting into thine,

I love with heart and mind and soul,
the God who is my highest goal.

**O Jesus, let the Fire of Joy,
consume the devil's subtle ploy,
transfigured is our planet earth,
the golden age is given birth.**

Sealing

In the name of the Divine Mother, I call to Mother Mary for the sealing of myself and all people in my circle of influence in the creative flow of the Divine Mother, the River of Life. I call for the multiplication of my calls by all representatives of the Divine Mother, so that we form the perfect figure-eight flow of "As Above, so below." Thus, I accept that this is fully manifest, because the mouth of the Lord, the Divine Mother that I AM, has spoken it. Amen.

7 | GRASPING THE PROGRESSIVENESS OF REVELATION

I AM the Ascended Master MORE, or as I have been known in previous dispensations: El Morya, Master M, Bapu or just Morya, so I am a man of many names. I am more than a name, and therefore I try to stay ahead of the students who attach a certain idolatrous image to a particular name. I am fully aware that many students will and already have rejected anything I say today because I have changed the name from El Morya to Master MORE. This is, however, as it should be, for there are students who *should* reject what I am saying for they are not part of the mandala, the dispensation, for which I am saying this. Yet there are some students who can, if they are willing to open their minds, benefit from what I am saying.

Each time we sponsor an organization, and we have sponsored more than you know of (most of you), then there is a certain group of people, a certain mandala of people, for which we sponsor that organization. There are others that are not meant to be part of that organization. When we then move on to a new organization, it is fit and natural that those who were part of the mandala from the previous organization do not move on with us. Yet, there will always be in an organization some people who are not part of that mandala for which the organization was created and who, therefore, are free to move on with us when we move on.

The spiritual path then and now

Now my beloved, I would like to start by talking about the question that was asked last night about how we presented the spiritual path in the previous dispensation of the Summit Lighthouse, even going back to the I AM Movement. I will talk about the contrast between that and how we present it today with these latest teachings based on how to express Christhood but also the teachings on the primal self, the Conscious You, being a co-creator, expressing your creative potential—the teachings we have given over the last few years. As the messenger pointed out, there is no inherent contradiction but if you look at it from a certain perspective, there will be a contradiction. You understand that the previous dispensation of the Summit Lighthouse was created primarily to help a certain mandala of people pass certain initiations that for them were critical initiations.

It was critical for their personal growth that they would pass these initiations and it was critical for the planet that a certain number of people, a critical mass of people, would pass these initiations. The Summit Lighthouse attracted many more people than were part of that mandala. They benefited from the Summit Lighthouse, they added much to the organization, they added much to the momentum and actually ensured that we got more of a return from that organization than we could have gotten from the people in the mandala. There were also many spiritual people that did not come into the Summit Lighthouse, partly because we did not direct them to come into it. These are some of the topics that I wish to discuss here.

The last dispensation of the Piscean age

We begin with the fact that the Summit Lighthouse was, as Jesus has expressed previously, the last dispensation (or at least the last public dispensation) we could sponsor in the Piscean age. This does not mean, as some interpreted it to be, that it was the most important, final or absolute teaching on the Piscean age that was given. The Summit Lighthouse was created for a variety of purposes but the purpose I am discussing here, of the original mandala for which it was created, was a very specific purpose. It was to help a certain group of lifestreams pass the initiations of the Piscean age that they had not passed during the Piscean Age.

You could say it this way: When the planet moves into a new spiritual age, when the planet moved from the previous into the Piscean age, then there is a certain group of people that, from a certain perspective, we could say that they are driving the planetary growth for that 2,000-year period. In other words, they are at a level of their personal growth where they have the potential to pass the initiations of the coming age. Therefore, by taking embodiment in that age, they can drive the spiritual growth, the growth in the Christ consciousness for that age. However, for them to drive the collective consciousness, they have to pass the initiations of the age, the foundational initiations of the age.

Each age has certain foundational initiations. Two thousand years ago Jesus inaugurated the Piscean age; he set the foundation for the Piscean age. In his complete, original teachings he gave the initiations. Even in the public teachings preserved in the scriptures you can find at least a critical mass of these initiations described, sometimes between the lines and sometimes in a more direct manner.

I am not here going to say that the scriptures about Jesus' life and words describe these initiations in their complete form, they certainly do not. But Jesus did give a certain matrix that could have been developed into the kind of movement that he envisioned, a movement that was based on the Holy Spirit, based on the Living Word being spoken. This could have driven the Piscean age, the growth in the collective consciousness.

People did not pass the Piscean initiations

As it happened, there were not enough people among that original mandala that were able to pass the initiations in the early centuries of that age. That is why it was possible for the fallen beings to step in, turn the Christian movement into the state religion of the Roman empire and from that moment on Christianity was basically damaged beyond repair. This meant that there was no public teaching available for how people could pass the initiations of the Piscean age.

This was, of course, not the original plan but as we always do, we respect free will (and I am saying "we" as the ascended masters because, obviously, during the Piscean Age I was not myself an ascended master, so

I was not part of these deliberations). The ascended masters always look at how people respond to the initiations. No matter how people respond or do not respond, we always seek to come up with something that can help them come up higher.

During the Piscean Age there was a certain inspiration and sponsorship for certain organizations. These were during the time when the Catholic church was persecuting all "non-believers." They were secret organizations: the Rosicrucians, the Freemasons have been mentioned among others. We also sponsored initiatives and organizations in other parts of the world where the Catholic influence was not so strong. I do not want you to limit your view of this to think that there were only these few organizations that we worked with. We worked, as we always do, with many individuals and groups of people who are open to our teachings at some level.

Nevertheless, what I wish to make you aware of here is that as we came closer to the end of the Piscean Age, it became clear that there was not a critical mass of that original Piscean mandala, there was not a critical mass of those lifestreams, who had passed the initiations of Pisces. It was determined (and this time I was part of the deliberations, as I had ascended) that we would start another organization for the primary purpose of helping these lifestreams master the initiations of Pisces. When you look at the Summit Lighthouse, it was primarily set up to give this particular group of lifestreams the initiations they needed at the end of the Piscean Age.

Was I myself part of the mandala at the beginning of the Piscean Age? Yes, I Was. So was Kuthumi, so was Saint Germain, so, of course, was Mother Mary. Mother Mary ascended very quickly, Saint Germain took longer. Kuthumi and I formed the rear and took a long time to ascend but nevertheless we ascended. Therefore, it was determined that I would be the main sponsor of the organization of the Summit Lighthouse.

You realize that the entire purpose (or at least the primary purpose) was to look at this specific mandala of lifestreams, those who had not passed the initiations of Pisces. This was, if you want to use a modern terminology, a form of crisis management. In other words, we were nearing the end of the Piscean Age, the sand in the hourglass was running out, these lifestreams had not passed the initiations. I am not saying that all of the lifestreams in that original mandala of Pisces had to pass the initiations during the 2,000-year period. I am saying that a critical mass had to pass them and we had not reached that critical mass at the time. As a form of crisis management, we deliberated and determined what could we do to help these lifestreams (at least a critical mass of them) get over the hump

7 | *Grasping the progressiveness of revelation*

and pass the initiations of Pisces. Those deliberations were the foundational matrix for the Summit Lighthouse and basically everything that took place in that organization in some ways relates to this purpose.

The Piscean initiations

What were the initiations that people had to pass, and not just that original mandala but mankind as a whole, during Pisces? Well, you can look at Jesus' life and you can look at the matrix he set. Then, you can look at the teachings we have given you and, of course, my beloved, you could express this in a variety of ways. There is not just one way to explain this in words, there is a variety of ways. You could use different vocabulary. I do not wish to give the impression that the way I will express it here is the only way that this could be expressed.

Certainly, one way to express it is to say: During the Piscean Age people were meant to free themselves from being dominated and enslaved by the fallen beings. How do you free yourself from the fallen beings? Only by attaining the Christ consciousness. The Christ consciousness is the mediator between Spirit and matter, it is the one sent. Why? Not to save you, as the Christian churches claim, but to give you a frame of reference so that when you, not *understand* but *experience* the Christ consciousness, you have that frame of reference. You can compare all of the lies and illusions sent at you, programmed into your subconscious minds by the fallen beings, to that rock of Christ.

You see that all of these illusions and philosophies and theories and –isms are just sand that is blowing in the wind. You can compare it to the rock that is immovable in the sense that it is not dualistic. It is, of course, not immovable because the Christ is moving with the upward movement of the entire universe so, in a sense, the Christ is always moving on. For you who are in embodiment on an unnatural planet dominated by duality, it is the rock that you can lean upon that is your firm foundation for evaluating the ideas of the fallen beings.

We could say, then, that the initiations that people were meant to pass during Pisces was that people would follow the example set by Jesus, believe on him, do the works that he did and then eventually do greater works than he did. As we have said many times before, follow the example rather than expecting Jesus to come and save them in the end. The question now becomes: "How can people actually follow the example of

Jesus?" You can look back and you can argue that because people did not have a written record of Jesus' true teachings, they had no ability to follow his example, they could not pass the initiations—there was a gap.

The gap between teaching and application

This is a topic I wish to discourse on: the gap. The question becomes: Let us assume here that there was no interference from the fallen beings. In other words, there was nothing that prevented the ascended masters from bringing forth into the physical octave exactly what we wanted to bring forth. Would it be possible for us to bring forth a teaching that was so complete that anyone who followed and applied the teaching would attain the Christ consciousness?

Many of you, if you examine your reaction to this question, will find that in your consciousness there is somewhere the belief that: Yes, this should be possible. Now, my beloved, again we are not seeking to blame you or make you feel bad, but I must be straightforward with you and say that this belief is an illusion and it is a potentially dangerous illusion. It is actually the illusion that is the primary reason so many people from the original mandala of Pisces did not pass the initiations of Pisces.

I wish to give you a slight historical overview here. There are people who have said: "Why didn't Jesus write down his true teachings so that people had a complete written record and therefore they had something they could take and use?" Well, this question I will answer later but we can see, as a historical fact, that Jesus *did not* write down his complete teachings, he did not leave a written record.

For the first several hundred years, Christianity was a somewhat chaotic, diversified movement with many different groups and sects, partly because of the lack of communication at the time and partly because it was meant to be that different people, different groups of people, would experiment with Christianity in their own ways.

Then, comes that critical moment in history where the fallen beings in the identity realm managed to convince a fallen being in embodiment that he had had a vision of Christ and therefore he turned the Christian movement into the state religion of the Roman Empire. From that moment on, the fallen beings were firmly in control of Christianity. You can see throughout the Middle Ages how they used that control of the Christian religion to exert influence and control over Western Europe or European society. What happened during that time is that certain organizations sprang up in secret: the Rosicrucians, the Freemasons and so on. These organizations were based on a gradual path, a step-by-step path that would lead you towards higher levels of consciousness or at least higher levels of initiation. We then see that gradually there came this point where the influence of the Catholic church began to decline. Science sprang up, materialism soon became another tool used by the fallen beings. But the fallen beings could not hold back a growing awareness of the need to walk a path of initiation, a gradual path of initiation leading towards higher levels.

The fallen beings could not stop this even though they would ideally have liked to do so. There came a point where there was a growing awareness of this need, and that is what opened up the possibility that we of the ascended masters could step forward and reveal our assistance publicly and therefore also begin to give teachings about a path of initiation.

Limitations of sponsored messengers

You could say that once we have a sponsored messenger, surely we can say anything we want through that messenger. This is both true and untrue in a sense that even though many in the previous dispensations will be reluctant to admit it, there is a limitation to what we can say even through a sponsored messenger. There are two limitations to this. One is that the messenger's level of consciousness determines how high a teaching that the messenger's mind is able to allow to go through. In other words, if a messenger has not passed certain initiations, then it is difficult for the messenger's mind to even receive the matrices and turn into words the teachings about higher initiations.

This is not necessarily that there is something wrong with the process because, my beloved, what would be the point in giving a teaching at a certain high level if no one in embodiment was at a level where they could grasp the teaching? In other words, we are always looking at a sponsored messenger and considering: "Are there enough people to receive a certain level of teaching?" If there is not, then we do not give that teaching at that point. That is, of course, why we have given you the concept of *progressive* revelation.

It is an irony that there are people in previous ascended master organizations who believe that their organization, and perhaps even several previous organizations, were part of this process of progressive revelation sponsored by us, but, lo and behold, this progressive revelation came to a halt with the end of their organization. When their organization no longer had a messenger, then progressive revelation somehow stopped. This is a great irony, a great irony to ponder. I know that the students who are actually trapped in this irony are not likely to ponder it but nevertheless, it needs to be stated and projected into the collective consciousness.

The important thing for those of you who are open is that progressive revelation is an ongoing process and we do not foresee that it will stop during the Aquarian Age. There will be ongoing progressive revelation, perhaps there can be some breaks for a variety of reasons but there will be progressive revelation throughout the next 2,000 years of the Aquarian Age. It is therefore futile in the Aquarian Age to ever consider that a certain teaching is somehow the ultimate, absolute or final teaching. It is a teaching that is a stepping stone in the process of progressive revelation that spans the entire Aquarian Age. Exactly how this will go will depend on how people respond and it will depend on what Saint Germain determines should be brought forth in the age for which he is the primary leader.

The path to Christhood is not mechanical

Going back to my original idea here, would it be possible for us, even today when we have a sponsored messenger, to bring forth a path of initiation, a systematic teaching that outlines practices and initiations and steps you can take that were so complete that anyone who sincerely followed that path and applied it would be guaranteed to attain the Christ consciousness? Even if there was no interference, there were no limitations of the collective consciousness, even if we had what you might call "ideal conditions" (even though such conditions are really meaningless to define), we would not be able to bring forth a path that would guarantee the result. The reason for this is that the path to Christhood, my beloved, it is not mechanical, it is not automatic. There may be automatic writing but there is no automatic Christhood.

My beloved, the fallen beings, from the moment we began to bring forth teachings about a path of initiation, have attempted to pervert it. They have been able to do this to a large degree because of what they created during the Piscean Age. If you look at what the fallen beings did with the formation of Christianity, you will see that they denied the path to Christhood but they knew they had to give some people something instead. In other words, they knew that they would not be able to make all people deny God or deny that there is a spiritual side to life. They attempted to do this, as I will explain, but what they started out doing with the Christian religion was that they realized: "There are some people who believe in some kind of God, in some kind of spiritual realm and in some kind of afterlife. We cannot destroy this in the short run so we must give them something." What they gave people was (in essence) a mechanical, automatic path to salvation.

What is the Christian religion? It is the promise of a guaranteed, automatic salvation—if you follow certain outer rules defined by the outer church. You see, they removed the true inner path to Christhood and instead they gave people the outer, mechanical, automatic salvation. What happened when we started giving teachings about a path of initiation? Many people interpreted this based on what they had been programmed to think during Pisces, that this meant that if you follow this path of initiation rigorously, then you would be guaranteed to achieve the result. There are today, for example, people in the Freemasons who believe that if they follow the thirty-three steps of that organization, they will have reached some higher level of consciousness. You see, my beloved, the reality is that although a certain path may have the goal to bring you to a higher state of consciousness, taking the initiations of the outer path is not the same as attaining that higher state of consciousness.

My beloved, listen very, very carefully to what I am saying because I am giving you critical keys for understanding what it takes to be the Living Christ in action. You cannot define how the Living Christ *should* and *should not* behave. You cannot come up with a definition that says: This is how the Living Christ *is*, this is what the Living Christ *does* and this is what the Living Christ *does not* do.

Of Course, you can come up with certain things. The Living Christ is not likely to go around and shoot people, to put it in an extreme manner. There are things that the Living Christ would not do because the Living Christ does not act from selfishness, does not act from fear and does not act to prove anything. You cannot come up with a definition of exactly how the Living Christ should act. That is why you cannot come up with a path that automatically, mechanically brings you to the point of Christhood.

Going back to my concept of the gap, what I am saying here is this: Why did Jesus not write down his teachings? Because if he had written down his teachings, many people would have taken those scriptures and used them to define an outer, mechanical, automatic path to Christhood. In other words, they would have thought that they could use these teachings (supposedly being the official teachings of Jesus) to define a mechanical path. This is something that the fallen beings would have used from the very beginning but many people, especially at that time, were open to this. That is why, for example, the Jews were open to the idea that in order to be saved, you had to wash away your sins and you did that with the blood of sacrificed animals. Well, how mechanical is that!

You see even today how the Jews are mechanically following certain outer rules for behavior. You see that there has always been this tendency for people who want this mechanical path and why is it? Because they do not want to do what Jesus told people to do: Look at the beam in your own eye instead of looking at the splinter in the eye of your brother.

Stop projecting problems outside yourself

What is another way to describe the initiation, the critical initiation, of Pisces? It is to say that people should stop looking at the splinter in the eye of their brothers and sisters and instead start looking for the beam in their own eye. In other words, people should stop projecting that the problem is *out there*, that their suffering is caused by external conditions. Instead, they should take responsibility for themselves, look at their own reactions, realize that their reactions spring from some kind of structure in their psychology and then vigorously continue pursuing this self-observation, this completely honest self-observation, until they had seen what was limiting them and could therefore let go of it.

There were people who were able to do this during the Piscean Age. Some of them had grown up in a Christian environment and had looked at even the incomplete scriptures about Jesus but still had understood the need to look at themselves, to look into their own consciousness. What is the critical, decisive change that needs to happen if you are to pass the initiations of Pisces? It is that you have to stop projecting *out*. You have to take responsibility for yourself and go *within*.

How did Jesus achieve Christhood? Well, of course, this is not described in the scriptures but he went through a process. You can, if you look carefully, even see certain hints of this and how, for example, at the wedding of Cana, Mother Mary had to push him to step forward and start his public mission. You can see how he withdrew into the wilderness for forty days, which was a period of intense self-observation. You will know, of course, from the teachings we have given that he also travelled in the East and therefore subjected himself to various forms of initiations there, followed a certain path. What Jesus, first of all, did (and which would have been difficult for him to describe at that time because of people's lack of knowledge of psychology), was to observe himself, his own reactions, constantly looking at himself, looking at his psychology and what were the limitations.

My beloved, I have said that we cannot come up with a teaching that guarantees results, that there will always be a gap. What is the gap? It is whether people will approach the teaching in a mechanical way and want to follow it as an outer path, or whether they will step up, take responsibility for themselves and use the teachings to observe themselves and their reaction. Can a teacher force a student to practice self-observation? No, you cannot. As a spiritual teacher, especially an ascended teacher, you have absolute respect for free will. You cannot force and you do not want to force the student. You can give teachings, you can give hints. If you look at the previous dispensations, you will find those hints but many people were not able to find them.

The gap in people's minds

We perfectly understand, my beloved, that if you look back at the Summit Lighthouse, the I AM movement, Theosophy and other organizations we have either sponsored or been somewhat involved with (and there are many more), then we perfectly understand that there was a gap in the minds of the students. They were willing to come into the teaching. They were willing to study the teaching. They were willing to practice the practices we gave them. Many of them were very eager and became very fired-up, very zealous, about doing their practices. Yet how will giving ten hours of violet flame help you practice self-observation, if you think all you need to do is the outer practice?

In other words, it is possible to take the teaching, take the practices we have given, and still project out, still think it is an outer path and even construct in your mind the belief that: "I do not actually have to look at myself. I just have to give enough violet flame." Or you might gradually construct an even more dangerous belief, which we saw many students in the Summit Lighthouse do.

You see, my beloved, you come across a certain teaching—and I freely admit that we ourselves sort of added fuel to the fire here. Jesus has earlier given the image that we are like used-car salesmen who must use the "bait-and-switch" tactic. We must give an outer teaching that appeals to what people can accept and deal with and what they need with their present level of consciousness. Then, we must hope that once they come into the teaching, they are willing to step beyond that level of consciousness and then receive a deeper understanding of the teaching.

The mandala for the Piscean age

What did people need at the time? Well, here is where you need to look at the people who were in that original mandala at the start of the Piscean Age. These lifestreams obviously had not manifested Christhood but they had the potential to manifest Christhood. It was a *potential*—they were not there. During the Piscean age, these lifestreams reincarnated, most of them almost continuously, in different contexts. Because they were at a certain level at the start of the Piscean Age, each time they incarnated they had a certain sense that there was something they had to do, something they had to accomplish, something they had to find. They had to find the path, they had to make progress on that path. In the most general terms, they came in with this sense. Those of them who eventually found the inner path did not have a great sense of lack.

They followed the inner path but there were some of them that could not (or I should say, *would* not) discover the inner path, apply the inner path, acknowledge the inner path. As they continued to incarnate during the Piscean Age, they built a certain frustration because they knew they were not where they should be. At the same time, my beloved, they also started realizing that they did have a higher level of consciousness than many people around them. Some of them had realized that from the very beginning and carried that sense with them.

The combination of the frustration that there was a certain inner knowing that they were not making the progress they were supposed to, combined with the knowledge or the observation that they were still more advanced than the people around them, created in these students a certain sense, a certain need, to feel two things: First of all they needed to have a validation that they were more advanced than other people. Second of all, they needed to have a sense that they were doing something important on this planet. Again, I am not blaming, I am not criticizing. I am simply describing the mechanism in the minds of these students.

When we founded the Summit Lighthouse, we knew that they had these needs and we gave certain teachings that catered to those needs. That is why certain statements were made that made people believe that this would be an absolute, final revelation that was given, that it would be the main teaching for the next 2,000 years and that this meant that because they could recognize the teaching, they were surely very advanced students.

Many of them *were* advanced compared to most people on earth but really, that is not a very high standard of comparison so it should not be the cause of spiritual pride. Of course, it does not matter to spiritual pride what the level of comparison is, all that matters is: "Am I higher than those other people?" You see this all over the world where people find ways to feel they are superior based on some artificial criteria.

The need to do something important

Now, the other need that the students had was the sense that they were doing something important. We fulfilled this through the decrees and having them decree for many of these world issues. Now, take care here: Decrees have an effect, there is no question about this. There is no question that the students of the Summit Lighthouse had a critically important impact on the planet and the progress of the planet. I am in no way seeking to dishonor or downplay the importance of the work that was done.

You understand that this will, then, feed the sense in these people (if they were to even hear or read this) of how important they are. Whatever we say, people can always dis-interpret what we are saying, so that is a risk we have to run. Nevertheless, there were many people that were not part of the original mandala who came into the Summit Lighthouse and gave their decrees and it was a magnificent service. However, for those in the original mandala, there were some who managed to take the teachings and the practices of the Summit Lighthouse and make the leap, close the gap and step onto the inner path. There were some who did this but there were others who were not able to do it.

They actually used the teachings of the Summit Lighthouse to reinforce what Kuan-Yin and Jesus explained: As a result of your primal self, you have created this other self that wants to feel, not only that it has an understanding of how the universe works but that it is safe and secure.

There were students in the Summit Lighthouse who took our teachings and used them to reinforce that self.

However, they also faced a certain initiation that most of them are not aware of. You see, my beloved, there was a certain idea in the Summit Lighthouse that you could fail an initiation and that this could have drastic consequences—and there is some validity to this. I am not saying that you who are in a different dispensation should pay too much attention to it, but it is helpful for you to understand it.

As I said, there is a reality here that there was a mandala of lifestreams at the beginning of Pisces who had the potential to drive this growth in the collective consciousness but only if they passed the initiations of Pisces. If they would not pass those initiations, then it could be somewhat problematic for them at the end of the Piscean Age.

You have to realize here that when we create an organization in order to help students who have not passed the initiations during a certain age, we have to run a certain risk. The risk we run is that we have to put people in an all-or-nothing situation. You understand that during the 2,000 years of the Piscean Age, people had time. If you, in a certain embodiment, did not pass the initiation, then you had an opportunity in your next embodiment. Now you are coming to the end of the Piscean age. Now you have a certain group of students who were in the last embodiment they could have in the Piscean age. Either they would pass the initiations in that embodiment or it would be very difficult for them to embody again in the Aquarian Age. This is not the case for all people on the planet but it is the case for the members of that original mandala. They had the opportunity to manifest Christhood in the Piscean age and if they did not, it would be difficult for them to incarnate in Aquarius.

This is not a disaster in the sense that if you cannot embody on earth, there are certainly other planets you can embody on. It was preferable for a variety of reasons that these students would at least come to a point where they had balanced enough of their karma that they did not need to come back into embodiment.

There were certain matrices and there was a certain release of Light given through the Summit Lighthouse that was an attempt to help people master this initiation. In other words, to close the gap, step onto the inner path and therefore pass the initiation of Pisces. Let me give you a more nuanced view.

High and low potential of Pisces

The highest potential for Pisces is that you manifest Christhood but there is always a *high* potential and a *low* potential. The lowest potential was that you would put yourself firmly on the inner path. You could say that for that original mandala, the bottom line for them was that at the end of the Piscean Age, they should have stepped onto the inner path. If they did not, it would be difficult for them to embody in Aquarius. This is what we wanted to achieve: to get them to that point.

The Summit Lighthouse presented people with certain critical initiations that in a sense put them in an all-or-nothing situation. These students would either pass the initiations or they would fail the initiations, there was no in-between there. If they did not step up to the inner path, they would fail. If they did not manifest Christhood but stepped onto the inner path, they could move on. They would not have fulfilled their highest potential, but they could move on. If not, they would fail the initiation of that cycle of Pisces and therefore they could not embody again on earth, at least for some time.

What was it that we observed in the students? Well, many students did pass those initiations and at the very least put themselves on the inner path. This means that the purpose of the Summit Lighthouse was actually fulfilled. We did manage to get a critical mass of that original mandala to pass at least the lowest initiations of Pisces and step onto the inner path. With that, we can say that the purpose was fulfilled but the highest potential was not fulfilled because there were not very many students who actually attained or dared to express Christhood.

The interesting thing that I will discourse on here is why this did not happen. The reason for this, I have already given you the keys to. It is that there were still so many students in the Summit Lighthouse who approached this as an outer path, as a somewhat mechanical path: If you gave enough decrees, then you did not really have to look at your psychology.

We did give teachings about the need to resolve your psychology, although we could not give them at the level that we are doing now. The teachings were there and there were tools there. We did give teachings, often between the lines, about the inner path. People had what they needed if they were willing to look for it, but there was a certain group of students that were not willing to look for this. This goes back to what I said that these students during Pisces had built the sense of inner frustration but also the sense of superiority.

Being judgmental towards others

Now, the combination of the inner frustration (of not knowing where you are at or knowing that you are not where you should be at) combined with the desire for superiority brings some students into a particular state of mind. It is actually what you saw that the scribes and the Pharisees were in during Jesus' time and that he challenged many times.

This was the state of mind of being very judgmental of others based on an outer structure of rules and regulations and even a concept of a path of initiation, of certain critical initiations, that you are supposed to pass, even an image of how you are supposed to walk and behave and act as an ascended master student. These students wanted to believe that by following the outer rules and practices religiously, you might say even *fanatically* or with the obsessive-compulsive disorder (that has become a catch phrase in this age), they would automatically make progress.

Now, you have a certain group of students who came into the organization, many of them at a relatively early age. They decided to come on staff and work for the organization and they had been on staff for many years, faithfully done whatever they were told, practiced the outer practices. Gradually, they started to build the idea that because they had done all of these outer things, they should have attained a certain level of authority. Therefore, they should have the ability to judge others and the authority to express that judgment.

Students lost to El Morya

My beloved, there is nothing I could do or say that would help these students. I must, as an ascended master who put a lot of my spiritual attainment into sponsoring that organization, I must admit freely and honestly that I lost these students. Despite my efforts to sponsor that organization and give teachings, I lost them. I could not help them. I am not saying this with regret but it is important for a variety of reasons to state this in the physical. I simply accept the outplaying of free will. I accept that I, as the sponsoring master of that organization, could not help these students. I am not looking at myself and saying I failed in the sense that I was not good enough or there was something else I could have done. I simply state the facts, I make the observation. I have nothing to say to or about such students—they would not be willing to hear it anyway. I wish to describe this to those of you who are open because it is important that you look at this. You can look at the Piscean Age and you can look at many spiritual and religious organizations, but also political organizations, and you will see this pattern of judging others based on outer criteria, criteria defined on earth. These criteria, as we have now given you many teachings on the duality consciousness and the fallen beings, are, of course, defined by the fallen beings.

Stepping onto the inner path

The important point for you to take from this is that the path to Christhood is not mechanical. It is not a matter of following a certain teaching, a certain practice, passing certain initiations—it is a matter of stepping onto the inner path. Once you step onto the inner path, you are beyond this whole idea that you could fail your test. If you are observing your own reactions, you cannot fail your test. There may be something you do not see yet, but you do not see it *yet*. If you are willing to observe yourself, you are on the inner path and it is just a matter of how much progress you make and how quickly. Sometimes, you make progress more quickly and for others it takes time to process a certain issue.

Certainly, with the teachings you now have about the primal self, you have the potential to make very quick progress and get to the point where you are not only on the inner path, you are really free of this reactionary self. Of course, that is the primary condition for being on the path to Christhood or being the Living Christ, namely that you are not reacting to things on earth.

You can look at all of these organizations and you could look at the tendency to judge, the tendency to judge other people. Look for example in this part of the world how, during the Soviet era, many people in the Soviet Union believed that because they were members of the Soviet Union, they were superior to those outside. They were very judgmental of the decadent West and whatever you have. Look at how many people even today have this certain judgment. Many people in the United States believe that America is the greatest country in the world and are very judgmental toward other nations, failing to see the beam in the eye of the American psyche. You see many, many examples of this around the world. Look how in the early parts of the previous century, the sense of superiority found in Germany, France and England precipitated first the First World

War and then the Second. It could have precipitated a third if it had not been for certain stop-gap measures that we managed to take, including the many decrees given through the Summit Lighthouse.

The self that deals with being judged

Those of you who are or have been aware of and affiliated with the Summit Lighthouse, and who are open to the teachings I am giving here, can use this as a way for you to make peace with your experience of that organization. Some of you will have certain wounds you received during that time in the Summit Lighthouse, first of all by being exposed to these very judgmental people. As I even said during the Summit times, there were many students that we did not dare bring into the organization. A primary reason was that these were more innocent souls and we did not want them to be exposed to this very judgmental consciousness that was dominating the organization and is still influencing it today.

You can, then, use these teachings to come to realize, my beloved, as this messenger just realized before this dictation, that in order to deal with that consciousness (not only in the Summit Lighthouse but from the fallen beings in general and from other organizations you have been involved in during Pisces, such as the Catholic church), you have built a self to deal with the judgment of others, the condemnation from others. It is very important for you to come to the point where you identify this self, you see that it is there, it is individual for each one.

The question to ask yourself: "When someone judges and condemns me and accuses me of having done something wrong, how do I deal with that? What is it I feel? What is my feeling? What is the belief behind it?" Then, you can continue to track this up to the identity body and you can see how it sprang from the primal self and how you reacted when the fallen beings put you down. This will, then, allow you to identify this self, separate yourself from it, look at it and see that whatever problem your individual self presents that you have to solve or whatever conditions you have to fulfill in order to avoid this judgment, it is unreal, it is an illusion. Even if you fulfilled the condition, the fallen beings would still condemn you, they will *always* condemn you. Once you realize that, you can take that very, very important step and depersonalize your path. We have said this before but I wish to give you a different perspective on it.

Depersonalizing your path

My beloved, consider the situation of an avatar who has spent a long time on a natural planet where there are no fallen beings. You have not been exposed to this condemnation, ever, on a natural planet. Now, you come to earth and in probably your first embodiment, you are exposed to this very intense, direct attack of condemnation by the fallen beings. What is it that actually happens in this process? Well, on a natural planet you are in a state of mind that is what we in comparison to what you experience here on earth could call "impersonal."

You are not so focused on yourself, you are focused on being part of a whole, working for the whole, raising up the whole. That is the natural state on a natural planet. Now, you come down here to earth and you come here with the intention that you are wanting to work for the whole and raise up the whole. You are used to that when you do this, you receive a positive reaction. At least, you are not put down for it. Suddenly, you experience that the fallen beings are accusing, attacking, condemning, judging you, putting you down. You experience the shock that: "But hey, it's me they are doing this to. It's me they are saying there's something wrong with. I've never experienced this before. Why would they say there's something wrong with me? I came here with the best of intentions. I'm only here to help and they are saying I'm wrong, there's something wrong with me?"

All of a sudden, for the first time in your existence, you are facing the question. Because you are the kind of lifestream you are, you are actually used to looking at yourself and your reactions, you are just not used to condemning or being condemned. You are looking at yourself, naturally you are going to look at yourself and say: "But, could they possibly have a point? Have I done something wrong on this planet?" Suddenly, you are propelled into this doubt and now you are forced to react to this. What is it you are doing? We have said you are creating a self, the primal self.

Yes, but what is it that the primal self is? It is a *personal* self. All of a sudden, from being impersonal on a natural planet, you come to earth, you go through the trauma and now you are looking at your life on earth from your self in a very personal way. On a natural planet your sense of self is vast, but on an unnatural planet you are forced into a very narrow sense of self where now you are the center of your personal universe. It is as if you are looking at everything from that center, you are looking out from that center. All of a sudden, it has become *personal* on this planet. Suddenly, there is the possibility that you could have failed, that you could have done something wrong on this planet. Built into the primal self is this fear of failure and that is why you take everything so personally.

We have tried to give you teachings that say this is an unnatural planet, nothing here is permanent, it is like playing in the sand box. We have given you these teachings but we know that we face the same situation we have always faced, of the gap. As long as you have not seen and resolved the primal self, you cannot depersonalize your life on earth. You cannot look at life on earth and say: "Hey, I'll just build another sand castle or I'll just wipe out the old one and the sand will go back to its pure condition." It is like hitting water with a stick. No matter how hard you hit the water, it will always go back to being calm.

My beloved, what age are we moving into: the Aquarian age. Be like water if you want to pass the initiations of Aquarius. You see, my beloved, when you look at that self and look at how you react to judgment, then when you can let that self die, suddenly, life is no longer so personal. There is no reason to judge yourself because you realize *we* do not judge you. We can tell you we do not judge you but as long as you have that self, you cannot really grasp the teaching. You certainly cannot accept it. When you are free of that self, you can experience what Jesus gave you yesterday: the unconditional acceptance that we have for you.

The impostor of El Morya created by students

My beloved, why did I come up with the idea to change my name? Because in the Summit Lighthouse, people had built an image of El Morya as being this strict disciplinarian. There were people who actually believed that they had the attainment and even the obligation to go around and "blue-ray" other students (as they called it) by telling them what they thought El Morya would have told them about their dweller or their ego. They perpetrated this image that I was this strict disciplinarian that had so many conditions you had to fulfill.

That image had become so strong that I decided that I simply wanted to accomplish two things. Either I wanted to shake up those students who had that image so they could begin to free themselves from the image. Or I would attract new students who had a new name (Master MORE) and therefore did not need to go into that previous matrix that was still there. The reality is that the students of the Summit Lighthouse created a false El Morya, an imposter of El Morya, as that very judgmental disciplinarian.

They have maintained that imposter to this day. Some of them worship that imposter and think it is the real me and it has hereby been stated that it is not. You have lost me, and I have lost you. I accept this. I know that these students will not accept it because if they had accepted, it they would have to change. They would have to actually look at themselves, realize how judgmental they are and it would be almost impossible for them to do this.

Do you understand, my beloved, why it would be almost impossible for these students to do this? It is very, very simple. If you had built a momentum of judging other people because they have done this or that mistake, what happens if you acknowledge that you are wrong for judging other people? Well, you can only judge this in terms of right and wrong. You must admit you are wrong. If you admit that you are wrong, then you still have that momentum of judgment. So now, instead of always looking at the splinter in the eye of your brothers and judging *them*, once you recognize the beam in your own eye, you will have to judge *yourself* as you have been judging others, perhaps for the past 2,000 years or even beyond. These students would not be able to psychologically bear experiencing that self-condemnation.

A few people have made the switch and have gone almost insane or had severe psychological problems as a result. Of course, I do not wish that upon anyone. If the students could embrace the teachings we have given, they would actually be able to see that it is not they who have been judging other people. It is a separate self they have created and they created this separate self as a result of the birth trauma they were exposed to by the fallen beings.

Therefore, they would be able, if they were willing to embrace these teachings and use the tools, to separate themselves from that self and say: "Yes, I recognize that this should not have happened but it *did* happen, but it was not truly *me* who did this, it was that separate self and I now know I am more than the separate self. Therefore, I can separate myself from it and I can look at it and I can say: 'I am letting you die.'" They could realize, if they would really embrace these teachings, that they do not need to compensate for their judgment. They do not need to change anything in the outer or make things right or solve any problem. They only need to identify the self and let it die. Of course, they also need to do a certain amount of decrees to transmute the energy misqualified through that self but that is something that they are very capable of doing.

All have a way out

There is a way out for all of the students of the ascended masters who wish to take it. There *is* a way out. You can overcome *anything* because anything you have ever done, that you may feel is not the way it should be, was done through a separate self. When you let that self die, you are reborn, you are a new being in Christ. You may still have other separate selves so you should not get into the illusion that you are now ego-free, perfect or enlightened. You are a new being in Christ. Every time you let go of one self, you are reborn into a higher sense of identity. That is all I desire, my beloved. That is all any ascended master desires to see for you, that you enter the process of being continually reborn.

Closing the gap

Again, and I know I am testing your endurance, the gap! We know that even the teachings we have given through this messenger, many people have taken the teachings, done the practices, they still feel the gap. They look at this goal of Christhood and they see it as being *up there,* they see themselves as being *down here,* there is a gap between where you are, where you should be and they do not see how to close the gap.

They look at the teachings and they study the teachings and they think there must be something they have overlooked and they cannot figure out what it is. We have now given you these teachings of how to close that gap with the primal self, these other separate selves.

The key ingredient here is to recognize that you cannot *solve* any problem projected at you by the separate self—you can only let the self die. That is why we have said you cannot actually step onto the path of Christhood as long as you are trying to do it through one of these reactionary selves. You cannot be the Christ through a self that is reacting to the fallen beings.

Once you overcome at least some of these selves, so that you have achieved some depersonalization of your life, you can start being the Christ. Now, you are not in it to feel safe, to feel superior, to solve any problem, to compensate for any mistake you have made, to get validation or acknowledgment. You are, again, back to where you were on a natural planet, working for the whole, at least as you see it at the present moment, and that is what you did on a natural planet. You were not enlightened on a natural planet. You were not ascended on a natural planet. You were not in the highest state of consciousness you can be in on a natural planet but you had that state of life was not so personal.

Words have reached their limitation. I can only offer to give you something beyond words and that is the love I have for each and every one of you. My beloved, nothing on earth is truly personal to you because nothing on earth is directed at the Conscious You, which is beyond form.

There are some conditions, characteristics, energies, matrices that are personal to you. Jesus' unconditional acceptance of you is personal to you. My love for you is personal to you, the real you. Even the "you" that you are in your present state of consciousness, I love you as you are right now but I will love you more each day. You cannot accept that more unless you become more each day by letting go of the selves that are less.

I love you with those selves but you cannot experience my love through the self. Only when you let the self die, then you will experience that I love you more, not because I really love you more but because you experience it more. With this, enough words, enough words, my beloved. No amount of words can close the gap, only a switch in the mind will close the gap.

8 | INVOKING THE CLOSING OF THE GAP

In the name I AM THAT I AM, Jesus Christ, I call to all representatives of the Divine Mother, especially Master MORE, to help me overcome the illusions that prevent me from accepting progressive revelation by making me cling to some idea or belief, including…

[Make personal calls.]

Part 1

1. Master MORE, help me see if I have not passed the initiations of Pisces. Help me free myself from being dominated and enslaved by the fallen beings.

> Master MORE, come to the fore,
> we will absorb your flame of MORE.
> Master MORE, our will so strong,
> our power centers cleared by song.

> **Master MORE, your Sacred Heart,**
> **from this we will no more depart,**
> **we are forever in your flow,**
> **of Diamond Will that you bestow.**

2. Master MORE, help me see that I free myself from the fallen beings only by attaining the Christ consciousness.

> Master MORE, your wisdom flows,
> as our attunement ever grows.
> Master MORE, we have a tie,
> that helps us see through Serpent's lie.

> **Master MORE, your Sacred Heart,**
> **from this we will no more depart,**
> **we are forever in your flow,**
> **of Diamond Will that you bestow.**

3. Master MORE, help me see that when I, not *understand* but *experience* the Christ consciousness, I have a frame of reference. I can compare all of the lies and illusions sent at me, programmed into my subconscious mind by the fallen beings, to that rock of Christ.

> Master MORE, your love so pink,
> there is no purer love, we think.
> Master MORE, you set us free,
> from all conditionality.

> **Master MORE, your Sacred Heart,**
> **from this we will no more depart,**
> **we are forever in your flow,**
> **of Diamond Will that you bestow.**

4. Master MORE, help me follow the example set by Jesus, believe on him, do the works that he did and then eventually do greater works than he did.

> Master MORE, we will endure,
> your discipline that makes us pure.

Master MORE, intentions true,
as we are always one with you.

**Master MORE, your Sacred Heart,
from this we will no more depart,
we are forever in your flow,
of Diamond Will that you bestow.**

5. Master MORE, help me see that there will be progressive revelation throughout the next 2,000 years of the Aquarian Age. It is therefore futile to think that a certain teaching is somehow the ultimate, absolute or final teaching.

Master MORE, our vision raised,
the will of God is always praised.
Master MORE, creative will,
raising all life higher still.

**Master MORE, your Sacred Heart,
from this we will no more depart,
we are forever in your flow,
of Diamond Will that you bestow.**

6. Master MORE, help me see that there is no automatic or mechanical path to Christhood. It is not possible to bring forth a path that would guarantee the result.

Master MORE, your peace is power,
the demons of war it will devour.
Master MORE, we serve all life,
our flames consuming war and strife.

**Master MORE, your Sacred Heart,
from this we will no more depart,
we are forever in your flow,
of Diamond Will that you bestow.**

7. Master MORE, help me see that when you started giving teachings about a path of initiation, many people interpreted this based on what they had been programmed to think during Pisces, namely that if you followed this path of initiation rigorously, then you would be guaranteed to achieve the result.

> Master MORE, we are so free,
> eternal bond from you we see.
> Master MORE, we find rebirth,
> in flow of your eternal mirth.
>
> **Master MORE, your Sacred Heart,**
> **from this we will no more depart,**
> **we are forever in your flow,**
> **of Diamond Will that you bestow.**

8. Master MORE, help me see that one cannot define how the Living Christ *should* and *should not* behave. One cannot come up with a definition that says: This is how the Living Christ *is*, this is what the Living Christ *does* and this is what the Living Christ *does not* do.

> Master MORE, you balance all,
> the seven rays upon our call.
> Master MORE, forever MORE,
> we are the Spirit's open door.
>
> **Master MORE, your Sacred Heart,**
> **from this we will no more depart,**
> **we are forever in your flow,**
> **of Diamond Will that you bestow.**

9. Master MORE, help me see that people want a mechanical path because they do not want to do what Jesus told people to do: Look at the beam in their own eyes instead of looking at the splinter in the eyes of their brothers.

> Master MORE, your Presence here,
> filling up the inner sphere.

Life is now a sacred flow,
God Power we on all bestow.

**Master MORE, your Sacred Heart,
from this we will no more depart,
we are forever in your flow,
of Diamond Will that you bestow.**

Part 2

1. Master MORE, help me see that the critical initiation of Pisces is that people stop looking at the splinter in the eye of their brothers and sisters and instead start looking for the beam in their own eye.

Master MORE, come to the fore,
we will absorb your flame of MORE.
Master MORE, our will so strong,
our power centers cleared by song.

**Master MORE, your Sacred Heart,
from this we will no more depart,
we are forever in your flow,
of Diamond Will that you bestow.**

2. Master MORE, help me see if I have a self that is projecting that the problem is *out there*, that my suffering is caused by external conditions. Help me take responsibility for myself, look at my own reactions.

Master MORE, your wisdom flows,
as our attunement ever grows.
Master MORE, we have a tie,
that helps us see through Serpent's lie.

**Master MORE, your Sacred Heart,
from this we will no more depart,
we are forever in your flow,
of Diamond Will that you bestow.**

3. Master MORE, help me realize that my reactions spring from some kind of structure in my psychology. Help me continue pursuing this self-observation, this completely honest self-observation, until I have seen what is limiting me and can let go of it.

> Master MORE, your love so pink,
> there is no purer love, we think.
> Master MORE, you set us free,
> from all conditionality.
>
> **Master MORE, your Sacred Heart,**
> **from this we will no more depart,**
> **we are forever in your flow,**
> **of Diamond Will that you bestow.**

4. Master MORE, help me see that the masters cannot come up with a teaching that guarantees results because there will always be a gap. The gap is whether people will approach the teaching in a mechanical way or whether they will take responsibility for themselves.

> Master MORE, we will endure,
> your discipline that makes us pure.
> Master MORE, intentions true,
> as we are always one with you.
>
> **Master MORE, your Sacred Heart,**
> **from this we will no more depart,**
> **we are forever in your flow,**
> **of Diamond Will that you bestow.**

5. Master MORE, help me see if I have selves that feel frustration, based on an inner knowing that I am not making the progress I am supposed to, combined with the observation that I am still more advanced than the people around me.

> Master MORE, our vision raised,
> the will of God is always praised.
> Master MORE, creative will,
> raising all life higher still.

> Master MORE, your Sacred Heart,
> from this we will no more depart,
> we are forever in your flow,
> of Diamond Will that you bestow.

6. Master MORE, help me see and surrender the self that has a need to have a validation that I am more advanced than other people.

> Master MORE, your peace is power,
> the demons of war it will devour.
> Master MORE, we serve all life,
> our flames consuming war and strife.

> **Master MORE, your Sacred Heart,
> from this we will no more depart,
> we are forever in your flow,
> of Diamond Will that you bestow.**

7. Master MORE, help me see and surrender the self that needs to have a sense that I am doing something important on this planet.

> Master MORE, we are so free,
> eternal bond from you we see.
> Master MORE, we find rebirth,
> in flow of your eternal mirth.

> **Master MORE, your Sacred Heart,
> from this we will no more depart,
> we are forever in your flow,
> of Diamond Will that you bestow.**

8. Master MORE, help me see and surrender the self that feels spiritual pride and needs to feel I am a very advanced student based on a comparison with other people.

> Master MORE, you balance all,
> the seven rays upon our call.
> Master MORE, forever MORE,
> we are the Spirit's open door.

> **Master MORE, your Sacred Heart,**
> **from this we will no more depart,**
> **we are forever in your flow,**
> **of Diamond Will that you bestow.**

9. Master MORE, help me see and surrender the self that thinks that if I give enough decrees, then I do not really have to look at my psychology. Help me pass the critical initiation of Pisces and anchor myself firmly on the inner path of self-observation.

> Master MORE, your Presence here,
> filling up the inner sphere.
> Life is now a sacred flow,
> God Power we on all bestow.

> **Master MORE, your Sacred Heart,**
> **from this we will no more depart,**
> **we are forever in your flow,**
> **of Diamond Will that you bestow.**

Part 3

1. Master MORE, help me see and surrender the self that is very judgmental of others, based on an outer structure of rules and regulations and even a concept of a path of initiation, even an image of how one is supposed to behave as an ascended master student.

> Master MORE, come to the fore,
> we will absorb your flame of MORE.
> Master MORE, our will so strong,
> our power centers cleared by song.

> **Master MORE, your Sacred Heart,**
> **from this we will no more depart,**
> **we are forever in your flow,**
> **of Diamond Will that you bestow.**

8 | Invoking the closing of the gap

2. Master MORE, help me fully accept that following the outer rules and practices religiously, even fanatically or with an obsessive-compulsive disorder will *not* automatically lead to progress.

> Master MORE, your wisdom flows,
> as our attunement ever grows.
> Master MORE, we have a tie,
> that helps us see through Serpent's lie.
>
> **Master MORE, your Sacred Heart,**
> **from this we will no more depart,**
> **we are forever in your flow,**
> **of Diamond Will that you bestow.**

3. Master MORE, help me see and surrender the self that thinks that because I have faithfully done the outer practices, I should have attained a certain level of authority and have the ability to judge others and the authority to express that judgment.

> Master MORE, your love so pink,
> there is no purer love, we think.
> Master MORE, you set us free,
> from all conditionality.
>
> **Master MORE, your Sacred Heart,**
> **from this we will no more depart,**
> **we are forever in your flow,**
> **of Diamond Will that you bestow.**

4. Master MORE, help me look at the Piscean Age and see how many spiritual organizations have this pattern of judging others based on criteria defined on earth, criteria defined by the fallen beings.

> Master MORE, we will endure,
> your discipline that makes us pure.
> Master MORE, intentions true,
> as we are always one with you.

> **Master MORE, your Sacred Heart,**
> **from this we will no more depart,**
> **we are forever in your flow,**
> **of Diamond Will that you bestow.**

5. Master MORE, help me truly accept that the path to Christhood is not mechanical. It is a matter of stepping onto the inner path. Once I step onto the inner path, I am beyond the risk that I could fail my test. If I am observing my own reactions, I cannot fail my test.

> Master MORE, our vision raised,
> the will of God is always praised.
> Master MORE, creative will,
> raising all life higher still.

> **Master MORE, your Sacred Heart,**
> **from this we will no more depart,**
> **we are forever in your flow,**
> **of Diamond Will that you bestow.**

6. Master MORE, help me see that when I am willing to observe myself, I am on the inner path and it is just a matter of how much progress I make and how quickly.

> Master MORE, your peace is power,
> the demons of war it will devour.
> Master MORE, we serve all life,
> our flames consuming war and strife.

> **Master MORE, your Sacred Heart,**
> **from this we will no more depart,**
> **we are forever in your flow,**
> **of Diamond Will that you bestow.**

7. Master MORE, help me use the teachings to free myself from this reactionary self and anchor myself on the path to Christhood. Help me see that the primary condition for being the Living Christ is that I am not reacting to things on earth.

> Master MORE, we are so free,
> eternal bond from you we see.
> Master MORE, we find rebirth,
> in flow of your eternal mirth.
>
> **Master MORE, your Sacred Heart,
> from this we will no more depart,
> we are forever in your flow,
> of Diamond Will that you bestow.**

8. Master MORE, help me make peace with my experience of a certain spiritual organization and being exposed to these very judgmental people. Help me realize that I have built a self to deal with the judgment of others, the condemnation from others.

> Master MORE, you balance all,
> the seven rays upon our call.
> Master MORE, forever MORE,
> we are the Spirit's open door.
>
> **Master MORE, your Sacred Heart,
> from this we will no more depart,
> we are forever in your flow,
> of Diamond Will that you bestow.**

9. Master MORE, help me identify this self and realize how I individually deal with and feel about the judgment from other people. Help me see the belief behind my reaction.

> Master MORE, your Presence here,
> filling up the inner sphere.
> Life is now a sacred flow,
> God Power we on all bestow.
>
> **Master MORE, your Sacred Heart,
> from this we will no more depart,
> we are forever in your flow,
> of Diamond Will that you bestow.**

Part 4

1. Master MORE, help me track this up to the identity body and see how it sprang from the primal self and how I reacted when the fallen beings put me down. Help me identify this self, separate myself from it.

> Master MORE, come to the fore,
> we will absorb your flame of MORE.
> Master MORE, our will so strong,
> our power centers cleared by song.
>
> **Master MORE, your Sacred Heart,**
> **from this we will no more depart,**
> **we are forever in your flow,**
> **of Diamond Will that you bestow.**

2. Master MORE, help me see that whatever problem my individual self presents that I have to solve, or whatever conditions I have to fulfill in order to avoid this judgment, it is unreal, it is an illusion. Even if I fulfilled the condition, the fallen beings would still condemn me.

> Master MORE, your wisdom flows,
> as our attunement ever grows.
> Master MORE, we have a tie,
> that helps us see through Serpent's lie.
>
> **Master MORE, your Sacred Heart,**
> **from this we will no more depart,**
> **we are forever in your flow,**
> **of Diamond Will that you bestow.**

3. Master MORE, help me take the very important step and depersonalize my path. Help me see how the fallen beings exposed me to intense condemnation, and this caused me to create the primal self, which is a *personal* self.

> Master MORE, your love so pink,
> there is no purer love, we think.

Master MORE, you set us free,
from all conditionality.

**Master MORE, your Sacred Heart,
from this we will no more depart,
we are forever in your flow,
of Diamond Will that you bestow.**

4. Master MORE, help me see how I shifted from being impersonal on a natural planet, to going through the trauma on earth and now I am looking at life from my self in a very personal way.

Master MORE, we will endure,
your discipline that makes us pure.
Master MORE, intentions true,
as we are always one with you.

**Master MORE, your Sacred Heart,
from this we will no more depart,
we are forever in your flow,
of Diamond Will that you bestow.**

5. Master MORE, help me see that on a natural planet my sense of self is vast, but on an unnatural planet I am forced into a very narrow sense of self where now I am the center of my personal universe. I am looking at everything from that center, I am looking out from that center.

Master MORE, our vision raised,
the will of God is always praised.
Master MORE, creative will,
raising all life higher still.

**Master MORE, your Sacred Heart,
from this we will no more depart,
we are forever in your flow,
of Diamond Will that you bestow.**

6. Master MORE, help me see how life became *personal* on this planet. Suddenly, there was the possibility that I could have failed, that I could have done something wrong on this planet. Built into the primal self is this fear of failure and that is why I take everything so personally.

> Master MORE, your peace is power,
> the demons of war it will devour.
> Master MORE, we serve all life,
> our flames consuming war and strife.
>
> **Master MORE, your Sacred Heart,**
> **from this we will no more depart,**
> **we are forever in your flow,**
> **of Diamond Will that you bestow.**

7. Master MORE, help me see and resolve the primal self so I can depersonalize my life on earth. Help me look at life on earth and say: "Hey, I'll just build another sand castle or I'll just wipe out the old one and the sand will go back to its pure condition."

> Master MORE, we are so free,
> eternal bond from you we see.
> Master MORE, we find rebirth,
> in flow of your eternal mirth.
>
> **Master MORE, your Sacred Heart,**
> **from this we will no more depart,**
> **we are forever in your flow,**
> **of Diamond Will that you bestow.**

8. Master MORE, help me see that whatever I do on earth is like hitting water with a stick. No matter how hard I hit the water, it will always go back to being calm. Help me see that we are moving into the Aquarian age. Help me be like water and pass the initiations of Aquarius.

> Master MORE, you balance all,
> the seven rays upon our call.
> Master MORE, forever MORE,
> we are the Spirit's open door.

> **Master MORE, your Sacred Heart,**
> **from this we will no more depart,**
> **we are forever in your flow,**
> **of Diamond Will that you bestow.**

9. Master MORE, help me look at the self and see how I react to judgment. Help me let that self die so that life is no longer so personal. Help me accept that there is no reason to judge myself because *you* do not judge me. Help me experience the unconditional acceptance that you have for me.

> Master MORE, your Presence here,
> filling up the inner sphere.
> Life is now a sacred flow,
> God Power we on all bestow.

> **Master MORE, your Sacred Heart,**
> **from this we will no more depart,**
> **we are forever in your flow,**
> **of Diamond Will that you bestow.**

Part 5

1. Master MORE, help me see if I have this tendency to judge everything. Help me see that it is not me who has been judging, it is a separate self. I have created this self as a result of the birth trauma I was exposed to by the fallen beings.

> Master MORE, come to the fore,
> we will absorb your flame of MORE.
> Master MORE, our will so strong,
> our power centers cleared by song.

> **Master MORE, your Sacred Heart,**
> **from this we will no more depart,**
> **we are forever in your flow,**
> **of Diamond Will that you bestow.**

2. Master MORE, I am willing to embrace these teachings and use the tools. Help me separate myself from that self and say: "Yes, I recognize that this should not have happened but it *did* happen, but it was not truly *me* who did this, it was that separate self and I now know I am more than the separate self. Therefore, I can separate myself from it. I can look at it and I can say: 'I am letting you die.'"

> Master MORE, your wisdom flows,
> as our attunement ever grows.
> Master MORE, we have a tie,
> that helps us see through Serpent's lie.
>
> **Master MORE, your Sacred Heart,**
> **from this we will no more depart,**
> **we are forever in your flow,**
> **of Diamond Will that you bestow.**

3. Master MORE, help me realize that I do not need to compensate for my judgment. I do not need to change anything in the outer or make things right or solve any problem. I only need to identify the self and let it die. Of course, I also need to use decrees to transmute the energy misqualified through that self.

> Master MORE, your love so pink,
> there is no purer love, we think.
> Master MORE, you set us free,
> from all conditionality.
>
> **Master MORE, your Sacred Heart,**
> **from this we will no more depart,**
> **we are forever in your flow,**
> **of Diamond Will that you bestow.**

4. Master MORE, help me truly accept that there is a way out for all of the students of the ascended masters who wish to take it. I can overcome *anything* because anything I have ever done was done through a separate self. When I let that self die, I am reborn, I am a new being in Christ.

> Master MORE, we will endure,
> your discipline that makes us pure.
> Master MORE, intentions true,
> as we are always one with you.
>
> **Master MORE, your Sacred Heart,
> from this we will no more depart,
> we are forever in your flow,
> of Diamond Will that you bestow.**

5. Master MORE, help me see that I may still have other separate selves, yet every time I let go of one self, I am reborn into a higher sense of identity. Help me see that the ascended masters desire that I enter the process of being continually reborn.

> Master MORE, our vision raised,
> the will of God is always praised.
> Master MORE, creative will,
> raising all life higher still.
>
> **Master MORE, your Sacred Heart,
> from this we will no more depart,
> we are forever in your flow,
> of Diamond Will that you bestow.**

6. Master MORE, help me see if I have a self that looks at the goal of Christhood and sees it as being *up there*, me as being *down here*, there is a gap between where I am, where I should be and the self does not see how to close the gap.

> Master MORE, your peace is power,
> the demons of war it will devour.
> Master MORE, we serve all life,
> our flames consuming war and strife.
>
> **Master MORE, your Sacred Heart,
> from this we will no more depart,
> we are forever in your flow,
> of Diamond Will that you bestow.**

7. Master MORE, help me recognize that I cannot *solve* any problem projected at me by the separate self—I can only let the self die. I cannot actually step onto the path of Christhood as long as I am trying to do it through one of these reactionary selves. I cannot be the Christ through a self that is reacting to the fallen beings.

> Master MORE, we are so free,
> eternal bond from you we see.
> Master MORE, we find rebirth,
> in flow of your eternal mirth.
>
> **Master MORE, your Sacred Heart,**
> **from this we will no more depart,**
> **we are forever in your flow,**
> **of Diamond Will that you bestow.**

8. Master MORE, help me overcome these selves and achieve some depersonalization of my life so I am not in it to feel safe, to feel superior, to solve any problem, to compensate for any mistake, to get validation or acknowledgment. Help me get back to where I was on a natural planet and work for the whole.

> Master MORE, you balance all,
> the seven rays upon our call.
> Master MORE, forever MORE,
> we are the Spirit's open door.
>
> **Master MORE, your Sacred Heart,**
> **from this we will no more depart,**
> **we are forever in your flow,**
> **of Diamond Will that you bestow.**

9. Master MORE, help me experience the love you have for me. Help me experience that nothing on earth is truly personal to me because nothing on earth is directed at the Conscious You, which is beyond form. Help me experience that your love for me is personal to me, the real me. Even the "me" that I am in my present state of consciousness, you love me as I am right now and you will love me more each day. I accept that more and I am willing to let go of the selves that are less so I can have the switch in the mind that will close the gap.

> Master MORE, your Presence here,
> filling up the inner sphere.
> Life is now a sacred flow,
> God Power we on all bestow.
>
> **Master MORE, your Sacred Heart,**
> **from this we will no more depart,**
> **we are forever in your flow,**
> **of Diamond Will that you bestow.**

Sealing

In the name of the Divine Mother, I call to Mother Mary for the sealing of myself and all people in my circle of influence in the creative flow of the Divine Mother, the River of Life. I call for the multiplication of my calls by all representatives of the Divine Mother, so that we form the perfect figure-eight flow of "As Above, so below." Thus, I accept that this is fully manifest, because the mouth of the Lord, the Divine Mother that I AM, has spoken it. Amen.

9 | IT IS TIME TO EXPRESS YOUR CHRISTHOOD

I AM the Ascended Master Jesus, and I come to give you another installment in what I have planned for this conference concerning how to be the Living Christ in action. Now, you have received a magnificent and multifaceted teaching from Master MORE earlier today. It has, indeed, many layers, many levels and much to ponder. In fact, you might say that dictation in itself is a complete description of the spiritual path. If you could fully internalize all aspects of it, then the question is whether you needed anything more.

Being the Christ without fanaticism

Of course, as it is Master MORE who gave it to you, there is more to be given. Naturally, the teachings on the primal self are essential for being the Christ in action. Consider a Christian crusader, a group of them sitting on their horses outside some village in the Middle East. They get themselves in an agitated state of mind and then they scream as with one voice: "God wills it." Then, they draw their swords, they ride into the village and kill men, women and children, believing they are doing this in the name of Christ and for the sake of Christ. Were they being the Christ in action? Well, of course, you know they were not. You nevertheless need to ask yourself: "How can I be the Christ in action without going into this unbalanced state of mind that is over-eager, over-zealous, bordering on the fanatical?"

Now, Master MORE talked about previous ascended master dispensations and how the students had reacted there. We have seen many ascended master students become so over-zealous, so unbalanced in their zeal to do something, that they simply went out in an unbalanced manner that was not being the Living Christ in action, even though some of these students were firmly convinced that this was expressing their Christhood.

We have, of course, already given you the essential key to avoiding this reaction. It is to overcome your primal self and the other selves that were created after it. The self that absolutely needs security, of course, can make you fanatical. Once you have built this sense of security based on some kind of outer system or belief, then you will not want that security to disappear. Therefore, you become fanatical in fighting anything that you see as a threat to the sense of security.

Indeed, you can also have another self, as we have explained, that is so concerned about not being wrong, not being proven wrong, never being wrong. Again, as the fallen ones made it seem like you were wrong in that first embodiment, this self is always wanting to do the right thing. Once it has convinced itself that it has done the right thing or is doing the right thing, then it is very, very reluctant to consider that it might not be the right thing at all.

Good people are the hardest to save

My beloved, 2,000 years ago I made the somewhat enigmatic statement that it is easier for a sinner to be saved than it is for a rich man to enter heaven. Obviously, when I said "rich" man, I did not necessarily mean a person who had money but a person who was rich in the sense that the person felt that he or she had done many good deeds. The paradoxical aspect of Christianity, other religions and even ascended master teachings is that sometimes the very, very hardest people for us to help are the ones who are absolutely convinced that they are good people and they have done a lot of good things.

Take what Master MORE said about students that became convinced that because they had been in an organization for a long time and faithfully followed all the outer practices and done everything they were told to do, they were entitled to some kind of position. You see an example of this, but you can also go to Christian churches and see those who for an entire lifetime have been convinced they have been doing Christian charity, doing what Christ told us to do by loving our neighbor, being good to all people, being engaged in some form of charity. There are many Christian ministers, and many people who are not ministers but who have been engaged in Christian forms of charity, who feel that because they have served and been so good and done so many good things for their entire lifetime, they are guaranteed to be saved based on the outer actions.

Of course, I made various statements that can be interpreted to unlock the understanding that this is not the case. The Kingdom of God is within you. *What* is within you? Your psyche. Well, if you do not resolve your psychology, overcome all of these selves, how can you enter the kingdom? You see, this, again, goes back to what Master MORE explained about the perversion of Christianity where they have to create the outer path, the dream of an automatic or guaranteed salvation. Many Christians are on this outer path because they have nothing else and they are absolutely convinced that when they are doing all these outer things, naturally they will be allowed into the kingdom at the end of this life.

This is not my primary concern here, I use it merely as an example. My primary concern is, of course, ascended master students. You need to recognize here that some of you, when you were exposed to the original birth trauma or the events that caused the trauma, the fallen beings made you feel that you had done something wrong or that you were wrong for being on earth, wrong for coming here.

Not wanting to be wrong

There was always a situation where the fallen beings made you feel that you had done something here on earth that was so wrong that you could never be redeemed. As we have said before, an aspect of the primal self is that you decide: "I never want to experience that again." What have you now done? You have created a separate self that is created to, is programmed to, make sure that you can never again be proven really wrong.

My beloved, what have some of you then done? You have, over many lifetimes, built a momentum of supposedly doing the right thing, by always doing what is defined as right in your culture, in your religion, by being charitable, by helping others and so forth and so on. Of course, based on the outer path of Christianity, some of you actually have a momentum from past lives, believing that if you do these outer things, if you give this service, then you *must* qualify for your ascension.

What have we said now, time and time again? When you stand there in front of the gate, if you want to use that image (and we realize you need some image but it is only an image), you are standing in front of the gate that leads to the ascended realm and you have to make a choice to go through it. You have to make a choice and it has to be a *free* choice, my beloved. How can you, the Conscious You, make a free choice? Only when you do not have any of these selves that are coloring your vision. This self that is programmed to make you to never again feel wrong by doing all these good things, it stands in the way of your ascension—if you cannot let go of it. You cannot ascend if you do not let go of it, and you cannot let go of it, if you have not looked at it. You cannot, of course, look at it if you are so afraid of seeing anything wrong in your being.

You see, my beloved, we have given you these teachings that we love you unconditionally. You have our unconditional acceptance, but as long as you have the self that never wants to be proven wrong again, you cannot really accept our acceptance, our love. You will always have the fear of being wrong, the sense that certain conditions can make you wrong, even the entire idea that *you* could be wrong. You cannot transcend it as long as you have that self because the self cannot question the basic programming, the basic illusion, out of which it was created.

The self cannot question it. As long as you are seeing yourself through the filter of that self, *you* cannot question it either. You can, as the Conscious You, step outside of that and I give you this specific teaching to help the Conscious You step outside of that self and realize that there are two ways to prevent yourself from ascending. One is to be in a very negative, self-centered, selfish state of mind, always battling other people, doing whatever you want without considering the consequences. In other words you are what some of you would call a bad person. There is another way to prevent yourself from getting into heaven, and that is to be what some of you see as a good person and wanting to maintain that image to the point where you will not question that there could be something in you that is not "right," in the sense that it will not allow you to go into the ascended state.

When you see yourself through that self, you will think that if there is something in you that is not *right,* then it must be *wrong.* Then, that must mean that *you* are wrong and therefore you cannot look at it. The only thing that can break this deadlock is that the Conscious You is somehow inspired, propelled to go outside of that self and see that it is just a self. It is just a self, and it is only this self that believes that by doing good things, you will automatically go to heaven. It is just a self and as all selves, it is based on an illusion. When you, the Conscious You, recognize this, then you can realize that this self is not you. You can realize that you cannot take this self with you into the ascended realm.

Why can you not take it with you? Because you did not bring it with you when you came here. No man can ascend back to heaven save he that descended from heaven. No self – no you – can ascend back to heaven except the you that descended from the I AM Presence. It is *that* simple. This is just another self, but I need some of you to recognize that being good and thinking you are good and have been good can also be a hindrance to your ascension. It is just another self that needs to go. As long as you are trying to do good based on such a self, you cannot be the Christ in action. You are seeking to do good in order to prevent yourself from being proven wrong. In other words, what you are doing is self-centered. It is centered around this lower self, not really your real self but the lower self. This is your motivation and it is not Christhood it is not the Christ consciousness.

You are already the Christ in action

This being said, I want to move into a new phase. I recognize that, as Master MORE said, anytime we give you a teaching, there are many of you that will sit there, you will study the teaching but you will have this sense of a gap. We have given you the tools of how to overcome the primal self and these other selves and when you do, the gap will disappear. I still want to make a few comments here because I want you to recognize that all of you are already, to some degree, the Christ in action and you have been the Christ in action, most of you, for this lifetime. It is just that you have not been conscious of it and it has not been something that has happened all the time. It has happened once in a while, maybe for some of you just a few times but you have all already been the Christ in action.

This, then, has to do with another aspect of the false Christianity, which is the enormous idolatry built around my person. Jesus is up there on the pedestal being the Son of God, being perfect from the beginning and so forth and so on. There has been created this very, very powerful beast in the collective consciousness that in order to be the Christ, you practically have to be perfect.

Some of you have also created this self, a self that is like this. In fact, most of you have an aspect of the thinking that you can only be saved, go to heaven or make your ascension when you live up to this almost superhuman standard. Therefore, you feel that as long as you do not live up to this standard, or if you do not live up to it all the time, well, then you cannot be the Christ.

What is the entire idea of the Christ as it was originally meant? What does it mean that the Christ takes incarnation, comes into flesh and blood? It means that the Christ consciousness can be expressed through a vehicle that is not yet completely free of all these outer selves.

As we have said, the Conscious You can step outside of your current sense of self. When that happens, you can be the open door for the Christ consciousness to flow through you, to express itself through you. As I said: "I can of my own self do nothing, it is the father (the I AM Presence, the Holy Spirit) that does the work." It does the work when you have an opening in your consciousness.

You cannot force this, as we have said before. There is nothing you can really *do*. You cannot create a mechanical path that automatically takes you to the point where you are the open door. You do not need to force it, you just need to stop forcing it away. The reality is that it rains upon the just and the unjust. The Spirit is constantly descending from Above. As I said: I will ask the Father and he will send you another comforter. When I ascended, there was a part of my momentum, my Spirit, that was released on earth and it has been descending for these past 2,000 years. It is not a matter of you somehow qualifying for it or forcing it to come through you.

The Spirit is constantly descending. It is only a matter of there being an opening in your four lower bodies through which the Spirit can flow. All of you have had glimpses of this where, for some reason or other, the outer self was set aside, the Conscious You could step out of its normal state of mind, its normal identification with one of these outer selves, and suddenly there was an inflow of something else. This "something else" is, of course, what it means to be the Christ in action. It is when you are the open door for expressing something that is beyond the normal state of awareness that most people are in. Most people have never experienced anything differently, anything higher. I talked about you giving the gift of acceptance to people but beyond that is any experience you give people where they experience something beyond their normal level of consciousness. This is an expression of Christ, this is being the Christ in action.

Beyond fixed images of Christ

It can take many forms, my beloved, and the real key to being open, to being the instrument for the expression of the Christ consciousness, is to not have all these expectations or pre-conceived opinions about how the Christ *should* or *should not* express itself. We have given you the concepts that there were many ways that I did it. One person I gave a cup of cold water because that was what he needed at that time, but then I gave him the feeling of being accepted, which he had never had before and that was the extra beyond the vehicle.

So many spiritual students, and especially ascended master students, have used our teachings to reinforce one of the outer selves that is an offspring of their primal selves. They have created this very, very, very fixed image of what it means to be the Christ in action both for themselves and also how I was when I was in embodiment. Many of them would be shocked to actually encounter me as I was when I was in embodiment. Many of them would have their faith shaken, as many Christians would have their faith shaken if they saw me as I really was.

What you can do is, with the Conscious You, look in your being and see what pre-conceived opinions and expectations you have about how the Christ should or should not be. You will see it in the scriptures how there were people who rejected me because I drank wine, I was from Nazareth, I did this, I did that. There were those who rejected me because of my looks, because of my dress, because of my behavior, because of the way I talked.

My beloved, there are always people who are seeking to find fault with the messenger, with the representative of Christ. This, of course, goes back to the fallen beings who have a constant judgment of the Living Christ. It is really the fallen beings and their attitude that has created this very judgmental culture that you find in so many spiritual organizations, including, of course, what Master MORE exposed earlier. You need to honestly look at whether you have a self that has some kind of judgment about how the Living Christ should be, because this will then be one of the most subtle and effective ways to close off yourself from having the Christ flow through you. If you feel that the expression of Spirit needs to conform to your standard, the standard you have in that self, then the Holy Spirit cannot flow. It bloweth where *it* listeth, not where *you* listeth, not where your outer self listeth and certainly not where the fallen beings want it to flow—because they do not want it to flow at all.

Basically, the enigma here is that you could say that the fallen beings do not want the Spirit to flow at all and they have largely been successful in stopping it. Why does the Spirit not do something about that, as was expressed in a question today? "Why doesn't God then change his plans based on my view of the universe?" This is essentially the fallen consciousness: "Why doesn't God change so that *I* don't have to change?" You could say that the Spirit should have done something to overcome this gridlock that the fallen beings have the planet in.

The Spirit respects free will, and therefore you could say that the statement: "The Holy Spirit bloweth where it listeth" is not the full understanding. It was given to show that the Holy Spirit does not flow according to human opinions, expectations and standards. On the other hand, as I just said, the Holy Spirit is constantly flowing, it is just that when there is no opening, it cannot come to expression in the physical octave and for that matter not in the other three octaves either.

That is why the Spirit waits until someone creates an opening and then it flows. When the opening is there, the flow is there. We have given you many thoughts, many tools and when you combine them with the tools of the birth trauma and the primal self, then you can make very, very significant progress. You can come to the point where you start becoming more of the open door and you do not have a compulsion to express your Christhood. You do not feel you have to, you are not afraid of it, you are not concerned about it. You just let it happen and you recognize that when you let it happen, when you are in a neutral frame of mind, then not only will the flow be there, you also do not have all of these concerns about whether you did the right thing or whether this was okay or whether this was good enough.

Over-analyzing yourself

Now, in the beginning you may indeed have some of these concerns come up and many of you have experienced this. You have a situation, you feel there was some extraordinary flow through you that is not your normal awareness. Then, afterwards you go into analyzing, evaluating: "Was it okay what I did? Was it the highest possible expression of Christ? Was it really Christ? Should I not have done this? Should I not have said this?"

You need to be prepared that as you begin to dare to express yourself more and more, you will have this sort of challenge come up afterwards. Then, you use that as an opportunity to realize it is another outer self that is causing this reaction in you. Then, you follow the formula: Identify the self, separate yourself from it and you let it die—*you let it die*, my beloved.

You see, when you come to the point where you are beginning to be more open to the flow of the Christ, then all of these concerns of whether you did the right thing or not will fade away. You will come to a point where you recognize that: "It was what it was."

No ultimate expression of Christ

There is an important step to take before you can get there and that is to recognize that there is no ultimate or absolute expression of Christ possible, for the very simple reason that this is an unnatural planet. An expression of Christ will always happen in a particular situation. It is expressed to people at a certain level of consciousness. It is not meant to raise them up to the highest level of consciousness, it is meant to raise them to the next step up, my beloved.

Now, what does this mean? This means that when you have any expression of Christ possible on earth, it is possible for the mind of antichrist to look at it, to analyze it, and to find fault with it. This is part of what Master MORE expressed this morning, that some students had gone into this judgmental attitude, which is really that they were using the mind of anti-christ to find fault. You will see that some of the questions asked this afternoon were asked from that level of consciousness, of actually attempting to find fault with the teaching or the teacher. This is, of course, what the mind of anti-christ always does.

You need to recognize here that beyond your own selves, that you have in your four lower bodies, is this planetary momentum of anti-christ that will always seek to come in and challenge any expression of Christ, attempting to put it down. Its purpose is two things. You have a person who is the open door for the expression of Christ and you have one or more people receiving that expression. The forces of anti-christ, the mind of anti-christ, wants to sow doubt in the mind of the people receiving the gift so that they will start doubting it and maybe even reject it. It wants to sow doubt in the mind of the person being the open door for giving the gift so that the person will doubt its own ability to be the instrument for the Christ in the future and perhaps, therefore, gradually decide to shut it off or impose some outer standard upon it.

You need to simply recognize that this force can, of course, magnify or work through whatever selves you have. You actually need to recognize that even when you have overcome the selves you have in your four lower bodies, this force can still project at you from without. You need to simply come to recognize and be aware that this force is there. It will always project at you.

Then, you need to recognize that there is nothing you need to do about this. You do not need to defend yourself. You do not need to try to refute this. You do not need to try and answer the questions that are asked from this state of mind because, as I said earlier today, they can never be answered. If you try to answer one question, seven more will come up. You just need to be aware that this is there, recognize it for what it is and let it pass through you. As long as you have the unresolved selves, then it cannot pass through you, it will hit one of those selves and magnify it. When you have resolved the selves, you just let it pass through you. As I said: "What is that too thee, follow thou me." In the beginning, it can help you to turn to me and really envision how you just let this pass through you and you are focusing your attention on me. You do not even pay attention to this.

Now, of course, this is a delicate balance because your ego would love to think that it is infallible and therefore you never need to pay attention to criticism. Sometimes, you may need to pay attention to what people are giving you of feedback. You can learn to discern between when people are simply expressing whatever concerns they have and, then, when it actually comes through the mind of anti-christ. You can learn to identify the difference. People might have feedback that shows you how they reacted at their level of consciousness. It might help you refine the next expression of how you approach these people, based on understanding their level of consciousness. When you feel that this simply comes from the anti-christ that is seeking to put you down, you just let it pass through you.

When I say that you should be open to feedback from people, that is also said with a caution because you cannot go into over-analyzing yourself. You have to be the *open* door, be neutral, in a neutral frame of mind and allow the Spirit to express itself. This is, quite frankly, the greatest challenge when you begin to have more Christhood. It is to not be completely closed but not over-analyze and therefore lose the spontaneity. It is a delicate balance. I faced it when I was in embodiment, we have all faced it before we ascended. *You* need to face it and you need to go through it in your own way but it is (again) not that there is one absolute expression of Christhood. Therefore, you need to recognize here that whatever expression of Christhood you were able to bring forth, there was nothing wrong with it. It may be that there can be a higher expression of Christhood but it does not mean that the other one was wrong. There is no reason to go into this mindset of: "Was this wrong?"

This needs to drop, my beloved, and there actually comes a point where, even though you have dissolved a certain self, you need to make a conscious decision: "I am not engaging this anymore, I am not even putting my attention on it. I am focused on being the open door and I am allowing other people to react to it however they want to react."

Wanting to help people too much

It can be a hindrance when you attain some Christhood that you really want to help other people and so you are in this mode of: "How can I help other people." This messenger has been in this mode for many lifetimes and was in this mode in this lifetime even after becoming a messenger. How could he best help other people and how could he not stand in the way of the expression of the Spirit through him?

It is, of course, valid to consider this but you have to find this very delicate balance. You, first of all, have to work on overcoming these outer selves so that you are actually free of them and not compelled to react to other people. You have to come to a point where you are not actually reacting to other people and how they accept or do not accept what is offered through you. You are observing, you might learn from what you observe but you are not reacting. You are not feeling that you *have* to change yourself based on their reactions because you acknowledge that their reactions are a product of their level of consciousness, including the selves they have that are unresolved.

Many people will come to you when you attain some degree of Christhood and they have an unresolved self that is coloring their view of the spiritual path. They have used the teachings on the spiritual path to validate and reinforce that self. Now, they come to you and they want you to validate that self as well. Sometimes they become angry, sometimes they become disappointed, sometimes they start accusing you of not being a true representative of Christ because you are not validating the self that they are not willing to separate themselves from and give up. You need to be aware of this.

My beloved, I realize, once again, that we are throwing a lot of concepts at you. You do not all need to pay attention to everything I say at this point. You need to find one thing in a dictation that you feel applies to you right now and then you internalize it. You accept that other things I said are for other people at different levels of consciousness. Sometimes some of the things I say no longer apply to you because you have risen above that level of consciousness. Sometimes there are things that will apply to you in the future when you rise to a certain level of consciousness.

No gap between you and Spirit

As Master MORE said, there is a limit to what can be given through words. Truly, you need to come to the point where you are not seeking to be the Christ based on a sense of distance, based on a gap. When you overcome the primal self and other selves, when you come to the point that Master MORE described where you have depersonalized the path, there is not a mechanism in the mind that seeks to filter what is coming from Spirit. There is not even the sense that you are "here" or that Spirit is "up there." Spirit is sending something to your mind that is then flowing through it. You can overcome the sense of separation. Many of you cannot grasp what I am saying here but some of you *can*. *All* of you will eventually be able to grasp this.

There comes that point where there is no structure in the mind that makes you think you should be a certain way when you are the Living Christ. Therefore, you are not looking at it through the mind, you are simply experiencing that the opening is there, that the flow is there and then you experience the flow as it is happening.

This messenger has many times been asked how he experiences a dictation and he has tried to explain the same thing. It is not that he sees himself as being here, and I am up there and I am releasing words from the ascended realm and he hears them in his mind and expresses them. No, we achieve a state of Oneness and the words are flowing through the messenger's mind and he is hearing them as they are being spoken because there is no gap. Therefore, when there is no gap, there is no room for your consciousness, the consciousness of other people or the fallen consciousness to interfere with the process. There is no gap there. There is no structure, there is no mechanism. It is a direct flow, a direct expression and you do not analyze it before it is happening, so why would you analyze it afterwards? Just let it flow and then afterwards let it be, let yourself be, let other people be. Let them react the way they react. If you are neutral when the gift is given, then it is the worthy offering.

Of course, people can only receive it fully when they are neutral but it is your responsibility to keep *yourself* neutral. It is not *your* responsibility to keep other people neutral. Your responsibility is to give the gift, to be the open door for the giving of the gift. It is not your responsibility how other people receive it. That is *their* responsibility. When you are clear on that in your mind, then you can avoid all of these very, very subtle temptations and projections from the fallen beings who will want you to get to the point where one expression of Christhood becomes the last one you dare to ever let happen through you.

Expressing Christhood online

I actually have one more thing I wish to give you and that is that we have reached a point now where we have given enough teachings through this messenger. There is a certain number of you who are following this teaching, some of you are new, some of you have been with this teaching for a while but you are ready to start expressing your Christhood in a more direct manner. There are, of course, many, many ways this can be done but certainly one of the ways it can be done is through the Internet.

Now, in my Christhood course [*Master Keys to Personal Christhood*] I gave you the task, those of you who have completed the course, to write your life story. With the modern phenomenon of blogging, why not write that story as a blog?

Why not create some website or a blog that takes the teachings of the ascended masters and applies them to a specific area? You could even take a specific area, you could search through all the teachings we have given, find all the things we have said and then put those ideas on a website. You can do it in your own words where you do it in a neutral way so that people are not required to believe in ascended masters or you can give the quotes, as long as you acknowledge where they came from. There are a myriad of ways that you can use the Internet to express your Christhood and thereby reach more people than you reach personally. It can also be a good way for you to practice expressing your Christhood and observing the reactions you have in yourself to this. You can also form, if you want, some kind of groups to help each other. Some of you have computer experience and can help those who have less experience and therefore you can begin to support each other. You can also help each other evaluate each other, give each other feedback and thereby begin to share many, many things. You can create a presence on the Internet that is not there today, that has never been seen there because you are coming from many different backgrounds, yet there will be some commonality, some deeper oneness to what you are expressing when you come from some degree of clarity and wholeness and having healed your psychology, letting go of these outer selves.

It is time for us to encourage you to do this. You have, of course, free will. You are not meant to be forced. We do not want you to force yourself to do this but there are certainly some of you who are ready to do this in some way. It is time for you to step up and stop thinking that the messenger is the one who has to create all the websites. Realize that you too have the potential and you have the experience and the attainment to do something. Again, be clear. What you can express now is not an ultimate expression of Christ but by expressing it now, you will be able to refine it. If you do not express it now, then you will not be able to refine it and you will not grow.

Go back to the situation of the wedding in Cana. I am standing there at one of these crossroads in my life. Will I start my public mission or will I postpone it? Well, if Mother Mary had not pushed me, I would not have done it. I am now pushing *you*. If I had not accepted it and dared to do it, would there have been an example set at the beginning of the Piscean Age? Well, maybe I would have done it later—*maybe*.

You cannot know what tomorrow will bring. You can only know the now, you can only act in the now. Maybe now is the "now" for you to step forward and turn the water of the human consciousness in some area of life on earth into the wine of the Christ consciousness flowing through you!

With this my beloved, I thank you for your attention, for your willingness to be the magnifiers for radiating this into the collective consciousness of the planet, which will have far-ranging effects, more than you will ever know with the outer mind. Truly, you could say that my public mission 2,000 years ago formed the alpha polarity and what we are giving now through this progressive revelation, not only through this messenger but

9 | It is time to express your Christhood

through other messengers as well, is the omega polarity. The beginning of the Piscean Age—the ending of the Piscean Age, but really, the Piscean Age cannot come to a full end until there has been a public expression of the true teachings of Christ.

You can be part of that expression, part of that public wave where suddenly everybody has an opportunity to encounter the true teachings of Christ, an opportunity that they have not been given during the Age of Pisces. When they have received that opportunity, *then* the end will come, not the end of the world but the end of the Piscean Age. Then, the planet can move more fully into Aquarius. We can start focusing on building the Golden Age of Saint Germain instead of playing catch-up, trying to fulfil all the things that were not fulfilled during Pisces.

You may have concerns about whether you are ready for this, whether you are worthy for this. These concerns come from your primal self and other selves. Therefore, I can only say: "Leave your nets and follow me and I will make you fishers of men, women and children."

10 | INVOKING THE VISION TO EXPRESS MY CHRISTHOOD

In the name I AM THAT I AM, Jesus Christ, I call to all representatives of the Divine Mother, especially Jesus, to help me overcome the illusions that prevent me from expressing my Christhood, including…

[Make personal calls.]

Part 1

1. Jesus, help me see if I have become so over-zealous in my zeal to do *something,* so that I have acted in an unbalanced manner that is not being the Living Christ in action.

> O Jesus, blessed brother mine,
> I walk the path that you outline,
> a great example to us all,
> I follow now your inner call.

> O Jesus, let the Fire of Joy,
> consume the devil's subtle ploy,
> transfigured is our planet earth,
> the golden age is given birth.

2. Jesus, help me see if I have a self that is concerned about not being wrong, and once it has convinced itself that it has done the right thing, then it is very reluctant to consider that it might not be the right thing at all.

> O Jesus, open inner sight,
> the ego wants to prove it's right,
> but this I will no longer do,
> I want to be all one with you.

> **O Jesus, let the Fire of Joy,**
> **consume the devil's subtle ploy,**
> **transfigured is our planet earth,**
> **the golden age is given birth.**

3. Jesus, help me see that it is very difficult for you to help people who are absolutely convinced that they are good people and they have done a lot of good things.

> O Jesus, I now clearly see,
> the Key of Knowledge given me,
> my Christ self I hereby embrace,
> as you fill up my inner space.

> **O Jesus, let the Fire of Joy,**
> **consume the devil's subtle ploy,**
> **transfigured is our planet earth,**
> **the golden age is given birth.**

4. Jesus, help me recognize if the fallen beings made me feel that I had done something here on earth that was so wrong that I could never be redeemed. Help me see if I created a separate self that is programmed to make sure that I can never again be proven really wrong.

O Jesus, show me serpent's lie,
expose the beam in my own eye,
as Christ discernment you me give,
in oneness I forever live.

O Jesus, let the Fire of Joy,
consume the devil's subtle ploy,
transfigured is our planet earth,
the golden age is given birth.

5. Jesus, help me see if this self has caused me to build a momentum of supposedly doing the right thing, by always doing what is defined as right in my culture or religion.

O Jesus, I am truly meek,
and thus I turn the other cheek,
when the accuser attacks me,
I go within and merge with thee.

O Jesus, let the Fire of Joy,
consume the devil's subtle ploy,
transfigured is our planet earth,
the golden age is given birth.

6. Jesus, help me see that when I am standing in front of the gate that leads to the ascended realm, I have to make a free choice to go through it. My Conscious You can make a free choice only when I do not have any of these selves that are coloring my vision.

O Jesus, ego I let die,
surrender ev'ry earthly tie,
the dead can bury what is dead,
I choose to walk with you instead.

O Jesus, let the Fire of Joy,
consume the devil's subtle ploy,
transfigured is our planet earth,
the golden age is given birth.

7. Jesus, help me see that the self that is programmed to make me never be wrong, stands in the way of my ascension. I cannot ascend if I do not let go of it, and I cannot let go of it, if I have not looked at it. I cannot look at it if I am so afraid of seeing anything wrong in my being.

> O Jesus, help me rise above,
> the devil's test through higher love,
> show me separate self unreal,
> my formless self you do reveal.
>
> **O Jesus, let the Fire of Joy,**
> **consume the devil's subtle ploy,**
> **transfigured is our planet earth,**
> **the golden age is given birth.**

8. Jesus, help me see that as long as I have the self that never wants to be proven wrong, I cannot accept your acceptance and love. I will always have the fear of being wrong. I cannot transcend it as long as I have that self because the self cannot question the basic programming.

> O Jesus, what is that to me,
> I just let go and follow thee,
> with this I do pass ev'ry test,
> to find with you eternal rest.
>
> **O Jesus, let the Fire of Joy,**
> **consume the devil's subtle ploy,**
> **transfigured is our planet earth,**
> **the golden age is given birth.**

9. Jesus, help me see that as long as I am seeing myself through the filter of that self, *I* cannot question it either. Help me, as the Conscious You, step outside of that self and realize that there are two ways to prevent myself from ascending.

> O Jesus, fiery master mine,
> my heart now melting into thine,
> I love with heart and mind and soul,
> the God who is my highest goal.

> O Jesus, let the Fire of Joy,
> consume the devil's subtle ploy,
> transfigured is our planet earth,
> the golden age is given birth.

Part 2

1. Jesus, help me see that one way to block my ascension is to be in a very negative, self-centered, selfish state of mind. The other way is to be a good person and wanting to maintain that image to the point where I will not question that there could be something in me that will not allow me to go into the ascended state.

> O Jesus, blessed brother mine,
> I walk the path that you outline,
> a great example to us all,
> I follow now your inner call.

> **O Jesus, let the Fire of Joy,**
> **consume the devil's subtle ploy,**
> **transfigured is our planet earth,**
> **the golden age is given birth.**

2. Jesus, help me realize that when I see myself through that self, I will think that if there is something in me that is not *right*, then it must be *wrong*. Then, that must mean that *I am* wrong and therefore I cannot look at it.

> O Jesus, open inner sight,
> the ego wants to prove it's right,
> but this I will no longer do,
> I want to be all one with you.

> **O Jesus, let the Fire of Joy,**
> **consume the devil's subtle ploy,**
> **transfigured is our planet earth,**
> **the golden age is given birth.**

3. Jesus, help me break this deadlock by inspiring the Conscious You to go outside of that self and see that it is just a self. It is only this self that believes that by doing good things, I will automatically go to heaven. It is just a self and as all selves, it is based on an illusion.

> O Jesus, I now clearly see,
> the Key of Knowledge given me,
> my Christ self I hereby embrace,
> as you fill up my inner space.
>
> **O Jesus, let the Fire of Joy,**
> **consume the devil's subtle ploy,**
> **transfigured is our planet earth,**
> **the golden age is given birth.**

4. Jesus, help me, as the Conscious You, recognize that this self is not me. Help me realize that I cannot take this self with me into the ascended realm because I did not bring it with me when I came here.

> O Jesus, show me serpent's lie,
> expose the beam in my own eye,
> as Christ discernment you me give,
> in oneness I forever live.
>
> **O Jesus, let the Fire of Joy,**
> **consume the devil's subtle ploy,**
> **transfigured is our planet earth,**
> **the golden age is given birth.**

5. Jesus, help me recognize that being good and thinking I am good and have been good can also be a hindrance to my ascension. As long as I am trying to do good based on such a self, I cannot be the Christ in action.

> O Jesus, I am truly meek,
> and thus I turn the other cheek,
> when the accuser attacks me,
> I go within and merge with thee.

**O Jesus, let the Fire of Joy,
consume the devil's subtle ploy,
transfigured is our planet earth,
the golden age is given birth.**

6. Jesus, help me see if I am seeking to do good in order to prevent myself from being proven wrong. Help me see that this is centered around this lower self, not my real self but the lower self. This is my motivation and it is not the Christ consciousness.

O Jesus, ego I let die,
surrender ev'ry earthly tie,
the dead can bury what is dead,
I choose to walk with you instead.

**O Jesus, let the Fire of Joy,
consume the devil's subtle ploy,
transfigured is our planet earth,
the golden age is given birth.**

7. Jesus, help me recognize that I am already, to some degree, the Christ in action and I have been the Christ in action for this lifetime. Help me become conscious of it and see that it has not been happening all the time.

O Jesus, help me rise above,
the devil's test through higher love,
show me separate self unreal,
my formless self you do reveal.

**O Jesus, let the Fire of Joy,
consume the devil's subtle ploy,
transfigured is our planet earth,
the golden age is given birth.**

8. Jesus, help me see if I have created a self that thinks I can only be saved when I live up to this almost super-human standard. The self thinks that as long as I do not live up to this standard, or if I do not live up to it all the time, then I cannot be the Christ.

> O Jesus, what is that to me,
> I just let go and follow thee,
> with this I do pass ev'ry test,
> to find with you eternal rest.
>
> **O Jesus, let the Fire of Joy,**
> **consume the devil's subtle ploy,**
> **transfigured is our planet earth,**
> **the golden age is given birth.**

9. Jesus, help me see that the idea of Christ taking incarnation means that the Christ consciousness can be expressed through a vehicle that is not yet completely free of all these outer selves. When the Conscious You can step outside of my current sense of self, I can be the open door for the Christ consciousness.

> O Jesus, fiery master mine,
> my heart now melting into thine,
> I love with heart and mind and soul,
> the God who is my highest goal.
>
> **O Jesus, let the Fire of Joy,**
> **consume the devil's subtle ploy,**
> **transfigured is our planet earth,**
> **the golden age is given birth.**

Part 3

1. Jesus, help me see that being the Christ in action means I am the open door for expressing something that is beyond the normal state of awareness that most people are in, such as giving the gift of acceptance to people.

> O Jesus, blessed brother mine,
> I walk the path that you outline,
> a great example to us all,
> I follow now your inner call.

> O Jesus, let the Fire of Joy,
> consume the devil's subtle ploy,
> transfigured is our planet earth,
> the golden age is given birth.

2. Jesus, help me see that the key to being open, to being the instrument for the expression of the Christ consciousness, is to not have all these expectations or pre-conceived opinions about how the Christ *should* or *should not* express itself.

> O Jesus, open inner sight,
> the ego wants to prove it's right,
> but this I will no longer do,
> I want to be all one with you.

> **O Jesus, let the Fire of Joy,**
> **consume the devil's subtle ploy,**
> **transfigured is our planet earth,**
> **the golden age is given birth.**

3. Jesus, help me see if I have used your teachings to reinforce one of the outer selves that is an offspring of my primal self. Help me see any fixed image of what it means to be the Christ in action both for myself and also how you were when you were in embodiment.

> O Jesus, I now clearly see,
> the Key of Knowledge given me,
> my Christ self I hereby embrace,
> as you fill up my inner space.

> **O Jesus, let the Fire of Joy,**
> **consume the devil's subtle ploy,**
> **transfigured is our planet earth,**
> **the golden age is given birth.**

4. Jesus, help me, with the Conscious You, look in my being and see what pre-conceived opinions and expectations I have about how the Christ should or should not be.

O Jesus, show me serpent's lie,
expose the beam in my own eye,
as Christ discernment you me give,
in oneness I forever live.

O Jesus, let the Fire of Joy,
consume the devil's subtle ploy,
transfigured is our planet earth,
the golden age is given birth.

5. Jesus, help me see if I have a self that has some kind of judgment about how the Living Christ should be. If I feel that the expression of Spirit needs to conform to my standard, the standard in that self, then the Holy Spirit cannot flow.

O Jesus, I am truly meek,
and thus I turn the other cheek,
when the accuser attacks me,
I go within and merge with thee.

O Jesus, let the Fire of Joy,
consume the devil's subtle ploy,
transfigured is our planet earth,
the golden age is given birth.

6. Jesus, help me see that the Holy Spirit does not flow according to human opinions, expectations and standards. The Holy Spirit is constantly flowing, it simply needs an opening in order to come to expression in the physical octave.

O Jesus, ego I let die,
surrender ev'ry earthly tie,
the dead can bury what is dead,
I choose to walk with you instead.

O Jesus, let the Fire of Joy,
consume the devil's subtle ploy,
transfigured is our planet earth,
the golden age is given birth.

7. Jesus, help me come to the point where I start becoming the open door and I do not have a compulsion to express my Christhood. I do not feel I have to, I am not afraid of it, I am not concerned about it. I let it happen.

> O Jesus, help me rise above,
> the devil's test through higher love,
> show me separate self unreal,
> my formless self you do reveal.
>
> **O Jesus, let the Fire of Joy,**
> **consume the devil's subtle ploy,**
> **transfigured is our planet earth,**
> **the golden age is given birth.**

8. Jesus, help me recognize that when I let it happen, when I am in a neutral frame of mind, the flow will be there and I do not have all of these concerns about whether I did the right thing or whether this was okay or whether this was good enough.

> O Jesus, what is that to me,
> I just let go and follow thee,
> with this I do pass ev'ry test,
> to find with you eternal rest.
>
> **O Jesus, let the Fire of Joy,**
> **consume the devil's subtle ploy,**
> **transfigured is our planet earth,**
> **the golden age is given birth.**

9. Jesus, help me see that there will be a temptation to analyze when I have felt the flow of the Spirit. Help me use that as an opportunity to realize it is another outer self that is causing this reaction in me. Help me identify the self, separate myself from it and let it die.

> O Jesus, fiery master mine,
> my heart now melting into thine,
> I love with heart and mind and soul,
> the God who is my highest goal.

**O Jesus, let the Fire of Joy,
consume the devil's subtle ploy,
transfigured is our planet earth,
the golden age is given birth.**

Part 4

1. Jesus, help me come to the point where I am beginning to be more open to the flow of the Christ, and all of these concerns of whether I did the right thing will fade away. Help me recognize that: "It was what it was."

> O Jesus, blessed brother mine,
> I walk the path that you outline,
> a great example to us all,
> I follow now your inner call.

> **O Jesus, let the Fire of Joy,
> consume the devil's subtle ploy,
> transfigured is our planet earth,
> the golden age is given birth.**

2. Jesus, help me recognize that there is no ultimate or absolute expression of Christ possible, for the very simple reason that this is an unnatural planet. An expression of Christ will always happen in a particular situation. It is expressed to people at a certain level of consciousness. It is not meant to raise them to the highest level of consciousness, it is meant to raise them to the next step up.

> O Jesus, open inner sight,
> the ego wants to prove it's right,
> but this I will no longer do,
> I want to be all one with you.

> **O Jesus, let the Fire of Joy,
> consume the devil's subtle ploy,
> transfigured is our planet earth,
> the golden age is given birth.**

3. Jesus, help me see that when there is any expression of Christ on earth, it is possible for the mind of anti-christ to look at it, to analyze it and to find fault with it. Help me recognize that beyond my own selves is the planetary momentum of anti-christ that will always seek to come in and challenge any expression of Christ, attempting to put it down.

> O Jesus, I now clearly see,
> the Key of Knowledge given me,
> my Christ self I hereby embrace,
> as you fill up my inner space.
>
> **O Jesus, let the Fire of Joy,**
> **consume the devil's subtle ploy,**
> **transfigured is our planet earth,**
> **the golden age is given birth.**

4. Jesus, help me see that he forces of anti-christ want to sow doubt in my mind so that I will doubt my own ability to be the instrument for the Christ in the future and decide to shut it off or impose some outer standard upon it.

> O Jesus, show me serpent's lie,
> expose the beam in my own eye,
> as Christ discernment you me give,
> in oneness I forever live.
>
> **O Jesus, let the Fire of Joy,**
> **consume the devil's subtle ploy,**
> **transfigured is our planet earth,**
> **the golden age is given birth.**

5. Jesus, help me recognize that this force can magnify or work through whatever selves I have. Help me see that even when I have overcome the selves I have in my four lower bodies, this force can still project at me from without. Help me recognize and be aware that this force is there and it will always project at me.

> O Jesus, I am truly meek,
> and thus I turn the other cheek,

when the accuser attacks me,
I go within and merge with thee.

O Jesus, let the Fire of Joy,
consume the devil's subtle ploy,
transfigured is our planet earth,
the golden age is given birth.

6. Jesus, help me recognize that there is nothing I need to do about this. I do not need to defend myself. I do not need to try to refute this. I do not need to try and answer the questions that are asked from this state of mind because they can never be answered. I just need to be aware that this is there, recognize it for what it is and let it pass through me.

O Jesus, ego I let die,
surrender ev'ry earthly tie,
the dead can bury what is dead,
I choose to walk with you instead.

O Jesus, let the Fire of Joy,
consume the devil's subtle ploy,
transfigured is our planet earth,
the golden age is given birth.

7. Jesus, help me build a habit of turning to you, envisioning how I let the projections pass through me and focusing my attention on you, saying: "Jesus, what is that to me, I will follow thee."

O Jesus, help me rise above,
the devil's test through higher love,
show me separate self unreal,
my formless self you do reveal.

O Jesus, let the Fire of Joy,
consume the devil's subtle ploy,
transfigured is our planet earth,
the golden age is given birth.

8. Jesus, help me find the delicate balance of not thinking I am infallible and realizing that I sometimes need to pay attention when people are giving me feedback. Help me learn to discern between when people are expressing concerns and when it comes through the mind of anti-christ.

> O Jesus, what is that to me,
> I just let go and follow thee,
> with this I do pass ev'ry test,
> to find with you eternal rest.
>
> **O Jesus, let the Fire of Joy,**
> **consume the devil's subtle ploy,**
> **transfigured is our planet earth,**
> **the golden age is given birth.**

9. Jesus, help me not go into over-analyzing myself. Help me be the *open* door, be neutral, in a neutral frame of mind and allow the Spirit to express itself. Help me to not be completely closed but not over-analyze and therefore lose the spontaneity.

> O Jesus, fiery master mine,
> my heart now melting into thine,
> I love with heart and mind and soul,
> the God who is my highest goal.
>
> **O Jesus, let the Fire of Joy,**
> **consume the devil's subtle ploy,**
> **transfigured is our planet earth,**
> **the golden age is given birth.**

Part 5

1. Jesus, help me recognize that whatever expression of Christhood I was able to bring forth, there was nothing wrong with it. It may be that there can be a higher expression of Christhood but it does not mean that the other one was wrong.

O Jesus, blessed brother mine,
I walk the path that you outline,
a great example to us all,
I follow now your inner call.

**O Jesus, let the Fire of Joy,
consume the devil's subtle ploy,
transfigured is our planet earth,
the golden age is given birth.**

2. Jesus, help me see that even though I have dissolved a certain self, I need to make a conscious decision: "I am not engaging this anymore, I am not even putting my attention on it. I am focused on being the open door and I am allowing other people to react to it however they want to react."

O Jesus, open inner sight,
the ego wants to prove it's right,
but this I will no longer do,
I want to be all one with you.

**O Jesus, let the Fire of Joy,
consume the devil's subtle ploy,
transfigured is our planet earth,
the golden age is given birth.**

3. Jesus, help me see that wanting to help other people can be a hindrance on the path of Christhood. Help me come to a point where I am not reacting to other people. I am observing, I learn from what I observe but I am not reacting.

O Jesus, I now clearly see,
the Key of Knowledge given me,
my Christ self I hereby embrace,
as you fill up my inner space.

**O Jesus, let the Fire of Joy,
consume the devil's subtle ploy,
transfigured is our planet earth,
the golden age is given birth.**

4. Jesus, help me come to the point where I am not feeling that I have to change myself based on people's reactions. I acknowledge that their reactions are a product of their level of consciousness, including the selves they have that are unresolved.

> O Jesus, show me serpent's lie,
> expose the beam in my own eye,
> as Christ discernment you me give,
> in oneness I forever live.
>
> **O Jesus, let the Fire of Joy,**
> **consume the devil's subtle ploy,**
> **transfigured is our planet earth,**
> **the golden age is given birth.**

5. Jesus, help me see that some people will come to me with an unresolved self that is coloring their view of the spiritual path. They want me to validate that self, and sometimes they become angry when I am not validating the self that they are not willing to separate themselves from and give up.

> O Jesus, I am truly meek,
> and thus I turn the other cheek,
> when the accuser attacks me,
> I go within and merge with thee.
>
> **O Jesus, let the Fire of Joy,**
> **consume the devil's subtle ploy,**
> **transfigured is our planet earth,**
> **the golden age is given birth.**

6. Jesus, help me come to the point where I am not seeking to be the Christ based on a sense of distance, based on a gap. Help me overcome the sense that I am "here" or that Spirit is "up there." Help me overcome the sense of separation.

> O Jesus, ego I let die,
> surrender ev'ry earthly tie,
> the dead can bury what is dead,
> I choose to walk with you instead.

> **O Jesus, let the Fire of Joy,**
> **consume the devil's subtle ploy,**
> **transfigured is our planet earth,**
> **the golden age is given birth.**

7. Jesus, help me come to the point where there is no structure in the mind that makes me think I should be a certain way when I am the Living Christ. I am not looking at it through the mind, I am simply experiencing that the opening is there, and I experience the flow as it is happening.

> O Jesus, help me rise above,
> the devil's test through higher love,
> show me separate self unreal,
> my formless self you do reveal.

> **O Jesus, let the Fire of Joy,**
> **consume the devil's subtle ploy,**
> **transfigured is our planet earth,**
> **the golden age is given birth.**

8. Jesus, help me see that when there is no gap, there is no room for my consciousness, the consciousness of other people or the fallen consciousness to interfere with the process. Help me see that it is my responsibility to keep *myself* neutral. It is not *my* responsibility to keep other people neutral. My responsibility is to give the gift, and it is not my responsibility how other people receive it.

> O Jesus, what is that to me,
> I just let go and follow thee,
> with this I do pass ev'ry test,
> to find with you eternal rest.

> **O Jesus, let the Fire of Joy,**
> **consume the devil's subtle ploy,**
> **transfigured is our planet earth,**
> **the golden age is given birth.**

9. Jesus, help me see how I can use the Internet to express my Christhood and use the teachings given by the ascended masters in the area of expertise I have and that I have specified in my Divine plan for this embodiment.

> O Jesus, fiery master mine,
> my heart now melting into thine,
> I love with heart and mind and soul,
> the God who is my highest goal.
>
> **O Jesus, let the Fire of Joy,**
> **consume the devil's subtle ploy,**
> **transfigured is our planet earth,**
> **the golden age is given birth.**

Sealing

In the name of the Divine Mother, I call to Mother Mary for the sealing of myself and all people in my circle of influence in the creative flow of the Divine Mother, the River of Life. I call for the multiplication of my calls by all representatives of the Divine Mother, so that we form the perfect figure-eight flow of "As Above, so below." Thus, I accept that this is fully manifest, because the mouth of the Lord, the Divine Mother that I AM, has spoken it. Amen.

11 | THE DILEMMA OF BEING ON EARTH

I AM indeed the Dhyani Buddha known as Vairochana. I AM, of course, also, from your perspective, the Ascended Master Vairochana. I come to give you some perspective on how you can move closer to being the Buddha in action on a planet as dense as earth. For this purpose we of the Dhyani Buddhas have previously given the concept that what prevents you from being the Buddha in action is that there are certain spiritual poisons. The antidote to those poisons is the particular flames of wisdom that we represent. Of course, this is in no way incompatible with the teaching you have now been given on the primal self and the many other separate selves that spring from that. Certainly, you could say that any self is based on one, or perhaps even more than one, of these spiritual poisons.

Ignorance of who you are

Some of you will know that the poison that I am the antidote for is ignorance and that my antidote, my wisdom, is the All-Pervading Wisdom. What is ignorance? Well, it has, of course, myriad forms and shapes and we can express it in many ways in words. One way to describe it is, certainly, to say that it is the ignorance of self, the ignorance of who you are.

This, of course, presents somewhat of a paradox. We have given you these teachings about the Conscious You descending into the four levels of this unascended sphere. This is a very profound teaching. Some of you have studied it to the point where you feel you understand it intellectually and you almost take it for granted. You are not quite aware of how profound this teaching is, in fact, how *revolutionary* it is compared to most of the teachings that have been available on this planet throughout history.

It is almost as if you can use a spiritual teaching to create a new form of ignorance where, in your outer mind, you feel you know the teaching. Therefore, you do not look for a deeper understanding or rather a deeper *experience*. It is as if for you, the Conscious You has become just another concept.

When you truly look at the teaching on the Conscious You, if you truly grasp it, when you experience the reality of it, you realize, you *experience* that the Conscious You is just a concept but it is more than a concept. You cannot fully internalize the teaching while looking at the Conscious You through the outer mind, especially the intellectual, analytical mind. You can only appreciate the teaching when you *experience* yourself as a formless being. When you have that experience, then you appreciate, you have fully internalized and made use of the teaching. As long as you are sitting there in your mind, having formulated a concept of the Conscious You and you see it from a distance, you have not made use of the teaching.

We could say that with any teaching that has ever been given throughout history, including the teachings given by Gautama 2,500 years ago, if you use it to create a concept that actually validates your sense of distance, then you have misused the teaching—at least, if you do not strive for more.

From teaching to experience

What would be the byword, the motto, the catchphrase of a true spiritual student? Well, first of all, you need to know that it is not enough to *understand* the teaching, you need to *experience* the reality behind the teaching. A teaching that is expressed in words is, of course, in a certain way only a way-shower, a symbol that points the way to an experience that is beyond words. Only when you have the experience, have you made full use of the teaching. This is perhaps the greatest problem of ignorance among spiritual students. They think the outer teaching, and understanding it with the outer mind, is enough. They do not go beyond to the experience. The first

11 | The dilemma of being on earth

byword is: "Go beyond the teaching to the experience." The real catchphrase that you might adopt as a spiritual student is this: "There is always *more* to experience." There is always more to *experience!*

I AM the Dhyani Buddha that has the antidote—in fact, I *am* the antidote to the poison of ignorance. If you tune in to me, experience my Presence, you can overcome all ignorance. Theoretically, you could tune in to me, come into oneness with me, and in a split second, all your ignorance could be burned away by my Presence. We do not advocate this because you are here to have an experience, a variety of experiences.

We have given the teaching that when you first descend to earth, you go through the immersion phase of immersing yourself in this realm. Then, you go through the awakening phase and the experience that you are here to have is of gradually descending, gradually immersing and then gradually awakening. You are not here to have the experience of awakening in a split second. You are here to have the experience of gradually awakening, awakening in increments by rising up to the 144th level of consciousness.

We might say that the awakening phase starts at the 48th level and then you gradually awaken until you are at the 144th level. It is not that you have fully awakened at the 144th level but you have reached the highest level of awakeness possible on earth. Then, you can ascend from earth and go into a new spiral of awakening to higher and higher levels of awareness as an ascended master. We of the ascended masters are constantly growing in consciousness. Even at our level of the Dhyani Buddhas, there is growth. That is why I say, if you want to take an important step towards overcoming ignorance, then fixate in your mind that whatever experience you are having right now, there is always more to experience.

Defining ignorance

What is ignorance? On a natural planet is there ignorance? Well, yes, there is ignorance in the sense that as you start as a new being on a natural planet, you start with a point-like sense of awareness. You are gradually expanding that sense of awareness. You could say that even in the ascended realm there is ignorance, in the sense that I have the self-awareness at the level of a Dhyani Buddha but I am not the Creator. I am not at the level of self-awareness of a Creator so I am ignorant of what you experience from the level of self-awareness of a Creator. Yet you need to understand that in the ascended realm, and even on a natural planet, there are not the kind of barriers to knowledge that you have on earth.

In the ascended realm there are really no barriers to knowledge. You can go anywhere you want to go. That is why, when Mark Prophet ascended as the Ascended Master Lanello, his first exclamation was: "I am everywhere in the consciousness of God." He realized that now that he was no longer in embodiment on a dense planet, he could go everywhere in the consciousness of God. There are no barriers to where you can go. Of course, there is, again, the process in the ascended realm of gradually raising your self-awareness. No one can switch from even an ascended master level to the Creator level in one step.

On a natural planet you also have a greater access to knowledge, to experience, to information. You can go and explore anything at that level of awareness of a natural planet. On earth, however, which has become an unnatural planet, there are many barriers to what you can know even what you can experience. We might say that if you look behind me there is a big screen. How do you create ignorance on earth? Well, we have said that as you descend to the 48th level of consciousness, you take on an illusion for each level of consciousness you descend, starting with the illusion corresponding to the 144th level, the 143rd and so on. For each of these illusions, it is as if you put up a screen like the one behind me.

What does this screen do? When you are standing on this side of the screen, you cannot see what is behind it. This is, in a sense, the entire function of a dense-matter planet. It allows you to have a sense of self where there are certain things you cannot see. What is the purpose of this? The purpose is to allow you to explore the full range of what is possible with self-awareness and free will.

Free will gives you the right to have any experience you want. How do you have an experience? By creating a self and experiencing the world, life and yourself through that self. On a natural planet there are certain types of selves you cannot create, for you have a higher awareness on a natural planet. You cannot believe, for example, that you are a completely separate being surrounded by other separate beings.

You cannot believe that if you harm another separate being, it will not affect yourself. On a natural planet you experience that you are part of a whole and that whatever you do, affects the whole. Whatever anyone else does, affects you. There are certain experiences of self that you cannot have on a natural planet. It is therefore perfectly within the range of free will that you have unnatural planets where those who wish to experience a more limited sense of self can descend and take embodiment.

We can say in the most general way that ignorance is when there is a barrier to what you can see, what you can know, what you can experience. You are creating a limited self by taking on these illusions, setting up these barriers in your mind, so there are certain things you cannot see. This is how you have an immersion experience. Free will allows you to go as far as you can imagine on that path of limiting your sense of self. However, we have said so far that you will experience the consequences of your choices by the Ma-ter light outpicturing what you are projecting upon it through your sense of self. Yes, that is indeed correct but there is another side to this. It is that you will also experience yourself.

Experiencing yourself

There are two aspects, we might say, an alpha and an omega to being a co-creator. So far, we have to a large extent focused on free will. You have free will, you have the will to make choices. You have the will to project onto the Mother light and co-create. The alpha aspect is that you have self-awareness. Obviously, self-awareness can mean many different things.

The self-awareness you have in the ascended realm is far higher than what you have on a natural planet, which is far higher than what you have on earth. Nevertheless, whatever kind of self you create, regardless of the degree of ignorance that this self has, you can never quite lose self-awareness. You can limit it, you can limit the *self* part, we might say, but you will have some form of *awareness*. You are not only experiencing that the Ma-ter Light out-pictures what you project upon it through your self but you are experiencing yourself through that self.

We might say that the Conscious You, being pure awareness, actually needs to go through a process. When the Conscious You is created, it does not know what to do with itself as a formless being. It needs the experience of taking a journey where it immerses itself in a more limited form of self and then gradually awakens from it. Only when it has gone through this process of immersion and awakening, can it fully accept itself as a formless being. Only when it again experiences itself as a formless being, and is able to fully accept itself as a formless being, can it ascend. In other words, the Conscious You could not be created and then immediately decide to ascend.

The entire idea of the Conscious you is that it explores the realms of free will until it has had enough of the level of expressing your free will that is possible in an unascended sphere—and then it ascends. Now, it starts a whole new level of exploring free will, this time in oneness with the I AM Presence. The I AM Presence has a whole different perspective by sending part of itself into the unascended sphere, a perspective it could never get from the ascended sphere. This might be said to be the entire purpose of creating these unascended spheres, even creating them with greater density because it gives you a different perspective. The I AM Presence gains a different perspective by sending part of itself to experience the denser realms from the inside.

Giving people a frame of reference

Why are people on earth ignorant? Well, because they are still in the immersion phase. Now, as this magnificent invocation you gave before this dictation tells you, and of course the dictation by Gautama Buddha upon which it is based, is that many of you came as avatars to earth. You came from natural planets. You came to earth and when you came to earth, you had in your mind the idea that you were here to set people free from their suffering, from their ignorance. You saw from a natural planet that on an unnatural planet, people have a much lower sense of self. They are trapped in a form of ignorance that creates suffering.

On a natural planet there is not that suffering and so you thought that: "People are trapped by their ignorance and I need to come, I *want* to come down here to help them be free of that ignorance." As Gautama was teaching you in his dictation [Published in the book *Healing Your Spiritual Traumas*, which also contains the invocation mentioned], before you can actually ascend as an avatar, you need to overcome this. You need to make peace with free will. You need to make peace with the fact that people have a right to choose to be in a certain sense of self that limits what they can see. They have a right to have that experience. You are not here to change their experience, to force them to change. You are here to give them a frame of reference.

This is an essential realization on your path to Buddhahood because as long as you maintain the idea that you (as the being you see yourself as) are here to create a change or to force a change on earth, you cannot be the Buddha as you cannot be the Living Christ. You will be acting through these outer selves. My beloved, you need to realize that when you descended, when you were exposed to the birth trauma and you created your primal self and other selves, the primal self and all selves that spring from it were created out of ignorance.

You have heard Jesus' statement about the blind leading the blind. Well, as long as you are acting through the primal self and other separate selves, you are the blind attempting to lead the blind. They may be more blind than you are but, really, that distinction is a relative distinction that has relatively little value. As long as you are blinded by this primal self (that is a reactionary self that is reactionary to the conditions you experienced on earth), you are not free of the conditions on earth. My beloved, if you are not free of the conditions on earth, how can you help other people become free?

You are seeking to raise them out of *their* form of ignorance and take on *your* form of ignorance. This is not the Buddha. The Buddha is the one who, first of all, works on himself or herself and overcomes the ignorance that you have taken on after you came to earth. Again, there is no blame. It is not wrong of you. It was simply so that for an avatar to embody on earth, for you to serve as an example, you must immerse yourself on earth. You do this by creating that primal self as a result of the shocking experience you have of experiencing the contrast between a natural planet and an unnatural planet.

The birth trauma was inevitable

We have given the concept that many of you were exposed to very aggressive attacks from the fallen beings. This is true but even on an unnatural planet with no fallen beings, an avatar descending to such a planet will still experience a birth trauma because the contrast between a natural planet and an unnatural planet is so big that you cannot prepare yourself for it from a natural planet. You simply cannot, on a natural planet, experience what it is like to be on an unnatural planet. You have to go into embodiment on an unnatural planet in order to experience it, and it *will* be a shock for you.

Many of the original inhabitants of the earth have not had this kind of a shock because they have been on earth and they have experienced a gradual descent to the point where the fallen beings could incarnate here. Their shock, their earth trauma, was encountering the fallen beings. Even if you had not encountered the fallen beings as an avatar, you would still have received a birth trauma from taking embodiment on an unnatural planet.

There is no reason to have any regret about this. It is a matter of realizing that until you awaken yourself from the illusions of the primal self, you cannot fulfil your reason for being on this planet. You cannot be the Christ in action, you cannot be the Buddha in action. You cannot bring the light, you cannot serve as an example, you cannot give people a frame of reference. You cannot help them out of their ignorance because you are trapped in your own form of ignorance.

What is it that the primal self allows you to do? It allows you to ignore the shock of being on earth, whether it was a trauma given to you by the fallen beings or whether you simply experienced a contrast. The shock was so great that it made you feel, it made you think: "Why did I come to this planet?" You were not at peace with it but you could not resolve it at the time and so you created the primal self as a screen, as a barrier.

Now, as long as you look at life on earth through the primal self, you do not see the shock, you do not see the trauma. Of course, it is still there. That is why you cannot fulfil your reason for coming here until you now use the greater experience you have on earth and the growth you have experienced on earth to go back into that birth trauma, to look at it and to make peace, in your own personal way, with being on earth.

Resolving the dilemma about being on earth

In a sense, we could say that before you descended to earth as an avatar, you had a reason in your mind for why you wanted to come here. When you descended and experienced what life was like here, you started to doubt that reason. What you need to do now at your present level is to go back, look at your reason for coming here and resolve the dilemma that being here presents. What this basically means is that you have to come to see your reason for coming here in a new light. You have to come to see that certain aspects of your reason were based on what Gautama in his dictation called inordinate desire. You have to come to the point where you can let this go, you can give it up, you can surrender it so that you are non-attached to what you accomplish or do not accomplish on earth.

As Gautama said, your sense of self-worth was still tied to your performance, to you doing something, to you producing a result. Now, that you have experienced the density of earth, you realize that it is impossible to produce the result you thought you could produce before you came here. Instead of being frustrated about this, you need to come to the point where you make peace with the fact that you came here to grow and this was the fastest way for you to grow, given the state of mind you were in before you descended here. You need to make peace with having come here, make peace with having been here, make peace with being here. Until you have made peace with coming here, being here, you cannot make peace with leaving because you think there is something you should have accomplished that you have not accomplished. As long as you have that feeling, as the very eager conscientious co-creator that you are, you cannot leave.

When you descend as an avatar, it is because you have a great desire to grow and that means you can never leave anything unfinished, unfulfilled. If you have set yourself a goal at a lower level as an avatar, you think the goal must be fulfilled before you can move on. What we are calling to you to do is to come up to the more mature level as an avatar, of realizing that there are two ways to move on from a goal. One is to fulfil it to where you have had enough of the experience, another is to look at the goal and realize it was not the highest goal. It was not really an expression of who you are. Therefore, you now see that when you give up that goal, you see a higher goal. You see that the highest goal is always your growth in self-awareness. This is when you can come to that point of making peace with the fact that your self-worth is based on who you are, based on your I AM Presence not on your accomplishments, whether it be here on earth or even on a natural planet.

Your accomplishments in this unascended sphere do not define your self-worth. It is who you are that defines your self-worth. This is a specific form of ignorance that you had before you came here. You did not fully grasp and accept that your self-worth comes from being who you are and not from what you do.

Now, we recognize that this is a very subtle challenge for co-creators. Naturally, you are created with a point-like sense of self. How do you expand your sense of self? By doing, by co creating. You will go through a phase where your sense of self-worth as a co-creator in the unascended sphere is tied to your co-creation, to the results you produce. What we are simply making you aware of is that there comes a time where you need to step up to that higher level of beginning to free yourself from this sense that your self-worth is tied to the results you produce. You need to come to the point where you can begin to enjoy the *process* of co-creation rather than the *result* of co-creation.

This is a topic that I will allow other masters to speak on, for I have given you what I desire to give you.

12 | INVOKING ALL-PERVADING WISDOM

In the name I AM THAT I AM, Jesus Christ, I call to all representatives of the Divine Mother, especially Vairochana, to help me tune in to your All-Pervading Wisdom and overcome the poisons, including…

[Make personal calls.]

Vairochana, release the All-Pervading Wisdom to give me awareness of self, awareness of who I am.

OM VAIROCHANA OM

Vairochana, release the All-Pervading Wisdom to give me awareness that it is not enough to study a spiritual teaching and understand it intellectually.

OM VAIROCHANA OM

Vairochana, release the All-Pervading Wisdom to give me awareness that it is possible to use a spiritual teaching to create a new form of ignorance where, in my outer mind, I feel I know the teaching. Therefore, I do not look for a deeper understanding or rather a deeper *experience*.

OM VAIROCHANA OM

Vairochana, release the All-Pervading Wisdom to give me awareness that the teaching on the Conscious You, when I experience the reality of it, is just a concept but it is more than a concept.

OM VAIROCHANA OM

Vairochana, release the All-Pervading Wisdom to give me awareness that I cannot fully internalize the teaching while looking at the Conscious You through the outer mind, especially the intellectual, analytical mind.

OM VAIROCHANA OM

Vairochana, release the All-Pervading Wisdom to give me awareness that I can only appreciate the teaching when I experience myself as a formless being.

OM VAIROCHANA OM

Vairochana, release the All-Pervading Wisdom to give me awareness that when I have that experience, then I appreciate, I have fully internalized and made use of the teaching.

OM VAIROCHANA OM

Vairochana, release the All-Pervading Wisdom to give me awareness that as long as I have formulated a concept of the Conscious You in my mind and I see it from a distance, I have not made use of the teaching.

OM VAIROCHANA OM

Vairochana, release the All-Pervading Wisdom to give me awareness that if I use any spiritual teaching to create a concept that validates my sense of distance, then I have misused the teaching—at least, if I do not strive for more.

OM VAIROCHANA OM

12 | Invoking All-Pervading Wisdom

Vairochana, release the All-Pervading Wisdom to give me awareness that the byword, the motto, the catchphrase of a true spiritual student is that it is not enough to *understand* the teaching, I need to *experience* the reality behind the teaching.

OM VAIROCHANA OM

Vairochana, release the All-Pervading Wisdom to give me awareness that a teaching that is expressed in words is only a way-shower, a symbol that points the way to an experience that is beyond words.

OM VAIROCHANA OM

Vairochana, release the All-Pervading Wisdom to give me awareness that only when I have the experience, have I made full use of the teaching.

OM VAIROCHANA OM

Vairochana, release the All-Pervading Wisdom to give me awareness that the greatest problem of ignorance among spiritual students is when we think the outer teaching, and understanding it with the outer mind, is enough and we do not go beyond to the experience.

OM VAIROCHANA OM

Vairochana, release the All-Pervading Wisdom to give me awareness that the first byword is: "Go beyond the teaching to the experience." The real catchphrase is: "There is always *more* to experience."

OM VAIROCHANA OM

Vairochana, release the All-Pervading Wisdom to give me awareness that you not only have the antidote, you *are* the antidote to the poison of ignorance. By tuning in to you, experiencing your Presence, I can overcome all ignorance.

OM VAIROCHANA OM

Vairochana, release the All-Pervading Wisdom to give me awareness that I am not here to have the experience of awakening in a split second. I am here to have the experience of gradually awakening, awakening in increments by rising to the 144th level of consciousness.

OM VAIROCHANA OM

Vairochana, release the All-Pervading Wisdom to give me awareness that whatever experience I am having right now, there is always more to experience.

OM VAIROCHANA OM

Vairochana, release the All-Pervading Wisdom to give me awareness that ignorance is like a screen in my mind that prevents me from seeing what is behind it. There is such a screen for each of the 144 levels of consciousness.

OM VAIROCHANA OM

Vairochana, release the All-Pervading Wisdom to give me awareness that the function of a dense-matter planet is to give me a sense of self where there are certain things I cannot see.

OM VAIROCHANA OM

Vairochana, release the All-Pervading Wisdom to give me awareness that the purpose is to allow me to explore the full range of experiences possible with self-awareness and free will.

OM VAIROCHANA OM

Vairochana, release the All-Pervading Wisdom to give me awareness that I have an experience by creating a self and experiencing the world, life and myself through that self.

OM VAIROCHANA OM

12 | Invoking All-Pervading Wisdom

Vairochana, release the All-Pervading Wisdom to give me awareness that there are certain experiences of self that I cannot have on a natural planet. It is therefore perfectly within the range of free will that there are unnatural planets for those who wish to experience a more limited sense of self.

OM VAIROCHANA OM

Vairochana, release the All-Pervading Wisdom to give me awareness that in a general way, ignorance is when there is a barrier to what I can see, what I can know, what I can experience.

OM VAIROCHANA OM

Vairochana, release the All-Pervading Wisdom to give me awareness that I am creating a limited self by taking on these illusions, setting up these barriers in my mind, so there are certain things I cannot see.

OM VAIROCHANA OM

Vairochana, release the All-Pervading Wisdom to give me awareness that free will allows me to go as far as I can imagine on the path of limiting my sense of self.

OM VAIROCHANA OM

Vairochana, release the All-Pervading Wisdom to give me awareness that I will experience the consequences of my choices by the Ma-ter light outpicturing what I am projecting upon it through my sense of self. I will also experience myself.

OM VAIROCHANA OM

Vairochana, release the All-Pervading Wisdom to give me awareness that the omega aspect of being a co-creator is that I have free will. The alpha aspect is that I have self-awareness.

OM VAIROCHANA OM

Vairochana, release the All-Pervading Wisdom to give me awareness that whatever kind of self I create, I can never lose self-awareness. I can limit it, I can limit the *self* part, but I will have some form of *awareness*.

OM VAIROCHANA OM

Vairochana, release the All-Pervading Wisdom to give me awareness that I am not only experiencing that the Ma-ter Light out-pictures what I project upon it through my self. I am experiencing myself through that self.

OM VAIROCHANA OM

Vairochana, release the All-Pervading Wisdom to give me awareness that when the Conscious You is created, it does not know what to do with itself as a formless being.

OM VAIROCHANA OM

Vairochana, release the All-Pervading Wisdom to give me awareness that I need the experience of taking a journey where I immerse myself in a more limited form of self and then gradually awaken from it.

OM VAIROCHANA OM

Vairochana, release the All-Pervading Wisdom to give me awareness that only when I have gone through this process of immersion and awakening, can I fully accept myself as a formless being.

OM VAIROCHANA OM

Vairochana, release the All-Pervading Wisdom to give me awareness that only when I again experience myself as a formless being, and am able to fully accept myself as a formless being, can I ascend.

OM VAIROCHANA OM

12 | Invoking All-Pervading Wisdom

Vairochana, release the All-Pervading Wisdom to give me awareness that the idea of the Conscious you is that I explore the realms of free will until I have had enough of the level of expressing my free will that is possible in an unascended sphere—and then I ascend.

OM VAIROCHANA OM

Vairochana, release the All-Pervading Wisdom to give me awareness that after I ascend, my I AM Presence has a different perspective by sending part of itself into the unascended sphere, a perspective it could never get from the ascended sphere.

OM VAIROCHANA OM

Vairochana, release the All-Pervading Wisdom to give me awareness that people on earth are ignorant because they are still in the immersion phase.

OM VAIROCHANA OM

Vairochana, release the All-Pervading Wisdom to give me awareness to see if I came as an avatar to earth. When I came to earth, I had in my mind the idea that I was here to set people free from their suffering, from their ignorance.

OM VAIROCHANA OM

Vairochana, release the All-Pervading Wisdom to give me awareness that before I came here, I thought that people are trapped by their ignorance and I need to come to help them be free of that ignorance.

OM VAIROCHANA OM

Vairochana, release the All-Pervading Wisdom to give me awareness that before I can ascend as an avatar, I need to overcome this, I need to make peace with free will.

OM VAIROCHANA OM

Vairochana, release the All-Pervading Wisdom to give me awareness that will help me make peace with the fact that people have a right to choose to be in a certain sense of self that limits what they can see. I am not here to change their experience, to force them to change. I am here to give them a frame of reference.

OM VAIROCHANA OM

Vairochana, release the All-Pervading Wisdom to give me awareness that as long as I maintain the idea that I am here to create a change or to force a change on earth, I cannot be the Buddha as I cannot be the Living Christ.

OM VAIROCHANA OM

Vairochana, release the All-Pervading Wisdom to give me awareness that when I was exposed to the birth trauma and created the primal self and other selves, these selves were created out of ignorance.

OM VAIROCHANA OM

Vairochana, release the All-Pervading Wisdom to give me awareness that as long as I am acting through the primal self and other separate selves, I am the blind attempting to lead the blind.

OM VAIROCHANA OM

Vairochana, release the All-Pervading Wisdom to give me awareness that as long as I am blinded by a self that is reactionary to the conditions I have experienced on earth, I am not free of the conditions on earth. If I am not free of the conditions on earth, how can I help other people become free?

OM VAIROCHANA OM

Vairochana, release the All-Pervading Wisdom to give me awareness that I am merely seeking to raise them out of *their* form of ignorance and take on *my* form of ignorance. This is not the Buddha.

OM VAIROCHANA OM

Vairochana, release the All-Pervading Wisdom to give me awareness that the Buddha is the one who, first of all, works on himself or herself and overcomes the ignorance that I have taken on after I came to earth.

OM VAIROCHANA OM

Vairochana, release the All-Pervading Wisdom to give me awareness that for an avatar to embody on earth, for me to serve as an example, I must immerse myself on earth. I do this by creating that primal self.

OM VAIROCHANA OM

Vairochana, release the All-Pervading Wisdom to give me awareness that I cannot, on a natural planet, experience what it is like to be on an unnatural planet. I have to go into embodiment on an unnatural planet in order to experience it, and it *will* be a shock for me.

OM VAIROCHANA OM

Vairochana, release the All-Pervading Wisdom to give me awareness that there is no reason to have any regret about this. It is a matter of realizing that until I awaken myself from the illusions of the primal self, I cannot fulfil my reason for being on this planet. I cannot be the Christ in action, I cannot be the Buddha in action. I cannot bring the light, I cannot serve as an example, I cannot give people a frame of reference. I cannot help them out of their ignorance because I am trapped in my own form of ignorance.

OM VAIROCHANA OM

Vairochana, release the All-Pervading Wisdom to give me awareness that the primal self allows me to ignore the shock of being on earth. The shock was so great that it made me think: "Why did I come to this planet?" I was not at peace with it but I could not resolve it at the time and so I created the primal self as a screen to hide the dilemma.

OM VAIROCHANA OM

Vairochana, release the All-Pervading Wisdom to give me awareness that as long as I look at life on earth through the primal self, I do not see the shock, I do not see the trauma.

OM VAIROCHANA OM

Vairochana, release the All-Pervading Wisdom to give me awareness that the trauma is still there, and that is why I cannot fulfil my reason for coming here until I use the greater experience I have on earth, and the growth I have experienced on earth, to go back into that birth trauma, to look at it and to make peace, in my own personal way, with being on earth.

OM VAIROCHANA OM

Vairochana, release the All-Pervading Wisdom to give me awareness that before I descended to earth as an avatar, I had a reason in my mind for why I wanted to come here. When I descended and experienced what life was like here, I started to doubt that reason.

OM VAIROCHANA OM

Vairochana, release the All-Pervading Wisdom to give me awareness that I need to go back, look at my reason for coming here and resolve the dilemma that being here presents.

OM VAIROCHANA OM

Vairochana, release the All-Pervading Wisdom to give me awareness that will help me see my reason for coming here in a new light. Help me see that certain aspects of my reason were based on inordinate desire.

OM VAIROCHANA OM

Vairochana, release the All-Pervading Wisdom to give me awareness that will help me let this go, give it up, surrender it so I am non-attached to what I accomplish or do not accomplish on earth.

OM VAIROCHANA OM

12 | Invoking All-Pervading Wisdom

Vairochana, release the All-Pervading Wisdom to give me awareness that it is impossible to produce the result I thought I could produce before I came here.

OM VAIROCHANA OM

Vairochana, release the All-Pervading Wisdom to give me awareness that will consume my frustration and help me make peace with the fact that I came here to grow and this was the fastest way for me to grow, given the state of mind I was in before I descended here.

OM VAIROCHANA OM

Vairochana, release the All-Pervading Wisdom to give me awareness that will help me make peace with having come here, make peace with having been here, make peace with being here.

OM VAIROCHANA OM

Vairochana, release the All-Pervading Wisdom to give me awareness that until I have made peace with coming here, being here, I cannot make peace with leaving because I think there is something I should have accomplished that I have not accomplished.

OM VAIROCHANA OM

Vairochana, release the All-Pervading Wisdom to give me awareness that when I descend as an avatar, it is because I have a great desire to grow and that means I can never leave anything unfinished, unfulfilled.

OM VAIROCHANA OM

Vairochana, release the All-Pervading Wisdom to give me awareness that if I have set myself a goal at a lower level as an avatar, I think the goal must be fulfilled before I can move on.

OM VAIROCHANA OM

Vairochana, release the All-Pervading Wisdom to give me awareness that will help me come up to the more mature level as an avatar, of realizing that my goal was not the highest goal. It was not really an expression of who I am.

OM VAIROCHANA OM

Vairochana, release the All-Pervading Wisdom to give me awareness that when I give up that goal, I see a higher goal. I see that the highest goal is always my growth in self-awareness.

OM VAIROCHANA OM

Vairochana, release the All-Pervading Wisdom to give me awareness that will help me make peace with the fact that my self-worth is based on who I am, based on my I AM Presence not on my accomplishments, whether it be here on earth or even on a natural planet.

OM VAIROCHANA OM

Vairochana, release the All-Pervading Wisdom to give me awareness that my accomplishments in this unascended sphere do not define my self-worth. It is who I am that defines my self-worth.

OM VAIROCHANA OM

Vairochana, release the All-Pervading Wisdom to give me awareness that this is a specific form of ignorance that I had before I came here. I did not fully grasp and accept that my self-worth comes from being who I am and not from what I do.

OM VAIROCHANA OM

Vairochana, release the All-Pervading Wisdom to give me awareness that this is a very subtle challenge for co-creators because I start out thinking that my sense of self-worth as a co-creator is tied to my co-creation, to the results I produce.

OM VAIROCHANA OM

Vairochana, release the All-Pervading Wisdom to give me awareness that it is time for me to step up to that higher level of freeing myself from this sense that my self-worth is tied to the results I produce.

OM VAIROCHANA OM

Vairochana, release the All-Pervading Wisdom to give me awareness that I need to come to the point where I can enjoy the *process* of co-creation rather than the *result* of co-creation.

OM VAIROCHANA OM

Sealing

In the name of the Divine Mother, I call to Mother Mary for the sealing of myself and all people in my circle of influence in the creative flow of the Divine Mother, the River of Life. I call for the multiplication of my calls by all representatives of the Divine Mother, so that we form the perfect figure-eight flow of "As Above, so below." Thus, I accept that this is fully manifest, because the mouth of the Lord, the Divine Mother that I AM, has spoken it. Amen.

13 | THE HIDDEN ANGER OF SPIRITUAL PEOPLE

I AM the Dhyani Buddha Akshobya. I AM the Ascended Master Akshobya but I am, of course, more than any name. The poison for which I have chosen to hold the balance for the earth is anger and hatred. What is anger? Well, words are limited for describing a feeling because feelings are often complex, they are more than just words.

Painting yourself into a corner

Let us focus on two types of beings. We have the fallen beings, we have avatars. The fallen beings have a deep anger against God, against other fallen beings, against human beings, against avatars, against Christed beings, against Buddhic beings. They basically have an anger against everything but themselves. Well, in reality their anger *is* an anger against themselves but they do not see this.

Now, if you take what was said earlier, you will see that ignorance creates a screen and you cannot see what is behind it. When an avatar comes to earth and begins to doubt, or receives the shock that your original purpose for coming here cannot be fulfilled, then you create that primal self that hides the shock of having to rethink your approach.

In the same way, in that first sphere where a being fell, the fallen being had built up this great sense of self for doing something good. When confronted by the ascended masters with the reality that it was not actually good, it was only self-centered, then that fallen being also experienced a shock and it created a self that has been hiding that shock ever since. The fallen being has been able to avoid rethinking its approach and coming to the point of looking at: "Oh, is there something in my attitude, my approach, my beliefs, my way of looking at things, my perception that was not the highest possible? Is it my perception that I have to change?"

You could say that with an avatar, you come to earth, you receive that shock of realizing that your reason for coming to earth cannot be fulfilled. You create that primal self to avoid having to deal with the question: "Was there something in my reason, in my attitude, in my perception of earth that needs to change?" You have created the self to avoid having to look at a deeper issue. Yet what happens as you continue embodying (whether it is as a fallen being in a higher sphere or as an avatar on earth) is that as you experience life, you experience that there are certain problems that you seemingly cannot solve.

The reason you cannot solve the problems is that you will not look at that original issue that is hidden by your primal self. By the very fact of creating this primal self, you are putting yourself in a limited perception and therefore there are certain problems that you cannot solve. As you continue to embody, you create more and more selves as an offspring of the primal self, and the selves create more and more limitations. For each time you create a self, you create a limitation. For each limitation, there is a problem you cannot solve until you resolve the self.

You could say that each self limits your perception. With a limited perception, there is a problem you cannot solve but what do you do? You cannot solve the problem but you have to react to the problem. How do you deal with that? You create another self based on another limitation and that creates another problem you cannot solve.

The build-up of anger

Gradually, things become more and more intense and that is why, as Master MORE said, that even spiritual students can build up this increasing frustration. You are experiencing that you are in an unpleasant situation. You feel limited, you feel boxed in. You are experiencing that you are boxed in by conditions that you have no power to change. You are limited by problems that you cannot solve—that is how it seems to you. The reason it seems that way is that you are looking at the problems through a certain self but you do not see this. Therefore, you are seeing that there is a problem that you cannot solve. Just as we have said before, it becomes personal to you because you are feeling boxed in and you are feeling you have no place to go. That is how anger builds up.

Anger builds because there are more and more problems you cannot solve. For every time you have to react to a problem, you create another self and that creates another problem and it seems like it will never end. It is the story of the monster in the cave where, when you cut off its head, seven more heads would grow out. This is what builds anger. It is a frustration, a build-up of energy, of tension that becomes more and more intense and that gives you that anger. That is when you, then, come to this point where it becomes so strong that you cannot help but express that anger. Of course, you do not express it towards yourself, you express it towards other people.

Now, here is where you can benefit from recognizing a difference between fallen beings and avatars. Fallen beings have had a much longer time to build up frustration and so their anger is stronger. Their anger has actually become so intense that it crosses the line and becomes hatred. The difference is subtle and not so important. Hatred is, of course, much more intense and much more directed against specific outer conditions that you identify as being the cause, the main cause of the problem. For many fallen beings it is God that they hate because they think God is the cause of their problems. What you have is that many fallen beings have this intense anger against God but since they cannot do anything to punish God (which is what they want), they then take out their anger against other people and seek to punish *them*. That is why, when you as an avatar came to earth, they saw you as a threat and they attempted to punish you.

Avatars are angry at themselves

What is it you are really doing with anger? Well, it comes from the frustration that you do not have power to solve a problem. The mechanism that comes in is that if you experience that you can take out your anger on another person (and make that person feel as bad as you feel about themselves, make that person feel as bad about themselves as you feel about yourself), somehow that gives you a sense of having some kind of power. You do not have power to solve the problem that made you angry but you have power to make another person feel bad. It gives you a momentary relief where you feel that, after all, you have *some* power.

That is why you see some people (you see it even in spiritual movements, as Master MORE talked about) who can express what they think is blue-raying another person in order to awaken that person, but it is in reality their own anger they are expressing. If you really go deep into the psychology, you will see that because the fallen beings have had such a long time to create more and more selves, they hate other people, God the Ma-ter light, whatever.

For many avatars their hatred or their anger is directed towards themselves. They feel a certain frustration, and in many cases, in your mind, it can be a frustration with certain conditions on earth. Many times, for example, you feel that it is certain conditions on earth that are limiting you and making you feel bad about yourself. In reality, if you go deeper, it goes back to that shock you received of realizing that your original goal for which you came to earth cannot be fulfilled. Therefore, you feel anger against yourself for making the choice to come here: "How could I be so stupid to choose to come to this planet?" Many of you will see that you have created both the primal self and other selves to hide that. Now, that we have given you these teachings, some of you have come to actually be willing to identify that in yourself and it is very important that you do this.

Creating selves to suppress anger

It is very important, as a spiritual person, that you allow yourself to recognize that you have these selves, that you have this frustration, that you have this anger. It is also important, as a spiritual being, that you accept that you have attempted to create selves to suppress your anger because you realize, at some level of your being, that as a spiritual person you should not feel angry. It is important, as my esteemed brother said, that you recognize that when you receive a spiritual teaching, you can actually create certain selves based on the teaching. You receive the teaching that the Buddha is at peace, the Buddha has non-attachment, so you feel that if you are a student of the Buddha, you have to create a self that suppresses your anger. You can go to the East and you can find many monks and nuns who have been faithful, devoted followers of Buddhism in this lifetime for many decades, maybe even for many lifetimes before this one. They seem to be very peaceful, very harmonious and some of them *are*. Many of them have actually created these very, very strong selves that are suppressing their anger so it never comes to expression—but it is still there. What we are calling you to do, you who are ascended master students and are open to this teaching, is to not be afraid to recognize that there is or there are certain selves in your being that have anger.

Some of you have experienced such intense suffering that you have taken on some of these projections from the fallen beings that you ask: "Why hasn't God changed the equation of free will, why does God allow us to suffer, why has God allowed *me* to suffer?" You feel a certain anger against God for giving you free will. You can feel (when you experience this intense suffering on earth that is never possible on a natural planet): "Why did God allow me to make the choice to go to earth? Why did God even give me free will?" This is something you have taken on as projections from the fallen beings but it is important to recognize that you have this self. Until you recognize that in your four lower bodies is a self that feels this anger, you cannot separate yourself from that self.

Overcoming anger

What can you, then, do? Well, of course, you can follow the process we have given you, coming to identify the separate self, realizing that the separate self that is angry is projecting a certain problem. It might, for instance, project a problem: "God should change his law and not allow free will to create such suffering." As long as you are inside that self, you are projecting out, you are thinking: "How can I make God see his mistake and change this?" Of course, you cannot. When you are in embodiment on a planet like earth, you cannot talk to your Creator and say: "Why don't you change your law?"

The Creator cannot hear you, you cannot reach the Creator consciousness. The self presents you with a problem that could never be solved. Any of these selves you have created, they are presenting you with a problem that could never be solved because the problem only exists due to the perception of that self, the limited perception. The problem is not a real problem, it is an artificially created problem, created from a limited perception. It could never be solved. The only way out is to see that this is a separate self that has a limited perception. It is not *you*. You are the Conscious You.

You have the ability to step outside of that self and receive a higher perception, which we have given you with the teachings on free will.

Therefore, you can come to see that the self is unreal, the problem is unreal, meaning you do not have to solve the problem. You do not have to make the Creator see that free will was a mistake. Therefore, you can come to that point where you see the illusion and you let go of the illusion. Then, you can look at that separate self and realize that the way to be free of it is *not* to solve the problem but to let the self die.

The antidote to anger

Now, we have given you the tools to do this, but I will still offer my help in terms of offering you the antidote that I have to the poison of anger. It is called the Mirror-Like Wisdom. My beloved, when I ask you to look at the fact that you have a self that has anger, you might at first feel very apprehensive about this. You are afraid that if you acknowledge that, as a spiritual student, you have anger, you will condemn yourself. Well, Master MORE gave you the keys to overcome the judgmental self.

If you focus on that first and get rid of that judgmental self, you will not have to judge yourself for having anger. You can look at it neutrally. What I offer you is this Mirror-Like Wisdom. If you will spend some time giving the mantra, tuning in to my Being, I will help you see this. I will help you tune in to this Mirror-Like Wisdom so you can come to the point where you just see in the mirror what you have in yourself but you are not imposing a judgment upon it.

Now, I know very well that you can look at planet earth, and perhaps women are more inclined to think this way than men. Many women do not like the mirror because it shows them as they really are, not as they feel they *should* be looking. You have a certain female trauma that has been created on earth but you can overcome this as well through my Mirror-Like Wisdom by asking yourself a question. My beloved, if you eat breakfast and there is a piece of food stuck in your teeth, would you rather walk around all day with this piece of food stuck in your teeth and have other people see it, or would you rather look in the mirror before you leave the house, see it, remove it and be free of it the whole day.

Naturally, it is the same here. You have a self that is angry. My beloved, it is inevitable that when you come to earth as an avatar, you build a self that is angry because it is such a low planet, such a dense planet you are on. It is inevitable. We all built this self, Jesus included, as is demonstrated by the book. Would you rather live the rest of your life having this angry self or would you rather look in the mirror that I offer you, see it, pull it out of your teeth, remove it from your four lower bodies, let it die and be free of it for the rest of your life?

Mirror-Like Wisdom does not judge

This ties in, again, with the unconditional acceptance that we do not judge you. I am a Dhyani Buddha, my beloved, I exist in a level of consciousness that is very, very much higher than the earth. There is absolutely nothing on earth that disturbs me. There is nothing on earth that affects me. Because there is nothing on earth that affects me, I do not feel threatened by anything on earth. Because I do not feel threatened, I do not need to judge anything on earth so I do not judge *you*. I have only the desire to set you free. I offer you the Mirror-Like Wisdom because unlike a mirror on earth, the Mirror-Like Wisdom that I am, offers you that when you tune in to it, you can see without judgment. You can see a self without seeing it through another self. In other words, you can see the angry self without seeing it through the judgmental self. You just see it.

That is what the Mirror-Like Wisdom is. It is not dualistic, it helps you see one dualistic condition without having to judge it through another dualistic condition or self. There is no other way to get beyond anger than to dissolve the self that is angry. When you have dealt with the primal self, it becomes much easier to look at the angry selves and dissolve them. Now, you can begin to look at: "Why did I come to earth? Did I have a realistic expectation, did I have a realistic desire or was it an unrealistic desire, an *inordinate* desire in the sense that it was an *impossible* desire, it could not be fulfilled."

Then, you can begin to look at: "Why would I need to change other people with free will?" Then, you can come to the point where you are not threatened by the fact that other people reject you, that they do not change. You are not having a self in you that feels bad because other people are still suffering. Therefore, you are not having to change them in order to avoid a feeling in yourself. You can let go of the judgment that suffering is wrong and these people should not be suffering.

Freeing your will from the will of others

You see my beloved, there is a self in you that is based on the perception you had before you came here but that was created after you saw how dense the planet is and you felt: "But I cannot possibly change other people, they wont listen to me, they are not responding." Then, you created this self that felt you should not have come here. Every time you experience that people are suffering, you are experiencing the frustration that springs from this self. You have compassion for people's suffering but you feel it is impossible to help them change and no longer suffer.

This makes *you* suffer. This makes you suffer because you feel it was futile for you to come here so it ties in with this entire frustration. The ultimate way to resolve anger is to come to see that self, and see that your feeling of how you experience being in embodiment on earth has so far been tied to other people and their suffering. The way you have felt about yourself and about being in embodiment on earth has been that, at some point, you made the decision that as long as other people are suffering, you cannot feel good about being on earth, you cannot feel at peace with being on earth. You cannot allow yourself to even feel joyful and happy as long as other people are suffering.

Well, now you can come to the point where you resolve your limited perception of free will. You realize that other people may choose to suffer for a long time until they have had enough of that experience and are willing to take responsibility for themselves. You still have your free will and it is actually not right for you, it is even not *lawful* for you, to tie your choices to the choices of other people. Taking responsibility for yourself as a spiritual student means that you stop letting your choices be affected or dependent upon other people. You stop letting your choices wait upon other people making certain choices. You realize that you need to completely (and this is your supreme responsibility when you are in embodiment on earth), free your own will from the will of other people.

You need to come to a point where you can make choices for yourself that are in no way dependent on other people. You need to recognize that you have a right to choose to be at peace, to choose to be happy on earth even if other people are still choosing to suffer. When you can recognize that, then you realize there is no reason for you to feel frustrated about being on earth. Then, you can look at the self that feels that free will is wrong, free will should be changed. You can look at the self (all of the selves that have the frustration, that have the anger) and you can let it go—you can let it die.

You can see that there is no problem that needs to be solved here. You can just let it die. You can let it die by looking into the mirror because the Mirror-Like Wisdom can help you not only see what you have in your own consciousness, but it can also help you look up and see that you are so much more than those selves. You are the Conscious You that is a formless being, therefore not trapped in these selves—unless you let yourself be trapped. You are more than that, you are the I AM Presence above, which is worthy in and of itself. Therefore, your self-worth on earth does not depend on the results you accomplish in terms of changing other people.

Again, you can come to the point of taking another step closer to focusing on the process rather than the result. This is something that other masters will say more about, as we are all building up to talking about process versus result.

As long as you are trapped in these selves that spring from the spiritual poisons, you cannot focus on the process instead of the result. You will be focused on the result because the selves project at you that there is a result that you *have* to manifest. It is an impossible result and that is what we are seeking to help you see by exposing the selves that spring from these poisons. With this, I have given you my gift.

14 | INVOKING MIRROR-LIKE WISDOM

In the name I AM THAT I AM, Jesus Christ, I call to all representatives of the Divine Mother, especially Akshobya, to help me tune in to your Mirror-Like Wisdom and overcome the poisons, including…

[Make personal calls.]

Akshobya, release the Mirror-Like Wisdom to give me awareness that when I came to earth and realized that my reason for coming could not be fulfilled, I created the primal self to avoid having to deal with the question: "Was there something in my reason, in my attitude, in my perception of earth that needs to change?"

OM AKSHOBYA HUM

Akshobya, release the Mirror-Like Wisdom to give me awareness that I have created the self to avoid having to look at a deeper issue.

OM AKSHOBYA HUM

Akshobya, release the Mirror-Like Wisdom to give me awareness that as I continue embodying, I experience that there are certain problems that I seemingly cannot solve.

OM AKSHOBYA HUM

Akshobya, release the Mirror-Like Wisdom to give me awareness that the reason I cannot solve the problems is that I will not look at the original issue that is hidden by my primal self.

OM AKSHOBYA HUM

Akshobya, release the Mirror-Like Wisdom to give me awareness that by the very fact of creating this primal self, I am putting myself in a limited perception and therefore there are certain problems that I cannot solve.

OM AKSHOBYA HUM

Akshobya, release the Mirror-Like Wisdom to give me awareness that as I continue to embody, I create more and more selves as an offspring of the primal self, and the selves create more and more limitations.

OM AKSHOBYA HUM

Akshobya, release the Mirror-Like Wisdom to give me awareness that for each time I create a self, I create a limitation. For each limitation, there is a problem I cannot solve until I resolve the self.

OM AKSHOBYA HUM

Akshobya, release the Mirror-Like Wisdom to give me awareness that each self limits my perception. With a limited perception, there is a problem I cannot solve.

OM AKSHOBYA HUM

Akshobya, release the Mirror-Like Wisdom to give me awareness that I cannot solve the problem but I have to react to the problem. I deal with that by creating another self based on another limitation and that creates another problem I cannot solve.

OM AKSHOBYA HUM

Akshobya, release the Mirror-Like Wisdom to give me awareness that gradually, things become more and more intense and that is why I build up this increasing frustration.

OM AKSHOBYA HUM

Akshobya, release the Mirror-Like Wisdom to give me awareness that I am experiencing that I am in an unpleasant situation. I feel limited, I feel boxed in.

OM AKSHOBYA HUM

Akshobya, release the Mirror-Like Wisdom to give me awareness that I am experiencing that I am boxed in by conditions that I have no power to change. I am limited by problems that I cannot solve—that is how it seems to me.

OM AKSHOBYA HUM

Akshobya, release the Mirror-Like Wisdom to give me awareness that the reason it seems that way is that I am looking at the problems through a certain self but I do not see this.

OM AKSHOBYA HUM

Akshobya, release the Mirror-Like Wisdom to give me awareness that I am seeing that there is a problem that I cannot solve. This becomes personal to me because I am feeling boxed in and I am feeling I have no place to go.

OM AKSHOBYA HUM

Akshobya, release the Mirror-Like Wisdom to give me awareness that this is how anger builds up. Anger builds because there are more and more problems I cannot solve.

OM AKSHOBYA HUM

Akshobya, release the Mirror-Like Wisdom to give me awareness that every time I have to react to a problem, I create another self and that creates another problem and it seems like it will never end.

OM AKSHOBYA HUM

Akshobya, release the Mirror-Like Wisdom to give me awareness that this is what builds anger. It is a frustration, a build-up of energy, of tension that becomes more and more intense—and *that* gives me anger.

OM AKSHOBYA HUM

Akshobya, release the Mirror-Like Wisdom to give me awareness that this is when I come to the point where it becomes so strong that I cannot help but express that anger. I do not express it towards myself, I express it towards other people.

OM AKSHOBYA HUM

Akshobya, release the Mirror-Like Wisdom to give me awareness that many fallen beings have this intense anger against God but since they cannot do anything to punish God, they then take out their anger against other people and seek to punish *them*.

OM AKSHOBYA HUM

Akshobya, release the Mirror-Like Wisdom to give me awareness that the mechanism that comes in, is that if I experience that I can take out my anger on another person, that gives me a sense of having some kind of power.

OM AKSHOBYA HUM

Akshobya, release the Mirror-Like Wisdom to give me awareness that I do not have power to solve the problem that made me angry, but I have power to make another person feel bad, and this gives me a momentary relief where I feel that, after all, I have *some* power.

OM AKSHOBYA HUM

Akshobya, release the Mirror-Like Wisdom to give me awareness that for most avatars the hatred or anger is directed towards ourselves.

OM AKSHOBYA HUM

Akshobya, release the Mirror-Like Wisdom to give me awareness that we feel a certain frustration, and it often seems to be a frustration with certain conditions on earth. In reality, it goes back to the shock we received of realizing that our original goal could not be fulfilled.

OM AKSHOBYA HUM

Akshobya, release the Mirror-Like Wisdom to give me awareness that I feel anger against myself for making the choice to come here: "How could I be so stupid to choose to come to this planet?"

OM AKSHOBYA HUM

Akshobya, release the Mirror-Like Wisdom to give me awareness that I have created both the primal self and other selves to hide that anger.

OM AKSHOBYA HUM

Akshobya, release the Mirror-Like Wisdom to give me awareness that will help me identify this in myself.

OM AKSHOBYA HUM

Akshobya, release the Mirror-Like Wisdom to give me awareness that will allow me to recognize that I have these selves, that I have this frustration, that I have this anger.

OM AKSHOBYA HUM

Akshobya, release the Mirror-Like Wisdom to give me awareness that will help me accept that I have attempted to create selves to suppress my anger because I think that as a spiritual person I should not feel angry.

OM AKSHOBYA HUM

Akshobya, release the Mirror-Like Wisdom to give me awareness that will help me recognize that when I receive a spiritual teaching, I can actually create certain selves based on the teaching.

OM AKSHOBYA HUM

Akshobya, release the Mirror-Like Wisdom to give me awareness that when I receive the teaching that the Buddha is at peace, the Buddha has non-attachment, I feel that if I am a student of the Buddha, I have to create a self that suppresses my anger.

OM AKSHOBYA HUM

Akshobya, release the Mirror-Like Wisdom to give me awareness that I have created very strong selves that are suppressing my anger so it never comes to expression—but it is still there.

OM AKSHOBYA HUM

Akshobya, release the Mirror-Like Wisdom to give me awareness that will allow me to not be afraid to recognize that there are certain selves in my being that have anger.

OM AKSHOBYA HUM

Akshobya, release the Mirror-Like Wisdom to give me awareness that I may feel a certain anger against God for giving me free will: "Why did God allow me to make the choice to go to earth? Why did God even give me free will?"

OM AKSHOBYA HUM

14 | Invoking Mirror-Like Wisdom

Akshobya, release the Mirror-Like Wisdom to give me awareness that this is something I have taken on as projections from the fallen beings but I have to recognize that I have this self.

OM AKSHOBYA HUM

Akshobya, release the Mirror-Like Wisdom to give me awareness that until I recognize that in my four lower bodies is a self that feels this anger, I cannot separate myself from that self.

OM AKSHOBYA HUM

Akshobya, release the Mirror-Like Wisdom to give me awareness that will help me realize that the separate self that is angry is projecting a certain problem, for instance: "God should change his law and not allow free will to create such suffering."

OM AKSHOBYA HUM

Akshobya, release the Mirror-Like Wisdom to give me awareness that as long as I am inside that self, I am projecting out, I am thinking: "How can I make God see his mistake and change this?" Of course, I cannot.

OM AKSHOBYA HUM

Akshobya, release the Mirror-Like Wisdom to give me awareness that the self presents me with a problem that could never be solved.

OM AKSHOBYA HUM

Akshobya, release the Mirror-Like Wisdom to give me awareness that any of these selves I have created, are presenting me with a problem that could never be solved because the problem only exists due to the limited perception of that self.

OM AKSHOBYA HUM

Akshobya, release the Mirror-Like Wisdom to give me awareness that the problem is not a real problem, it is an artificially created problem, created from a limited perception. It could never be solved.

OM AKSHOBYA HUM

Akshobya, release the Mirror-Like Wisdom to give me awareness that the only way out is to see that this is a separate self that has a limited perception. It is not *me*.

OM AKSHOBYA HUM

Akshobya, release the Mirror-Like Wisdom to give me awareness that I am the Conscious You. I have the ability to step outside of that self and receive a higher perception, which I have from the teachings on free will.

OM AKSHOBYA HUM

Akshobya, release the Mirror-Like Wisdom to give me awareness that the self is unreal, the problem is unreal, meaning I do not have to solve the problem.

OM AKSHOBYA HUM

Akshobya, release the Mirror-Like Wisdom to give me awareness that helps me see the illusion and let go of the illusion. Then, I can look at that separate self and realize that the way to be free of it is *not* to solve the problem but to let the self die.

OM AKSHOBYA HUM

Akshobya, release the Mirror-Like Wisdom to give me awareness that I might be afraid that if I acknowledge my anger, I will condemn myself.

OM AKSHOBYA HUM

Akshobya, release the Mirror-Like Wisdom to give me awareness that if I first get rid of that judgmental self, I will not have to judge myself for having anger. I can look at it neutrally.

OM AKSHOBYA HUM

Akshobya, release the Mirror-Like Wisdom to give me awareness that will help me come to the point where I just see in the mirror what I have in myself but I am not imposing a judgment upon it.

OM AKSHOBYA HUM

Akshobya, release the Mirror-Like Wisdom to give me awareness that it is inevitable that when I come to earth as an avatar, I build a self that is angry because it is such a dense planet.

OM AKSHOBYA HUM

Akshobya, I want to look in the mirror that you offer me, see the angry self, and remove it from my four lower bodies, let it die and be free of it for the rest of my life.

OM AKSHOBYA HUM

Akshobya, release the Mirror-Like Wisdom to give me awareness of your unconditional acceptance and that you do not judge me.

OM AKSHOBYA HUM

Akshobya, release the Mirror-Like Wisdom to give me awareness that you only have a desire to set me free.

OM AKSHOBYA HUM

Akshobya, release the Mirror-Like Wisdom to give me awareness that when I tune in to your wisdom, I can see without judgment. I can see a self without seeing it through another self. I can see the angry self without seeing it through the judgmental self.

OM AKSHOBYA HUM

Akshobya, release the Mirror-Like Wisdom to give me awareness that helps me see one dualistic condition without having to judge it through another dualistic condition or self.

OM AKSHOBYA HUM

Akshobya, release the Mirror-Like Wisdom to give me awareness that there is no other way to get beyond anger than to dissolve the self that is angry.

OM AKSHOBYA HUM

Akshobya, release the Mirror-Like Wisdom to give me awareness that when I have dealt with the primal self, it becomes much easier to look at the angry selves and dissolve them.

OM AKSHOBYA HUM

Akshobya, release the Mirror-Like Wisdom to give me awareness that I came to earth with an unrealistic expectation, an unrealistic desire, an inordinate desire in the sense that it was an impossible desire, it could not be fulfilled.

OM AKSHOBYA HUM

Akshobya, release the Mirror-Like Wisdom to give me awareness that I do not need to change other people because they have free will.

OM AKSHOBYA HUM

Akshobya, release the Mirror-Like Wisdom to give me awareness that I am not threatened by the fact that other people reject me, that they do not change.

OM AKSHOBYA HUM

Akshobya, release the Mirror-Like Wisdom to give me awareness that helps me come to the point where I am not having a self in me that feels bad because other people are still suffering.

OM AKSHOBYA HUM

Akshobya, release the Mirror-Like Wisdom to give me awareness that helps me come to the point where I do not have to change others in order to avoid a feeling in myself.

OM AKSHOBYA HUM

Akshobya, release the Mirror-Like Wisdom to give me awareness that helps me come to the point where I can let go of the judgment that suffering is wrong and these people should not be suffering.

OM AKSHOBYA HUM

Akshobya, release the Mirror-Like Wisdom to give me awareness that there is a self in me that is based on the perception I had before I came here, but it was created after I saw how dense the planet is and realized I cannot change other people because they are not responding.

OM AKSHOBYA HUM

Akshobya, release the Mirror-Like Wisdom to give me awareness that after I felt rejected, I created this self that felt I should not have come here.

OM AKSHOBYA HUM

Akshobya, release the Mirror-Like Wisdom to give me awareness that every time I experience that people are suffering, I am experiencing the frustration that springs from this self.

OM AKSHOBYA HUM

Akshobya, release the Mirror-Like Wisdom to give me awareness that I have compassion for people's suffering, but I feel it is impossible to help them change and no longer suffer.

OM AKSHOBYA HUM

Akshobya, release the Mirror-Like Wisdom to give me awareness that this makes *me* suffer because I feel it was futile for me to come here so it reinforces the entire frustration.

OM AKSHOBYA HUM

Akshobya, release the Mirror-Like Wisdom to give me awareness that the ultimate way to resolve anger is to come to see that self, and see that my feeling of how I experience being in embodiment on earth has so far been tied to other people and their suffering.

OM AKSHOBYA HUM

Akshobya, release the Mirror-Like Wisdom to give me awareness that the way I have felt about myself and about being in embodiment on earth is based on the decision that as long as other people are suffering, I cannot feel good about being on earth. I cannot allow myself to feel joyful and happy as long as other people are suffering.

OM AKSHOBYA HUM

Akshobya, release the Mirror-Like Wisdom to give me awareness that resolves my limited perception of free will because I realize that other people may choose to suffer for a long time until they have had enough of that experience and are willing to take responsibility for themselves.

OM AKSHOBYA HUM

Akshobya, release the Mirror-Like Wisdom to give me awareness that I still have my free will and it is not right for me to tie my choices to the choices of other people.

OM AKSHOBYA HUM

Akshobya, release the Mirror-Like Wisdom to give me awareness that taking responsibility for myself as a spiritual student means that I stop letting my choices be affected or dependent upon other people.

OM AKSHOBYA HUM

Akshobya, release the Mirror-Like Wisdom to give me awareness that helps me stop letting my choices wait upon other people making certain choices.

OM AKSHOBYA HUM

Akshobya, release the Mirror-Like Wisdom to give me awareness that helps me realize that it is my supreme responsibility to free my own will from the will of other people.

OM AKSHOBYA HUM

Akshobya, release the Mirror-Like Wisdom to give me awareness that helps me come to the point where I can make choices for myself that are in no way dependent on other people.

OM AKSHOBYA HUM

Akshobya, release the Mirror-Like Wisdom to give me awareness that I have a right to choose to be at peace, to be happy even if other people are still choosing to suffer.

OM AKSHOBYA HUM

Akshobya, release the Mirror-Like Wisdom to give me awareness that there is no reason for me to feel frustrated about being on earth.

OM AKSHOBYA HUM

Akshobya, release the Mirror-Like Wisdom to give me awareness that helps me look at the self that feels that free will is wrong. Help me let it go—let it die.

OM AKSHOBYA HUM

Akshobya, release the Mirror-Like Wisdom to give me awareness that there is no problem that needs to be solved here. I can just let the self die.

OM AKSHOBYA HUM

Akshobya, release the Mirror-Like Wisdom to give me awareness that I can let the self die by looking into the mirror because the Mirror-Like Wisdom can help me not only see what I have in my own consciousness, but also see that I am so much more than those selves.

OM AKSHOBYA HUM

Akshobya, release the Mirror-Like Wisdom to give me awareness that I am the Conscious You, that is a formless being. Therefore, I am not trapped in these selves—unless I let myself be trapped.

OM AKSHOBYA HUM

Akshobya, release the Mirror-Like Wisdom to give me awareness that I am more than these selves. I am the I AM Presence above, which is worthy in and of itself.

OM AKSHOBYA HUM

Akshobya, release the Mirror-Like Wisdom to give me awareness that my self-worth on earth does not depend on the results I accomplish in terms of changing other people.

OM AKSHOBYA HUM

Akshobya, release the Mirror-Like Wisdom to give me awareness that helps me take another step closer to focusing on the process rather than the result.

OM AKSHOBYA HUM

Akshobya, release the Mirror-Like Wisdom to give me awareness that as long as I am trapped in the selves that spring from the spiritual poisons, I cannot focus on the process instead of the result.

OM AKSHOBYA HUM

Akshobya, release the Mirror-Like Wisdom to give me awareness that I am focused on the result because the selves project at me that there is a result that I *have* to manifest.

OM AKSHOBYA HUM

Akshobya, release the Mirror-Like Wisdom to give me awareness that it is an impossible result and that I only need to let the selves die one by one.

OM AKSHOBYA HUM

Sealing

In the name of the Divine Mother, I call to Mother Mary for the sealing of myself and all people in my circle of influence in the creative flow of the Divine Mother, the River of Life. I call for the multiplication of my calls by all representatives of the Divine Mother, so that we form the perfect figure-eight flow of "As Above, so below." Thus, I accept that this is fully manifest, because the mouth of the Lord, the Divine Mother that I AM, has spoken it. Amen.

15 | EQUALITY VANISHES SUPERIORITY AND INFERIORITY

I AM Ratnasambhava. The poison for which I am the antidote is pride. What is pride? Well, naturally there are degrees of pride, there are variations of pride. It needs to be stated that there is pride even on a natural planet. It is simply because, when you start out as a co-creator, you have a very small (as we have said, a point-like) sense of self, which you are meant to gradually expand by experimenting. You are co-creating based on the self you have, experiencing the results, then expanding that self, co-creating something more and you keep doing this.

Natural and unnatural pride

It is both natural and inevitable that as you have done this for a long time, you experience that you have a certain mastery, a certain accomplishment. You have reached a certain ability to envision something and to manifest it, not only a thing but even life circumstances. It is almost inevitable (and, in fact, there is no blame here) that when you grow in your awareness to create, you develop a certain sense that you have accomplished something.

You have reached a certain level of maturity, a certain level of advancement and sophistication. Naturally, you can look back at the sense of self you had earlier and you can see how much you have expanded it, how much you have grown, how much you have a sense that you can actually manifest something.

You can take the teachings of Jesus: "I can of my own self do nothing." On a natural planet you are directly experiencing that you are not manifesting something as a separate self, you are part of the whole, your energy comes from your I AM Presence. You know it is not entirely by your own accomplishments that you are manifesting it but still, you develop this sense that you, as the self you see yourself as, have an ability to manifest. It is, of course, perfectly true—you *do*. You *have* expanded your sense of self and you *can* manifest something that you could not manifest in the beginning.

There is what we might call a natural pride of feeling good about your accomplishments and your abilities. Is it technically a spiritual poison? Well, certainly not the way we use the word on an unnatural planet because you do not see yourself as a separate being. You are not in duality and therefore you are not having the kind of pride that you see on earth.

It needs to be understood that those of you who came to earth as avatars, you did come with a certain sense of having accomplishment, having the ability to manifest something—even though, when you come into embodiment, you might lose the conscious awareness of this. You need to recognize here that you carry something with you from your time on a natural planet.

Avatars taking embodiment on earth

We have told you that when you descend into embodiment on earth, even as an avatar, regardless of your accomplishment, you must descend to the 48th level of consciousness, taking on all of the illusions down to that level. This means that at the conscious level, you are at the 48th level of consciousness.

What do you do on a natural planet? Well, you also build something there that is the equivalent of what we have called your four lower bodies on earth. You build a sense of identity, you build a certain understanding of how the co-creative process works and you build certain feelings. Those you can, at least to some degree, take with you and they are used to form your identity, mental and emotional bodies. In other words, when you come as an avatar to earth, you are not starting from nothing when you create the four lower bodies that you use to take embodiment here. You carry something with you from a natural planet. This means that even though, at the conscious level, you are at the 48th level of consciousness (and therefore you do not consciously remember coming from a natural planet), you still have certain sensations, certain memories. You even have certain abilities because it is, of course, much easier for you to begin to master the co-creative process on earth than it would be for an entirely new lifestream that was just created at that level.

When you come to earth, you experience that you are more sophisticated, you are more accomplished, you have greater abilities than most of the people who embody on earth. Now, where this can become tricky for an avatar is, of course, when you receive the birth trauma. What happens in that process is that the fallen beings attempt to put you down and tell you that you have no right to be on earth, and you should never have come here and so forth and so on. You now create the primal self, and therefore you do not see the dilemma that the fallen beings put you in. This causes you to create other selves that have this sensation that now you need to validate yourself on earth. You need to justify yourself, you need to explain yourself. You need to prove yourself that you are worthy, that you have a right to be on earth, that you are not a bad person and so forth.

Mutual respect with fallen beings

This can lead you to create these selves where you become very eager to attain some kind of accomplishment, some kind of special ability to do something in the physical, even to do something with the physical body. You see that many avatars have in various embodiments developed some mastery of the body. They have, in some cases, gone into martial arts and become great warriors. They have developed special abilities as artists, musicians, gymnasts or sports people or whatever you have.

When you have gone through several embodiments of seeking to justify yourself, there are two things that will happen. First of all, you will experience that in an outer sense, you can never really be satisfied with your accomplishments. You can never satisfy the fallen beings, you will never validate yourself in their eyes. Also, to most people on earth you will not validate yourself in their eyes. They might look at you admiringly because you have an ability they do not have, but it does not really satisfy you.

You are building up this certain frustration, and this means that in order to feel that you have accomplished something, you go into what they call a rat race or a treadmill. You have to run faster and faster, do more and more, accomplish more and more. In fact, you see this in many people even today where whatever they accomplish is not enough. No matter how much money they make, no matter how much accomplishment they have in some field, how much recognition they get, it is never quite enough.

For example, you see in some sports people that at a young age they go to the Olympics and they win several medals and they set world records. They feel on an absolute high because they feel ultimately validated. Then, suddenly this very merciless phenomenon of age creeps up on them and they can no longer achieve those results. Now, they go into a kind of depression because they have no validation anymore but they still feel that they need it.

Many avatars have gone through this from lifetime to lifetime, spending great effort to build up some kind of ability in that lifetime, only to then lose it again and ending the lifetime feeling on a low and feeling very insecure about themselves. This is what can cause some lifestreams to gradually develop a more permanent self that they create, that they carry over from lifetime to lifetime, and this is what gives them the sense of superiority. They now use the duality consciousness, which of course always implies or carries within it a value judgment. They are sort of tricked by the fallen beings into applying the duality consciousness to create a self that has this great sense of pride that they are somehow special, they are more advanced than other people and therefore they are entitled to a certain position, to certain privileges, to this and that.

What I am basically saying to you is that some avatars, because of this, become tricked into basically acting like the fallen beings. You can look back at the middle ages and some of the kings and the noble people who felt they were entitled to special privileges. Some of them were fallen beings and some of them were avatars. They often mixed together, as is described in the book *My Lives,* because you will often see that, in fact, fallen beings because of their long history also have a greater ability to manifest certain physical results. There is that sense of almost mutual respect that can develop between avatars and fallen beings because each of them realizes that the other has certain accomplishments.

Admitting that a self in you has pride

This, of course, does not apply to the fallen beings in the identity realm and it does not apply to all fallen beings on earth. But you can come into a situation where there are some fallen beings on earth (not necessarily the most evil ones) where you develop almost a camaraderie between them and avatars so they respect each others abilities to do something in the physical. Therefore, they reinforce each others sense of pride.

There are avatars that find it very difficult to break their ties to such lifestreams, to such fallen beings. It can be very, very hard for an avatar to break such a tie. It can be hard for you to actually admit that you have developed this admiration and respect for a fallen being. You can do this by recognizing that it was, of course, a self in you that had developed this and it was an offspring of the self that has given you this sense of pride.

Now, again, as with anger, there is no shame. There is no condemnation in admitting that you have a certain element of pride. When you look at the dynamic, the psychological dynamic of being an avatar, coming to a planet like earth, going through what you have gone through, it is inevitable that you develop such a self. Basically, you are on earth, you are in a physical body, you are exposed to the conditions on earth (which are, as we now have said many times, very difficult, very dense). As long as you are at a certain level of consciousness, you need to respond to these conditions with that level of consciousness. The only way to respond at the 48th level is to develop a self based on the illusion at the 48th level. Again, you can see that it is inevitable that you develop these selves. What we are simply calling you to recognize is that you have them and it is time to let them die. Again, we have given you the tools and the teachings to accomplish this.

The fallen beings, of course, have a pride that is much more ingrained, much more solidified than what an avatar has had time to develop. Even if you have reincarnated for two million years on earth, that is a very short time span compared to the time since the fallen beings fell in a previous sphere. What you realize here is that their pride is much more severe and it is very much tied to anger.

Of course, it is a very dense form of ignorance that they have. I am not saying that (even though there are some similarities and you can have a mutual respect with fallen beings) your pride is the same as that of the fallen beings. You can actually get out of it much more easily than the fallen beings could. Even though they, of course, also have the potential to go through the exact same process you are going through: identifying a self, letting it die. Of course, for a fallen being it is much more difficult to step outside of their current self, look at it from the outside, identify it as an unreal self and letting it die, but it is still possible and it is still the same basic process.

Equality dissolves pride

What I want to offer you is the gift of my wisdom, which is the Wisdom of Equality because this is the ultimate antidote to pride. This wisdom has, of course, many levels. At the very first level, as an avatar, let us say that you come to the conscious recognition that one of the spiritual poisons you have to overcome on earth is pride. You have developed a certain self that has this pride. What can you, then, do to begin to shift out of identification with that self?

Well, you begin by using the Wisdom of Equality to recognize what we have told you about the dualistic consciousness. The consciousness of duality has two opposite polarities but it always applies a value judgment to them: one is good, one is bad. You can use, you can tune in to and you can call forth my Presence with my mantra to really experience the unreality of duality.

Therefore, you can see that it is simply an illusion that one polarity is better than another, that one is good, that one is bad. You can see that there is something unreal about duality. I know very well that many of you have studied the teachings we have given on duality and there is what Master MORE called "the gap" between the teaching and your experiencing the reality of the teaching. That is where the Wisdom of Equality can be of help.

Let us go further in using the Wisdom of Equality. You are sitting here, you have your physical senses, you have your conscious awareness. I am asking you to look at earth, look at life and in your mind's eye. You see all of the varied conditions that you have experienced in your life. You see this incredible variety. You see how some people are suffering, some people are warring, some people are living peaceful lives and so forth and so on. Naturally, it is very hard to look at all this and not apply some kind of value judgment, saying that some things are not the highest because they cause suffering and other things must be higher because they do not cause people to suffer. Now, with the Wisdom of Equality, you can begin to step back from this very diversified scenario. I ask you to look at the fact that all of the material things you see on earth are made out of matter. What is matter made out of? Well, you know from science that it is made out of atoms. There are many different forms of matter phenomena but they are all made out of these basic building blocks of atoms.

You know there are 108 atoms—actually there are more but science has discovered 108. You know that any material phenomenon that you can detect with your senses is made out of these atoms, either one atom or a combination of several atoms. My beloved, when you look at the macroscopic level of your sensory experience, you can see that there may be a person who has an open wound and there is pus oozing out of the wound and there are flies and maggots all over it. This, to your normal awakened mind, seems like a travesty because it causes suffering.

Levels of meaningfulness

Now, allow yourself to see that this phenomenon is made out of matter, which is made out of atoms. If you could shift your vision so you only saw the atoms (in other words, instead of seeing an open wound you are seeing a certain combination of atoms, instead of seeing a maggot crawling around, you are seeing a combination of atoms), the value judgment you apply at the macroscopic level that this is bad, is that really relevant at the level of atoms? Do the atoms think that: "Oh, I have manifested a maggot and this is bad?" Well, of course they do not! They are just manifesting whatever matrix has been put upon them. What I am saying here is this: The value judgment of good and bad exists at that macroscopic level in the physical mind but it does not exist at the deeper level. It is meaningless at the deeper level.

What you also realize, when you tune in to the deeper level of atoms, is that atoms are not bound to a particular form. The atoms could easily be freed from the form of a maggot and form a beautiful flower. It is no more difficult for the atom to form one or the other. It is completely possible that the atoms forming a maggot could be set free and become part of forming a rose. In fact, the atoms that are now forming the maggot might at a previous time have formed a rose. You see that nothing that happens at the macroscopic level in the physical world is permanent. It is temporary. Now, you can, of course, go to an even deeper level. Atoms are made out of elementary particles. Elementary particles are on the borderline between matter and energy so they are really partly energy waves. You can go to an even deeper level and see just the energy waves. Everything is made up of energy waves, a very, very complex interference pattern of different energy waves. At the level of the energy waves, again the value judgments from the macroscopic level have no value, they have no relevance. It is just energy waves.

You can then look at all of the mighty empires built by men, all of the structures they have built to build up their pride, their sense of accomplishment, their sense of being special. Look at all these citadels of power and ask yourself: "At the level of the energy waves, do they have any permanence, do they have any power?" "Nay!"

You can realize that what is really happening on earth is just a game. It is a theatre performance that people are enacting in order to have certain experiences until they feel they have had enough of that experience. You can then, as a spiritual student, begin to consider: Do you actually really need to feel superior to others? Have you not had many lifetimes where you have had this experience and is it not time to consider: "Have I just had enough of it? Haven't I just had enough of this artificial, non-permanent, pointless game of superiority and inferiority?"

Inferiority is also pride

Now, some of you may have another self where you can identify that you do not actually have the sense of superiority, you have a sense of *in*feriority. My beloved, this is actually still a form of pride because you are still applying a value judgment to yourself. What are you thinking you can do here? You are thinking that you can know better than God that you are inferior. God did not create you inferior. You were not created as an inferior being but now you think you can know that you are actually an inferior being—and that is pride. You think you know better than your Creator, than your Source. You can come to this realization that you have just had enough of the inferiority, the superiority and any other kind of *-ority* that you can think up.

You can come to the point where, suddenly, your vision shifts and you see beyond this macroscopic level. You see that at a deeper level of atoms, of energy waves, of the Ma-ter light that this is all unreal, this is all pointless. Then, you can come to see that it is actually not *you* who believes this, it is a separate self. The separate self is just like a computer: It is also unreal.

Therefore, you can come to look at it and just say: "I let you die. I don't want you any more in my being, I am letting you die."

When that falls away from you, you will feel a great sense of freedom. Whether you feel inferior or superior, it has become, over the lifetimes you have had, gradually more and more difficult to uphold that sense, that illusion. You have had to work harder and harder to uphold it. This means that it has become more of a strain for you. You have to put more of your mental energy and your attention into this. Once you stop doing this, then suddenly your attention is freed up. Suddenly, you can feel a sense of peace that you cannot feel when you are in the inferiority-superiority dynamic.

This is the Wisdom of Equality that I offer to you. You can actually meditate on that Wisdom of Equality. You can go through the steps I have outlined or you can even go through a visualization. You visualize the earth with all of its mountains, all of its great cities. Then, you see how, if you could speed up time, then all of the mountains would be made low, all of the cities would fall apart, everything would be reduced to sand, to rubble, to atoms, to energy waves. In the end, there would be only the complete equality of the Ma-ter light.

We have said that the Ma-ter light can be raised up and become self-aware, but that is the Ma-ter light, not the structures built out of the Ma-ter light on a planet like earth. They will never attain permanence. Therefore, as the Ma-ter light becomes self-aware, it will shake off these forms. They will gradually crumble and be reduced to nothingness until only the pure light is left.

You can visualize and meditate on this, and it can help you free yourself from this dynamic of not only inferiority and superiority but also all the offsprings of the dualistic consciousness of putting things up and comparing one to another. With this, I thank you for your attention and for receiving my gift.

16 | INVOKING THE WISDOM OF EQUALITY

In the name I AM THAT I AM, Jesus Christ, I call to all representatives of the Divine Mother, especially Ratnasambhava, to help me tune in to your Wisdom of Equality and overcome the poisons, including…

[Make personal calls.]

Ratnasambhava, release the Wisdom of Equality to give me awareness that it is both natural and inevitable that as I have co-created for a long time on a natural planet, I experience that I have a certain mastery, a certain accomplishment.

OM RATNASAMBHAVA TRAM

Ratnasambhava, release the Wisdom of Equality to give me awareness that it is almost inevitable that when I grow in my awareness to create, I develop a sense that I have reached a certain level of advancement and sophistication.

OM RATNASAMBHAVA TRAM

Ratnasambhava, release the Wisdom of Equality to give me awareness that I know it is not entirely by my own accomplishments that I am manifesting it but still, I develop the sense that I, as the self I see myself as, have an ability to manifest.

OM RATNASAMBHAVA TRAM

Ratnasambhava, release the Wisdom of Equality to give me awareness that this is a natural pride of feeling good about my accomplishments and abilities. This is not a spiritual poison as the word is used on an unnatural planet because I do not see myself as a separate being.

OM RATNASAMBHAVA TRAM

Ratnasambhava, release the Wisdom of Equality to give me awareness that when I came to earth as an avatar, I did come with a certain sense of having accomplishment, having the ability to manifest something.

OM RATNASAMBHAVA TRAM

Ratnasambhava, release the Wisdom of Equality to give me awareness that when I descend to earth, even as an avatar, I descended to the 48th level of consciousness, taking on all of the illusions down to that level.

OM RATNASAMBHAVA TRAM

Ratnasambhava, release the Wisdom of Equality to give me awareness that when I come as an avatar, I am not starting from nothing when I create the four lower bodies that I use to take embodiment here.

OM RATNASAMBHAVA TRAM

Ratnasambhava, release the Wisdom of Equality to give me awareness that I carry something with me from a natural planet. Even though, at the conscious level, I am at the 48th level of consciousness, I still have certain sensations and memories.

OM RATNASAMBHAVA TRAM

16 | Invoking the Wisdom of Equality

Ratnasambhava, release the Wisdom of Equality to give me awareness that I have certain abilities because it is much easier for me to begin to master the co-creative process on earth than it would be for an entirely new lifestream.

OM RATNASAMBHAVA TRAM

Ratnasambhava, release the Wisdom of Equality to give me awareness that when I come to earth, I experience that I am more sophisticated and I have greater abilities than most of the people who embody on earth.

OM RATNASAMBHAVA TRAM

Ratnasambhava, release the Wisdom of Equality to give me awareness that this becomes difficult when the fallen beings put me down and I receive the birth trauma.

OM RATNASAMBHAVA TRAM

Ratnasambhava, release the Wisdom of Equality to give me awareness that I now create the primal self, and therefore I do not see the dilemma that the fallen beings put me in. This causes me to create other selves that have this sensation that now I need to validate myself on earth.

OM RATNASAMBHAVA TRAM

Ratnasambhava, release the Wisdom of Equality to give me awareness that these selves think I need to justify myself, I need to explain myself. I need to prove that I am worthy, that I have a right to be on earth, that I am not a bad person and so forth.

OM RATNASAMBHAVA TRAM

Ratnasambhava, release the Wisdom of Equality to give me awareness that this led me to create these selves where I became very eager to attain some kind of accomplishment, some kind of special ability to do something in the physical, even to do something with the physical body.

OM RATNASAMBHAVA TRAM

Ratnasambhava, release the Wisdom of Equality to give me awareness that I have gone through several embodiments of seeking to justify myself. Therefore, I experience that in an outer sense, I can never really be satisfied with my accomplishments.

OM RATNASAMBHAVA TRAM

Ratnasambhava, release the Wisdom of Equality to give me awareness that I also experience that I can never satisfy the fallen beings, I will never validate myself in their eyes. To most people on earth, I will not validate myself in their eyes. They might look at me admiringly because I have an ability they do not have, but it does not really satisfy me.

OM RATNASAMBHAVA TRAM

Ratnasambhava, release the Wisdom of Equality to give me awareness that I then build up a frustration, and this means that in order to feel that I have accomplished something, I have to accomplish more and more.

OM RATNASAMBHAVA TRAM

Ratnasambhava, release the Wisdom of Equality to give me awareness that many avatars have gone through this from lifetime to lifetime, spending great effort to build up some kind of ability in that lifetime, only to then lose it again and ending the lifetime feeling on a low and feeling very insecure about themselves.

OM RATNASAMBHAVA TRAM

Ratnasambhava, release the Wisdom of Equality to give me awareness that this can cause some avatars to develop a more permanent self that gives them a sense of superiority.

OM RATNASAMBHAVA TRAM

16 | Invoking the Wisdom of Equality

Ratnasambhava, release the Wisdom of Equality to give me awareness that as avatars we can be tricked by the fallen beings into applying the duality consciousness to create a self that has this great sense of pride that we are somehow special, we are more advanced than other people and therefore we are entitled to a certain position and privileges.

OM RATNASAMBHAVA TRAM

Ratnasambhava, release the Wisdom of Equality to give me awareness that some avatars become tricked into basically acting like the fallen beings, even mixing with the fallen beings, developing a mutual respect.

OM RATNASAMBHAVA TRAM

Ratnasambhava, release the Wisdom of Equality to give me awareness that will help me break any ties to fallen beings.

OM RATNASAMBHAVA TRAM

Ratnasambhava, release the Wisdom of Equality to give me awareness that will help me admit that I have developed this admiration and respect for a fallen being.

OM RATNASAMBHAVA TRAM

Ratnasambhava, release the Wisdom of Equality to give me awareness that will help me recognize that it was a self in me that had developed this, and it was an offspring of the self that has given me this sense of pride.

OM RATNASAMBHAVA TRAM

Ratnasambhava, release the Wisdom of Equality to give me awareness that there is no shame or condemnation in admitting that I have a certain element of pride.

OM RATNASAMBHAVA TRAM

Ratnasambhava, release the Wisdom of Equality to give me awareness that considering the psychological dynamic of an avatar, coming to a planet like earth, going through what I have gone through, makes it inevitable that I develop such a self.

OM RATNASAMBHAVA TRAM

Ratnasambhava, release the Wisdom of Equality to give me awareness that it is inevitable that I develop these selves, but now it is time to let them die.

OM RATNASAMBHAVA TRAM

Ratnasambhava, release the Wisdom of Equality to give me awareness that one of the spiritual poisons I have to overcome on earth is pride. I have developed a certain self that has this pride.

OM RATNASAMBHAVA TRAM

Ratnasambhava, release the Wisdom of Equality to give me awareness that will help me begin to shift out of identification with that self.

OM RATNASAMBHAVA TRAM

Ratnasambhava, release the Wisdom of Equality to give me awareness that the consciousness of duality has two opposite polarities but it always applies a value judgment to them: one is good, one is bad.

OM RATNASAMBHAVA TRAM

Ratnasambhava, release the Wisdom of Equality to give me awareness that will help me tune in to your Presence and really experience the unreality of duality.

OM RATNASAMBHAVA TRAM

Ratnasambhava, release the Wisdom of Equality to give me awareness that it is simply an illusion that one polarity is better than another, that one is good, that one is bad. There is something unreal about duality.

16 | Invoking the Wisdom of Equality

OM RATNASAMBHAVA TRAM

Ratnasambhava, release the Wisdom of Equality to give me awareness that it is very hard to look at the suffering on earth and not apply a value judgment. Yet with the Wisdom of Equality, I can step back from this very diversified scenario.

OM RATNASAMBHAVA TRAM

Ratnasambhava, release the Wisdom of Equality to give me awareness that all of the material things on earth are made out of matter. Yet all matter is made out of atoms.

OM RATNASAMBHAVA TRAM

Ratnasambhava, release the Wisdom of Equality to give me awareness that there are many different forms of matter phenomena but they are all made out of these basic building blocks of atoms.

OM RATNASAMBHAVA TRAM

Ratnasambhava, release the Wisdom of Equality to give me awareness that when I look at the macroscopic level of my sensory experience, a situation might seem like a travesty because it causes suffering.

OM RATNASAMBHAVA TRAM

Ratnasambhava, release the Wisdom of Equality to give me awareness that allows me to see that this phenomenon is made out of matter, which is made out of atoms.

OM RATNASAMBHAVA TRAM

Ratnasambhava, release the Wisdom of Equality to give me awareness that helps me shift my vision and see that the value judgment I apply at the macroscopic level is not relevant at the level of atoms.

OM RATNASAMBHAVA TRAM

Ratnasambhava, release the Wisdom of Equality to give me awareness that the atoms do not think that what they have manifested is bad. The value judgment of good and bad exists at the macroscopic level in the outer mind but it does not exist at the deeper level. It is meaningless at the deeper level.

OM RATNASAMBHAVA TRAM

Ratnasambhava, release the Wisdom of Equality to give me awareness that atoms are not bound to a particular form. The atoms could easily be freed from one form and manifest a different form.

OM RATNASAMBHAVA TRAM

Ratnasambhava, release the Wisdom of Equality to give me awareness that nothing that happens at the macroscopic level in the physical world is permanent. It is temporary.

OM RATNASAMBHAVA TRAM

Ratnasambhava, release the Wisdom of Equality to give me awareness that at a deeper level, atoms are made out of elementary particles. Elementary particles are really energy waves.

OM RATNASAMBHAVA TRAM

Ratnasambhava, release the Wisdom of Equality to give me awareness that everything is made up of energy waves, a very complex interference pattern of different energy waves.

OM RATNASAMBHAVA TRAM

Ratnasambhava, release the Wisdom of Equality to give me awareness that at the level of the energy waves, the value judgments from the macroscopic level have no value, they have no relevance. It is just energy waves.

OM RATNASAMBHAVA TRAM

16 | Invoking the Wisdom of Equality

Ratnasambhava, release the Wisdom of Equality to give me awareness that the mighty empires built by men, at the level of the energy waves have no permanence, no power.

OM RATNASAMBHAVA TRAM

Ratnasambhava, release the Wisdom of Equality to give me awareness that what is really happening on earth is just a game. It is a theatre performance that people are enacting in order to have certain experiences until they feel they have had enough of that experience.

OM RATNASAMBHAVA TRAM

Ratnasambhava, release the Wisdom of Equality to give me awareness that I do not really need to feel superior to others. I have had enough of this artificial, non-permanent, pointless game of superiority and inferiority.

OM RATNASAMBHAVA TRAM

Ratnasambhava, release the Wisdom of Equality to give me awareness that helps me see if I have a self that has a sense of *in*feriority.

OM RATNASAMBHAVA TRAM

Ratnasambhava, release the Wisdom of Equality to give me awareness that this is still a form of pride because I am still applying a value judgment to myself.

OM RATNASAMBHAVA TRAM

Ratnasambhava, release the Wisdom of Equality to give me awareness that the inferiority self thinks it can know better than God that I am inferior.

OM RATNASAMBHAVA TRAM

Ratnasambhava, release the Wisdom of Equality to give me awareness that God did not create me inferior. I was not created as an inferior being but now I think I can know that I am actually an inferior being—and that is pride.

OM RATNASAMBHAVA TRAM

Ratnasambhava, release the Wisdom of Equality to give me awareness that I have simply had enough of the inferiority, the superiority and any other kind of *-ority* that I can think up.

OM RATNASAMBHAVA TRAM

Ratnasambhava, release the Wisdom of Equality to give me awareness that shifts my vision so I see beyond the macroscopic level.

OM RATNASAMBHAVA TRAM

Ratnasambhava, release the Wisdom of Equality to give me awareness that at a deeper level of atoms, of energy waves, of the Ma-ter light that this is all unreal, this is all pointless.

OM RATNASAMBHAVA TRAM

Ratnasambhava, release the Wisdom of Equality to give me awareness that it is actually not *me* who believes this, it is a separate self. The separate self is just like a computer: It is also unreal.

OM RATNASAMBHAVA TRAM

Ratnasambhava, release the Wisdom of Equality to give me awareness that helps me see this self and say: "I let you die. I don't want you anymore in my being, I am letting you die."

OM RATNASAMBHAVA TRAM

Ratnasambhava, release the Wisdom of Equality to give me awareness that whether I feel inferior or superior, it has become gradually more and more difficult to uphold that sense, that illusion.

OM RATNASAMBHAVA TRAM

Ratnasambhava, release the Wisdom of Equality to give me awareness that I have had to work harder and harder to uphold it, meaning it has become more of a strain for me. I have to put more of my mental energy and my attention into this.

OM RATNASAMBHAVA TRAM

Ratnasambhava, release the Wisdom of Equality to give me awareness that once I stop doing this, then attention is freed up and I can feel a sense of peace that I cannot feel when I am in the inferiority-superiority dynamic.

OM RATNASAMBHAVA TRAM

Ratnasambhava, release the Wisdom of Equality to give me awareness that over time the mountains will be made low, all of the cities will fall apart, everything will be reduced to sand, to rubble, to atoms, to energy waves.

OM RATNASAMBHAVA TRAM

Ratnasambhava, release the Wisdom of Equality to give me awareness that in the end, there will be only the complete equality of the Ma-ter light.

OM RATNASAMBHAVA TRAM

Ratnasambhava, release the Wisdom of Equality to give me awareness that the structures built out of the Ma-ter light on a planet like earth will never attain permanence.

OM RATNASAMBHAVA TRAM

Ratnasambhava, release the Wisdom of Equality to give me awareness that as the Ma-ter light becomes self-aware, it will shake off these forms. They will gradually crumble and be reduced to nothingness until only the pure light is left.

OM RATNASAMBHAVA TRAM

Ratnasambhava, release the Wisdom of Equality to give me awareness that frees me from this dynamic of not only inferiority and superiority but also all the offsprings of the dualistic consciousness of putting things up and comparing one to another.

OM RATNASAMBHAVA TRAM

Sealing

In the name of the Divine Mother, I call to Mother Mary for the sealing of myself and all people in my circle of influence in the creative flow of the Divine Mother, the River of Life. I call for the multiplication of my calls by all representatives of the Divine Mother, so that we form the perfect figure-eight flow of "As Above, so below." Thus, I accept that this is fully manifest, because the mouth of the Lord, the Divine Mother that I AM, has spoken it. Amen.

17 | DISCERNMENT SHOWS YOU WHEN ENOUGH IS ENOUGH

I AM the Buddha Amitabha. The poison for which I am the antidote has been called envy, greed and lust. These are, of course, somewhat symbols for a complex phenomenon. What is greed? What is lust? Most people look at it as the physical lust, or the lusts of the physical body, or the greed for money but it is actually much more. It is really the sense that you cannot get enough of something and this will present somewhat of a paradox.

A poison becomes a treadmill

If you take the teachings we have given you, we have said that all self-aware beings have been given free will by their Creator. They have the right to create or to have any experience they want and continue to have it for as long as they want it until they have had enough of it. How can we say that it is a spiritual poison that you want more and more of something? Is it not actually okay to be greedy and want more and more money, if this is the experience you have? Is it not okay to lust for sex or food or whatever pleasures you can have with the physical body if this is the experience you want? You should just indulge in it, have as much as possible of what you want so that you can more quickly come to the point where you have had enough.

There are certain eastern schools of philosophy that say that there are two ways to enlightenment. One is to go the path of the sage where you withdraw from worldly pleasures, another path is to indulge in it until you have had enough. All of these things are valid concerns. However, the point of a poison (and the reason we call it a poison) is that it traps you. It traps you on this merry-go-round, this treadmill, where you are going round and round and you may be going faster and faster but you are not really getting anywhere. The thing is, if you could take a person who is indulging himself in the pleasures of the physical body, then if he was not affected by the poison of greed and lust, he may indeed come to the point within a few lifetimes where he has had enough of those pleasures and he could give them up.

The point is that over time, both on earth and even by the fallen beings, the poison has been created. When people take that poison into their beings, they cannot have enough. They cannot have the feeling of being full because what the poison of greed and envy does is, it blocks out the feeling of being full, of having had enough.

This, of course, ties in with the teaching we have given you on the selves that you have created. You can create a self that feels that it is inadequate on earth. As an avatar you often create such a self that feels inadequate on earth because of the birth trauma. You feel there is a certain lack, there is a certain emptiness, there is a certain deficit in your being. This self is basically programmed to seek to fill that void and it creates other selves that then say: "If you have enough money, you will fill the void." "If you have enough sex, you will fill the void." "If you have enough recognition, you will fill the void." "If you accomplish enough works, you will fill the void." "If you help change enough people, you will fill the void." "If you change this or that condition on earth, you will fill the void."

For an avatar, this is how it plays out: You came to earth to bring a positive change. You experience the trauma. It gives you the sense of void, of emptiness. You create selves that project at you that if you just have enough of this or that condition, you will feel full.

Of course, this ties into this collective momentum that started with the fallen beings in the fourth sphere when they first fell, and which has been built on to ever since. When you are affected by this poison, you cannot ever feel full. Well, you can feel *somewhat* full in brief moments when you have one of these very extreme experiences. Like my brother said, you have a sportsman who sets the world record and wins the Olympic medal and he feels a high for a brief period of time, but then it suddenly is not enough. He either needs more or he goes into the depression that is the follow-up to the high, the opposite polarity of the high. What goes up, must come down. That is why what is actually a legitimate desire to have a certain type of experience, becomes perverted by the poison into a never-ending quest for more and more that can never be enough, that can never fill you.

The Discerning Wisdom

There are many people on earth who are trapped in some of these desires (that avatars usually do not have) for physical pleasures, for indulging in various things on earth. This is not your concern as an avatar. These people will gradually be pulled up as the collective consciousness is raised and some of them will be able to overcome this and move on with it. As the collective consciousness is raised, people will actually be able to tune in to the Discriminating Wisdom and begin to ask themselves whether they could ever have enough. How much beer do you need to drink? How many handbags do you need to have in your closet and so forth and so on. You see, in fact, in the western world, where you have had the consumer culture now for decades, there are people who are beginning to ask these kind of questions and, of course, have been doing so for some time.

What I wish to give you as an avatar is to offer you my assistance with the wisdom that is my antidote to the poison. It is the Discriminating Wisdom or the Discerning Wisdom. There is a difference between value judgment and discrimination or discernment. Discrimination is used in the higher sense of the word, not in the commonly used word where you are discriminating against somebody based on their race, for example. That is why I prefer the word *discernment*, the Discerning Wisdom.

When you tune in to that Discerning Wisdom, then you can begin to ask yourself some of these questions. You can begin to identify that you have, for example, in your being a desire to see a certain change happen on earth. You desire to see people awaken and not indulge in a certain activity that causes them suffering. When you then tune in to the discerning wisdom, you can begin to draw on the teachings we have given on free will and ask yourself whether it is reasonable of you to have this desire to bring about a change, or to see brought about a change, that depends on the choices of other people.

You can use the teachings to tune in and experience the reality that you cannot, as an avatar, allow yourself to have a self that projects at you that your state of mind, your peace of mind, depends on the choices of other people. You can come to see that you may have a certain self that projects at you that you should help bring about a certain change and that you cannot feel full until people are no longer suffering from a certain disease, for example, or they are no longer being killed in war. This would in both cases essentially mean that you could not possibly feel full for the rest of this lifetime. It may not happen that war is eradicated or a certain disease is eradicated for the remainder of your lifetime, depending on how old you are at the present moment.

This would, then, mean that for the rest of this lifetime, you would have to live with this void. You can then come to realize that you do not want to do this. Then, again, you can draw from the teachings that what gives you the sense that this needs to be accomplished is a separate self. You can identify it, you can separate yourself from it and you can let it die.

You can also use the Discerning Wisdom to tune in, to meditate upon this wisdom. You may visualize it as a very thin, very sharp blade of a very hard material. Or you can visualize it as a laser light that will cut through the density of the duality consciousness and thereby separate the real from the unreal, allowing you to see what is an impossible desire, a desire that cannot be fulfilled.

Looking at your original motivation

You can, then, begin to look at your original motivation for coming here and, again, see that there was a certain desire you had before coming here that was impossible to fulfill. You could only fulfill it by affecting the free will of other people and that is neither lawful nor what you actually want to do. If you truly lock in to the Discerning Wisdom, you will be able to see that you do not actually have a true higher desire to change the choices of other people. It was an unlawful, an impossible, an unfulfillable desire based on a lower state of consciousness than what you have today.

You can begin, then, to separate these selves out, to separate yourself from them, to identify them, to see them for what they are. There may often be more than one. Some of them may require you to wrestle a little bit with this because, again, it ties in with this: You come to earth with the best of intentions. You receive the shock of beginning to doubt your intentions, doubt your original vision. It can require some work to come to the point where you can see and acknowledge that it was a lower vision. It was based on an illusion and you can therefore let it go. You can let go of the self that wants to defend your reason for coming here, wants to justify it, wants to explain it, wants to validate why it was not so bad what you did.

Truly, it *was* not bad what you did, but it was based on the state of consciousness you had at the time, and that was not the state of consciousness that was the highest possible. It was not the state of consciousness with which you can ascend. Because you have had this long sojourn on earth, you have now the potential to rise to a higher level of consciousness and thereby rise to the level of consciousness from which you *can* ascend.

You could not actually have ascended from a natural planet but you can ascend from the earth. That is why, in a sense, it was justified that you descended to earth. It was justified for your long-term growth. It is just that you need to see that the reason you had in your mind when you descended was not justified, it was not ultimate. The Discriminating Wisdom can help you cut through that dross in your own mind where there is also a self that feels it could never have enough of creating change on earth—unless all people were free and that, of course, is a very long-term proposition.

By using this wisdom, the Discriminating Wisdom, giving my mantra, tuning in to my Being, you can free yourself from these momentums that many of you have carried with you for two million years. You can overcome this and very quickly make progress and attain that greater sense of peace that we all want for you. My beloved, this is my gift for you.

18 | INVOKING DISCERNING WISDOM

In the name I AM THAT I AM, Jesus Christ, I call to all representatives of the Divine Mother, especially Amitabha, to help me tune in to your Discerning Wisdom and overcome the poisons, including…

[Make personal calls.]

Amitabha, release the Discerning Wisdom to give me awareness that greed and lust is really the sense that we cannot get enough of something.

OM AMITABHA HRIH

Amitabha, release the Discerning Wisdom to give me awareness that a spiritual poison traps me on this merry-go-round, this treadmill, where I am going round and round and I may be going faster and faster but I am not getting anywhere.

OM AMITABHA HRIH

Amitabha, release the Discerning Wisdom to give me awareness that if I am not affected by the poison of greed and lust, I may come to the point where I have had enough of those pleasures and give them up.

OM AMITABHA HRIH

Amitabha, release the Discerning Wisdom to give me awareness that when I take a poison into my being, I cannot have enough. I cannot have the feeling of being full because the poison of greed and envy blocks out the feeling of being full, of having had enough.

OM AMITABHA HRIH

Amitabha, release the Discerning Wisdom to give me awareness that as an avatar I have likely created a self that feels inadequate on earth because of the birth trauma. I feel there is a certain lack, there is a certain emptiness, there is a certain deficit in my being.

OM AMITABHA HRIH

Amitabha, release the Discerning Wisdom to give me awareness that this self is basically programmed to seek to fill that void and it creates other selves that then say: "If you have enough money, you will fill the void." "If you have enough sex, you will fill the void." "If you have enough recognition, you will fill the void." "If you accomplish enough works, you will fill the void." "If you help change enough people, you will fill the void." "If you change this or that condition on earth, you will fill the void."

OM AMITABHA HRIH

Amitabha, release the Discerning Wisdom to give me awareness that I came to earth to bring a positive change. I experienced the trauma and it gave me the sense of emptiness. I created selves that project at me that if I just have enough of this or that condition, I will feel full.

OM AMITABHA HRIH

Amitabha, release the Discerning Wisdom to give me awareness that when I am affected by this poison, I cannot ever feel full.

OM AMITABHA HRIH

Amitabha, release the Discerning Wisdom to give me awareness that what is a legitimate desire to have a certain type of experience, becomes perverted by the poison into a never-ending quest for more and more that can never be enough, that can never fill me.

OM AMITABHA HRIH

Amitabha, release the Discerning Wisdom to give me awareness that there is a difference between value judgment and discrimination or discernment. Discrimination is used in the higher sense of the word, not in the commonly used word where we are discriminating against somebody.

OM AMITABHA HRIH

Amitabha, release the Discerning Wisdom to give me awareness that I have a desire to see a certain change happen on earth. I desire to see people awaken and not indulge in a certain activity that causes them suffering.

OM AMITABHA HRIH

Amitabha, release the Discerning Wisdom to give me awareness that it is not constructive that I have this desire to bring about a change that depends on the choices of other people.

OM AMITABHA HRIH

Amitabha, release the Discerning Wisdom to give me awareness that as an avatar, I cannot allow myself to have a self that projects at me that my state of mind, my peace of mind, depends on the choices of other people.

OM AMITABHA HRIH

Amitabha, release the Discerning Wisdom to give me awareness that I have a self that projects at me that I should help bring about a certain change. I cannot feel full until people are no longer suffering.

OM AMITABHA HRIH

Amitabha, release the Discerning Wisdom to give me awareness that this essentially means that I could not possibly feel full for the rest of this lifetime.

OM AMITABHA HRIH

Amitabha, release the Discerning Wisdom to give me awareness that having this self means that for the rest of this lifetime, I will have to live with this void.

OM AMITABHA HRIH

Amitabha, release the Discerning Wisdom to give me awareness that I do not want to do this. The sense that this needs to be accomplished is from a separate self. I identify it, I separate myself from it and I let it die.

OM AMITABHA HRIH

Amitabha, release the Discerning Wisdom to give me awareness that is like a very thin, very sharp blade of a very hard material. It is like a laser light that will cut through the density of the duality consciousness and thereby separate the real from the unreal, allowing me to see what is an impossible desire that cannot be fulfilled.

OM AMITABHA HRIH

Amitabha, release the Discerning Wisdom to give me awareness that my original motivation for coming here was based on a certain desire that was impossible to fulfill.

OM AMITABHA HRIH

Amitabha, release the Discerning Wisdom to give me awareness that I could only fulfill this desire by affecting the free will of other people and that is neither lawful nor what I actually want to do.

OM AMITABHA HRIH

Amitabha, release the Discerning Wisdom to give me awareness that I do not have a true higher desire to change the choices of other people. It was an unlawful, an impossible, an unfulfillable desire based on a lower state of consciousness than what I have today.

OM AMITABHA HRIH

Amitabha, release the Discerning Wisdom to give me awareness that will allow me to separate these selves out, to separate myself from them, to identify them, to see them for what they are.

OM AMITABHA HRIH

Amitabha, release the Discerning Wisdom to give me awareness that my intentions for coming to earth were based on a lower vision. They were based on an illusion and I can therefore let it go. I let go of the self that wants to defend my reason for coming here, wants to justify it, wants to explain it, wants to validate why it was not so bad what I did.

OM AMITABHA HRIH

Amitabha, release the Discerning Wisdom to give me awareness that what I did *was* not bad, but it was based on the state of consciousness I had at the time, and that was not the highest possible state of consciousness.

OM AMITABHA HRIH

Amitabha, release the Discerning Wisdom to give me awareness that because I have had this long sojourn on earth, I have the potential to rise to a higher level of consciousness from which I can ascend.

OM AMITABHA HRIH

Amitabha, release the Discerning Wisdom to give me awareness that I could not have ascended from a natural planet but I can ascend from earth.

OM AMITABHA HRIH

Amitabha, release the Discerning Wisdom to give me awareness that it was justified that I descended to earth. It was justified for my long-term growth.

OM AMITABHA HRIH

Amitabha, release the Discerning Wisdom to give me awareness that the reason I had in my mind when I descended was not justified, it was not ultimate.

OM AMITABHA HRIH

Amitabha, release the Discerning Wisdom to give me awareness that can help me cut through the dross in my mind where there is also a self that feels it could never have enough of creating change on earth.

OM AMITABHA HRIH

Amitabha, release the Discerning Wisdom to give me awareness that can help me free myself from these momentums that I have carried with me for a very long time.

OM AMITABHA HRIH

Amitabha, release the Discerning Wisdom to give me awareness that can help me overcome this and very quickly make progress and attain that greater sense of peace that I really want.

OM AMITABHA HRIH

Sealing

In the name of the Divine Mother, I call to Mother Mary for the sealing of myself and all people in my circle of influence in the creative flow of the Divine Mother, the River of Life. I call for the multiplication of my calls by all representatives of the Divine Mother, so that we form the perfect figure-eight flow of "As Above, so below." Thus, I accept that this is fully manifest, because the mouth of the Lord, the Divine Mother that I AM, has spoken it. Amen.

19 | OVERCOMING ENVY
BE ACCOMPLISHING ALL THINGS

I AM the Buddha Amogasiddhi. The poison for which I am the antidote is envy. What is envy? Where does it come from? It originated, as the other poisons, with the fallen beings who after they fell experienced something they had not experienced before. Before they fell, they had in many cases a high attainment on co-creation, or at least on controlling the matter realm as it was in the sphere in which they fell, be it the fourth, fifth or the sixth. Some of these fallen beings had gone into using their co-creative abilities in a controlling manner, seeking to maintain something and maintain a certain state, instead of being willing to give up a limited state in order to co-create that which is more.

How envy originated

This is, as we have said before, the basic principle of co-creation. You create through your current sense of self. You experience the physical outpicturing of it. Then, you refine your sense of self, raise your sense of self, and co-create something more based on the new self. This process requires you to let the former self die. If you are not willing to do that, then you go into seeking to maintain either the former self or the state you have attained in the physical realm. As long as you have not fallen, you are still receiving light from your I AM Presence and you can actually use that light to seek to create that state of control.

Some of the primary fallen beings had built this sense that they were the highest, the most advanced, the most sophisticated, the most powerful beings in the little enclave they had created for themselves. They often had many followers who affirmed and validated that they were the superior ones, they were the leaders, the most powerful beings. They had that sense of identity of being the superior beings and as such they had no need for envy, for they were, as they saw it, the highest. This, of course, only took place on what you in your sphere would call planets. There were a limited number of planets where the fallen beings had been allowed to create their "sophisticated" civilizations.

It was not until the sphere was ready to ascend that the fallen beings were confronted with the ascended masters. It was not until then that they realized that their creation, their co-creation, had not been as high as they thought it was. The fallen beings, then, fall into the next sphere that is created. Now, they gradually realize, by interacting with both the new beings that were created in that sphere and certain other beings that they encountered (which are the equivalent of what we have called avatars here), that they had been cut off from their I AM Presences. Actually, the fallen beings did not realize this but they experienced that there were other beings who had more spiritual light, more co-creative energy than they themselves had.

In a sense, you could say that a fallen being is no longer a co-creator because they cannot co-create with the I AM Presence, as they are not receiving any creative energy from their I AM Presence with which to co-create. They can only de-create by taking light that is already brought into the realm, the sphere, where they exist. They cannot bring forth something new so they seek to, again, create some empire where they can set themselves up as being in control.

Those who fell with them as their followers once again validated them as their leaders and so they were able to build something like this. Every once in a while there was sent into these planets, into these empires, those who had spiritual light and who could therefore demonstrate to the fallen beings that they had something that these seemingly very powerful, sophisticated fallen beings did not have. That was the origin of envy. The fallen beings saw the light in others, in those who were still co-creators, and they envied that light. They realized at some level that they could not have it as long as they were in the fallen consciousness. They were not willing to give up the fallen consciousness so they could not have it.

Hatred of the light

This is what led them to actually hate the light, hate the avatars, hate those who had the co-creative abilities. Anger is an extreme feeling but hatred is more extreme. Anger makes you want to punish others and hatred makes you want to destroy them. The fallen beings developed this desire to destroy but it is very much tied to their envy because they think (or they experience, you might say) that they cannot have what co-creators and avatars have. They could, of course, have it if they were willing to give up the fallen self and engage in the process of gradually transcending their selves, rising to a higher level of consciousness where they could again receive light from their I AM Presences. If they are not willing to do that, then from their perspective they experience that they cannot have it.

As soon as the fallen beings came to a planet, such as when they came to earth, they introduced the duality consciousness. They created the value judgment between those who are right, those who are wrong, those who are higher, those who are lower, those who are most powerful, most sophisticated and those who are not. Now, you have an active force of the fallen beings who were not necessarily wanting to destroy the original inhabitants of the earth (because they actually wanted to control them), but they also wanted to have the original inhabitants of the earth feel envy of the fallen beings because of their power and a certain mastery they had of the matter realm.

They, of course, attempted to take the poison that they had brought with them and export it, so to speak, to all people on earth, putting everyone in this comparative frame of mind. Naturally, you can only have envy when you are in the duality consciousness and have the value judgment that makes you compare everything to this scale with two extremes where one is better than another. The entire idea that something is better than something else springs from the duality consciousness and the poison of envy.

Overcoming envy

The antidote that I embody to the poison of envy is or has been called the All-Accomplishing Wisdom. Naturally, from a certain perspective, from a certain level of consciousness, it will look like this: "I experience that there are other people on earth who have something I don't have. I want to have it. So if I get the All-Accomplishing Wisdom of Amogasiddhi, I should be able to get anything I want on earth and then I wouldn't have to feel envy toward anyone because no one would have more than me."

This is how people have reasoned many times since these teachings were given, and it is not exactly what the All-Accomplishing Wisdom is about. I wish to give you some thoughts on this. When you feel, as a person embodied on earth, envy, are *you* feeling the envy or is it a separate self? Based on our teachings, you, of course, know it is a separate self that feels this way. What have we told you about these separate selves? They project that there is a problem that needs to be solved. There is a condition that needs to be fulfilled and then you will feel something.

In other words, you are feeling envy but if you get what it is you envy, then you will no longer feel envy. Such is the reasoning of these selves. These selves will say: "Apply to Amogasiddhi, get the All-Accomplishing Wisdom so we can get the condition we want and then you will no longer feel envy. You will no longer feel envy when I, the separate self, get what I want."

The All-Accomplishing Wisdom, of course, allows you, as a Conscious You, to step outside of this self and see that what the self wants is another example of an impossible goal, an impossible desire. Even if you got what the self projects that you should have, you would not overcome the poison of envy because the poison is the poison.

The belief that you envy something and that you need to have something is just the illusion behind which the poison is hiding. This is a distinction that the self cannot make. It can only be as a computer, programmed to pursue a certain goal. You envy power, the self will project you need to get power. You will never be at peace until you have that power. The envy of those who have power is a poison, my beloved, it is a condition. To give you a visual analogy, let us say that in your house, your basement fills up with water but you do not realize that your basement is full of water. There is a person living in your house who is the only one who goes to the basement and he knows that the basement is full of water but he does not want you to know. He projects instead into your mind or tells you that your house needs a new roof and when you get the new roof, you will feel better.

We are assuming here that even though you do not consciously know your house is filled with water, you feel – suddenly – an unease about being in your house. This person projects that the cause of your unease is that your neighbor has got a beautiful new roof. You need to get an even better roof, then you will feel at ease again. But the cause of you feeling a lack of peace is that your basement is full of water. No matter how fancy a roof you put on your house, is it going to get the water out of the basement? It is not because the poison is still there and it is simply a self that is projecting the illusion that you need to get what the self envies.

If you have an envy of those who have a certain position or recognition in society, the self projects that you need to get that recognition, then you will be at peace. It is not the lack of recognition that makes you feel non-peace, it is the spiritual poison of envy that makes you feel this way. That is why getting the recognition will not remove the envy. Only removing the poison will remove the unease.

How do you remove the poison? Part of it is, of course, to come to see and understand what the poison is. You understand that there is a separate self that is using this poison to project that you should do something, and then you separate yourself from the self and let it go. Another part of it is to bring the antidote into your being that can consume, dispel, dissolve the poison. That is why we offer you our service, all of us, where you can tune in to our beings, open your mind, open your four lower bodies to an influx of the antidote that will then consume the poison. Everything revolves around free will. That is why you need to see certain things, come to certain realizations, which we will also help you reach and which you can reach by using the teachings that other masters have brought forth about the primal self, the separate self and so on.

Envy of the fallen beings

We have said that some avatars have actually entered into some sort of a relationship with certain fallen beings—developing a sense of mutual respect, admiring the fallen beings for their mastery of matter. There are certain avatars who have a sort of envy of certain fallen beings because they have that mastery of controlling matter, not co-creating but of controlling. That is why the All-Accomplishing Wisdom can help you see that controlling matter is not actually a very high accomplishment. It certainly will not be an all-accomplishing accomplishment, regardless of how impressive it may seem on a planet like earth what the fallen beings can do. There is a limit to what you can accomplish through the controlling mindset, the fallen mindset, the duality consciousness. Anything that you create – de-create – through the fallen consciousness, will be subject to the second law of thermodynamics, as we have called it, or the Wrath of Shiva, or the contracting force of the mother. In other words, it will have an opposite polarity. There will be a tension between them and eventually they will destroy each other.

The more power a fallen being has, the more opposition to its own power it creates. Therefore, it will eventually come to the point where its accomplishments will basically cancel out themselves. This is not true accomplishment. True accomplishment is attained through co-creation where you co-create through your current self, use the feedback to expand your sense of self and therefore co-create something that is more. You can continue this process indefinitely because you are not, when you are co-creating, creating an opposition to your creation.

The All-Accomplishing Wisdom will show you the difference between de-creation and co-creation and therefore help you see that you may have a genuine desire as an avatar to improve yourself, to expand your sense of self, to increase your accomplishments but this can only be attained through co-creation, not de-creation. The real sense of accomplishment you can have is, as Jesus demonstrated, that you can of your own self (your outer self, your limited self here on earth) do nothing. It is only by connecting to the higher self, the I AM Presence that you are truly co-creating.

Envy of Jesus

Another topic that I wish to mention here is that some co-creators, some avatars, have envy of other avatars. For example, it is not uncommon that avatars have a certain envy of Jesus or of the Buddha or of other people who have been publicly known for some positive reason or another.

Let us here focus on Jesus. An enormous idolatry of Jesus has been built by the Christian churches, instrumented and engineered by the fallen beings. Even many spiritual students, many ascended master students included, have still some idolatry of Jesus. The new book, *My Lives With Lucifer, Satan, Hitler and Jesus,* is an attempt to dispel that idolatry and help you see that Jesus was an avatar and you are an avatar and Jesus said: "The works that I do, you can do also." The ascended masters have always said: "What one has done, all can do." This must be understood in the context of the limitations of practical reality on a planet like earth.

What I am saying here is that even if you are not consciously aware that you are an avatar, you have a subtle sense, an inner sense, an intuitive sense: "Why was Jesus elevated to be the primary spiritual figure for the Piscean Age?" Many of you can sense in you that there is a certain self that says: "Why him and not me?" Now, understand here that the reason you can feel this way is that at some level of your being (not the conscious level), you realize that you are an avatar, Jesus was an avatar and so there was a potential for you to have filled the same position Jesus filled.

You know, at a certain level of your being, that it is not true what the fallen beings are saying that: "Jesus was so unique and so different that you couldn't possibly have done what he did." You have an inner sense that it was actually true when Jesus said that you could do the works that he did. This can have caused you, as a result of your birth trauma (as a result of your primal self, as a result of a sort of compensating for the loss you felt when you came to earth) to raise yourself up, validate yourself, validate why it was okay to come to earth. It can give you this sense of envy, of: "Why Jesus and not me?"

That is where you can use the All-Accomplishing Wisdom to realize that there is a certain practical reality on earth. There is a certain progression of cycles. At the inauguration of each cycle, at least at the inauguration of the Piscean Age, there was a need to have one person who sort of embodied the initiations of the Piscean Age.

We are moving into the Aquarian Age, which has been said to be the age of community. Therefore, there is not in the Aquarian Age the need to have one person be the superior example. There is actually a need to have many people be the example of how to be the Christ in the Aquarian Age. There was a need to have one person in the Piscean Age embody that potential of how to be the Christ in the Age of Pisces, given the state of the planet and the collective consciousness. For a variety of reasons, some of which we have actually described in the book about *My Lives*, Jesus was the one who was chosen and who himself chose to raise himself up to where he could fill the position. The all-accomplishing wisdom can help you see this practical reality, and it can also help you see beyond it and see that Jesus' accomplishment did not take anything away from you. You are part of the mandala of avatars that have come to this planet. Even though you may have come from different natural planets, you are all part of that mandala. This mandala is based on Oneness and what one member of the mandala accomplishes, raises up all. There is no reason for you as an avatar to have envy of Jesus' accomplishment because you are part of it—if you accept yourself as part of that mandala.

Therefore, there is also no reason for any of you to have any envy of each other. There are people who have come, experienced this messenger take a dictation and a part of their beings has felt: "Why him and not me?" Some have gone away because they could not deal with their envy, some have become angry, some have tried to put the messenger down and criticize him for this or that.

That is certainly the way it was in previous dispensations where actually, in the last dispensation, the messenger had to endure much more of this. Some people thought that they could be a better messenger than her or went into criticizing her for not being good enough, having this or that fault or this or that idiosyncrasy and so forth and so on. Some of these people have been fallen beings who were not willing to reform themselves but some of them have been avatars.

What you need to recognize here is that you have the potential to see that such envy comes from a separate self that you have created as a result of needing to compensate for the loss you felt when you came to earth. If you deal with that self and overcome it, then you can overcome the envy of the messenger. You can see that you are part of the mandala and therefore you have a unique gift to bring forth in the Aquarian Age. It may be in cooperation with the messenger, it may be that you go out in society and bring forth your own gift.

Focus on your own unique gift

You recognize here, when you use the All-Accomplishing Wisdom, that what you really came to earth to accomplish was not the goal that may be defined in any of the separate selves that spring from your primal self. These are all false goals that will not lead you to feel that you have fulfilled your reason for coming to earth.

You need to do what we have explained: Look at your motivation, realize it was not necessarily the highest motivation you had and then realize, first of all, that the real reason for your coming to earth was your growth in self-awareness. That was the immediate or the omega reason.

The alpha reason was to come to earth, be an open door for the I AM Presence whereby you can bring something into the physical octave that is absolutely unique to you. When you realize that the all-accomplishment for you is to bring forth your unique gift, then you also realize that there is absolutely no reason for you to have envy of another person who is expressing his or her unique gift.

Each and every one of you who have come as avatars, you have the potential to bring a gift to this planet that is absolutely unique to you. As we have said before: "In uniqueness there can be no comparisons and when there are no comparisons, there can be no envy." It is not that what Jesus did was more important or better than what you could bring forth. It is not that what this messenger is doing is more important or better than your gift. All of you—your gifts are equally important.

You might need to use the Wisdom of Equality to see that God does not discriminate and apply a value judgment to co-creators who are expressions of the One Mind. When you truly apply the Discriminating Wisdom, you can see that it is not so that one I AM Presence is better than another I AM Presence. There is no value judgment that can be applied to I AM Presences. Each is unique.

The only question – really – to apply to yourself is: "How open of a door am I to my I AM Presence?" If you look at someone else and you can see: "Oh, that person is more of an open door for his or her Presence than I am," then instead of going into envy of that, you say: "But then, I need to look at the separate selves that I have that are preventing me from being the open door, that are closing the opening, filtering out what is coming from my I AM Presence. When I get rid of those selves, then I can have the all-accomplishment of being the fully open door for my I AM Presence and this is how I have the ultimate sense of accomplishment on earth. All of these lesser goals defined by these separate selves are unreal goals and they will not give me the ultimate sense of accomplishment, the ultimate sense of fulfillment, the ultimate sense of being at peace with being on earth, having come to earth, having brought my gift and leaving earth behind forever in the ascension."

That is what I offer you, if you will tune in to me through that All-Accomplishing Wisdom. You can indeed accomplish all things on earth, not all things that your separate selves want, or that other people want, or that the fallen beings project that *you* should want. All things that your I AM Presence wants to accomplish through you and that you, as the Conscious You, want to accomplish when you realize you are a formless being and you are not identified with these separate selves—you let them die. It is not so, my beloved, that the Conscious You, when it becomes an open door for the I AM Presence, becomes a robot, a puppet on a string. It is so that there are still choices you make as the Conscious You: what you want to accomplish, what you want to experience, what you want to enjoy. You are not making these choices through an identification with a separate self. You are making a free choice as to what you as a formless being want to experience in form, what you want to accomplish in form, what you want to enjoy while you are still in a physical body. These are free choices and they are legitimate desires. There is nothing wrong with the Conscious You having a desire to experience some aspect of life on earth, to accomplish something on earth, to enjoy something on earth while you are still in embodiment. It is a free choice you are making. Not a choice you are compelled to make by a separate self through which you can never feel that sense of accomplishment, enjoyment and a sense of peace with being here.

This, my beloved, has given me a sense of accomplishment that I was allowed to bring forth this gift and that you were willing to receive it. The figure-eight flow has been closed and you have my gratitude for this.

20 | INVOKING ALL-ACCOMPLISHING WISDOM

In the name I AM THAT I AM, Jesus Christ, I call to all representatives of the Divine Mother, especially Amogasiddhi, to help me tune in to your All-Accomplishing Wisdom and overcome the poisons, including…

[Make personal calls.]

Amogasiddhi, release the All-Accomplishing Wisdom to give me awareness that the basic principle of co-creation is that I create through my current sense of self. I experience the physical out-picturing of it and refine my sense of self.

OM AMOGASIDDHI AH

Amogasiddhi, release the All-Accomplishing Wisdom to give me awareness that the co-creative process requires me to let the former self die. If I am not willing to do that, then I go into seeking to maintain either the former self or the state I have attained in the physical realm.

OM AMOGASIDDHI AH

Amogasiddhi, release the All-Accomplishing Wisdom to give me awareness that when I seek to maintain something, I cannot be creative at the same time. This opens me to being jealous of those who are still creative.

OM AMOGASIDDHI AH

Amogasiddhi, release the All-Accomplishing Wisdom to give me awareness that envy originated with the fallen beings who, after they fell, had less light than those who were still creative.

OM AMOGASIDDHI AH

Amogasiddhi, release the All-Accomplishing Wisdom to give me awareness that if I am no longer creative, it is very tempting to seek to attain a certain status through control rather than creativity.

OM AMOGASIDDHI AH

Amogasiddhi, release the All-Accomplishing Wisdom to give me awareness that the fallen beings introduced the duality consciousness and set up the value judgment between those who are right, those who are wrong, those who are higher, those who are lower.

OM AMOGASIDDHI AH

Amogasiddhi, release the All-Accomplishing Wisdom to give me awareness that the fallen beings have attempted to export the poison of envy to all people on earth, putting everyone in a comparative frame of mind.

OM AMOGASIDDHI AH

Amogasiddhi, release the All-Accomplishing Wisdom to give me awareness that I can only have envy when I am in the duality consciousness and have the value judgment that makes me compare everything to this scale with two extremes where one is better than another.

OM AMOGASIDDHI AH

Amogasiddhi, release the All-Accomplishing Wisdom to give me awareness that the entire idea that something is better than something else springs from the duality consciousness and the poison of envy.

OM AMOGASIDDHI AH

Amogasiddhi, release the All-Accomplishing Wisdom to give me awareness that your wisdom does not empower me to get anything I want on earth.

OM AMOGASIDDHI AH

Amogasiddhi, release the All-Accomplishing Wisdom to give me awareness that when I feel envy, *I* am not feeling the envy because is it a separate self feeling the envy.

OM AMOGASIDDHI AH

Amogasiddhi, release the All-Accomplishing Wisdom to give me awareness that this separate self projects that there is a problem that needs to be solved. There is a condition that needs to be fulfilled and then I will no longer feel envy.

OM AMOGASIDDHI AH

Amogasiddhi, release the All-Accomplishing Wisdom to give me awareness that the self projects that if I get what it is I envy, then I will no longer feel envy.

OM AMOGASIDDHI AH

Amogasiddhi, release the All-Accomplishing Wisdom to give me awareness that these selves will say: "Apply to Amogasiddhi, get the All-Accomplishing Wisdom, so we can get the condition we want and then you will no longer feel envy. You will no longer feel envy when I, the separate self, get what I want."

OM AMOGASIDDHI AH

Amogasiddhi, release the All-Accomplishing Wisdom to give me awareness that allows me, as a Conscious You, to step outside of this self and see that what the self wants is another example of an impossible goal, an impossible desire.

OM AMOGASIDDHI AH

Amogasiddhi, release the All-Accomplishing Wisdom to give me awareness that even if I got what the self projects that I should have, I would not overcome the poison of envy because the poison is the poison.

OM AMOGASIDDHI AH

Amogasiddhi, release the All-Accomplishing Wisdom to give me awareness that the belief that I envy something and that I need to have something is just the illusion behind which the poison is hiding.

OM AMOGASIDDHI AH

Amogasiddhi, release the All-Accomplishing Wisdom to give me awareness that if I have an envy of those who have a certain position or recognition in society, the self projects that I need to get that recognition, then I will be at peace.

OM AMOGASIDDHI AH

Amogasiddhi, release the All-Accomplishing Wisdom to give me awareness that it is not the lack of recognition that makes me feel non-peace, it is the spiritual poison of envy that makes me feel this way. That is why getting the recognition will not remove the envy. Only removing the poison will remove the unease.

OM AMOGASIDDHI AH

Amogasiddhi, release the All-Accomplishing Wisdom to give me awareness that I remove the poison by coming to see and understand what the poison is.

OM AMOGASIDDHI AH

Amogasiddhi, release the All-Accomplishing Wisdom to give me awareness that there is a separate self that is using this poison to project that I should do something.

OM AMOGASIDDHI AH

Amogasiddhi, release the All-Accomplishing Wisdom to give me awareness that helps me separate myself from the self and let it die.

OM AMOGASIDDHI AH

Amogasiddhi, release the All-Accomplishing Wisdom to give me awareness that I also need to bring the antidote into my being that can consume, dispel, dissolve the poison.

OM AMOGASIDDHI AH

Amogasiddhi, release the All-Accomplishing Wisdom to give me awareness that helps me tune in to your Being, open my mind, open my four lower bodies to an influx of the antidote that will then consume the poison.

OM AMOGASIDDHI AH

Amogasiddhi, release the All-Accomplishing Wisdom to give me awareness that will help me see certain things, come to certain realizations, by using the teachings about the primal self and the separate self.

OM AMOGASIDDHI AH

Amogasiddhi, release the All-Accomplishing Wisdom to give me awareness that some avatars have entered into a relationship with certain fallen beings—developing a sense of mutual respect, admiring the fallen beings for their mastery of matter.

OM AMOGASIDDHI AH

Amogasiddhi, release the All-Accomplishing Wisdom to give me awareness that some avatars have envy of certain fallen beings because they have the mastery of controlling matter with force.

OM AMOGASIDDHI AH

Amogasiddhi, release the All-Accomplishing Wisdom to give me awareness that helps me see that controlling matter is not a very high accomplishment. It certainly will not be an all-accomplishing accomplishment, regardless of how impressive it may seem on a planet like earth.

OM AMOGASIDDHI AH

Amogasiddhi, release the All-Accomplishing Wisdom to give me awareness that there is a limit to what I can accomplish through the controlling mindset, the fallen mindset, the duality consciousness.

OM AMOGASIDDHI AH

Amogasiddhi, release the All-Accomplishing Wisdom to give me awareness that anything that I create – de-create – through the fallen consciousness, will be subject to the second law of thermodynamics. It will have an opposite polarity, there will be tension between them and eventually they will destroy each other.

OM AMOGASIDDHI AH

Amogasiddhi, release the All-Accomplishing Wisdom to give me awareness that the more power a fallen being has, the more opposition to its own power it creates. It will eventually come to the point where its accomplishments will cancel out themselves.

OM AMOGASIDDHI AH

Amogasiddhi, release the All-Accomplishing Wisdom to give me awareness that true accomplishment is attained through co-creation where I co-create through my current self, use the feedback to expand my sense of self and therefore co-create something that is more. I can continue this process indefinitely because I am not creating an opposition to my creation.

OM AMOGASIDDHI AH

Amogasiddhi, release the All-Accomplishing Wisdom to give me awareness of the difference between de-creation and co-creation.

OM AMOGASIDDHI AH

Amogasiddhi, release the All-Accomplishing Wisdom to give me awareness that helps me see that I may have a genuine desire as an avatar to improve myself, to expand my sense of self, to increase my accomplishments but this can only be attained through co-creation, not de-creation.

OM AMOGASIDDHI AH

Amogasiddhi, release the All-Accomplishing Wisdom to give me awareness that the real sense of accomplishment I can have is that I can of my own self (my outer self, my limited self here on earth) do nothing. It is only by connecting to the higher self, the I AM Presence that I am truly co-creating.

OM AMOGASIDDHI AH

Amogasiddhi, release the All-Accomplishing Wisdom to give me awareness that some avatars have envy of other avatars, such as Jesus, the Buddha or other people who have been publicly known.

OM AMOGASIDDHI AH

Amogasiddhi, release the All-Accomplishing Wisdom to give me awareness to see if I have the sense: "Why was Jesus elevated to be the primary spiritual figure for the Piscean Age? Why him and not me?"

OM AMOGASIDDHI AH

Amogasiddhi, release the All-Accomplishing Wisdom to give me awareness that I may feel this way at some level of my being. I realize that I am an avatar, Jesus was an avatar and so there was a potential for me to have filled the same position Jesus filled.

OM AMOGASIDDHI AH

Amogasiddhi, release the All-Accomplishing Wisdom to give me awareness to see if I have an inner sense that it was true when Jesus said that I could do the works that he did.

OM AMOGASIDDHI AH

Amogasiddhi, release the All-Accomplishing Wisdom to give me awareness to see if this caused me, as a result of my birth trauma, to seek to raise myself up and validate why it was okay to come to earth. This can give me this sense of envy of Jesus.

OM AMOGASIDDHI AH

Amogasiddhi, release the All-Accomplishing Wisdom to give me awareness that there is a certain practical reality on earth. There is a certain progression of cycles. At the inauguration of the Piscean Age, there was a need to have one person who embodied the initiations of that age.

OM AMOGASIDDHI AH

Amogasiddhi, release the All-Accomplishing Wisdom to give me awareness that we are moving into the Aquarian Age, which is the age of community. There is no need to have one person be the superior example, but to have many people be the example of how to be the Christ in the Aquarian Age.

OM AMOGASIDDHI AH

Amogasiddhi, release the All-Accomplishing Wisdom to give me awareness to see this practical reality, and then see beyond it and see that Jesus' accomplishment did not take anything away from me.

OM AMOGASIDDHI AH

Amogasiddhi, release the All-Accomplishing Wisdom to give me awareness that I am part of the mandala of avatars that have come to this planet.

OM AMOGASIDDHI AH

Amogasiddhi, release the All-Accomplishing Wisdom to give me awareness that this mandala is based on Oneness and what one member of the mandala accomplishes, raises up all.

OM AMOGASIDDHI AH

Amogasiddhi, release the All-Accomplishing Wisdom to give me awareness that there is no reason for me as an avatar to have envy of Jesus' accomplishment because I am part of it—if I accept myself as part of that mandala.

OM AMOGASIDDHI AH

Amogasiddhi, release the All-Accomplishing Wisdom to give me awareness that there is also no reason for me to have envy of any other person.

OM AMOGASIDDHI AH

Amogasiddhi, release the All-Accomplishing Wisdom to give me awareness that such envy comes from a separate self that I have created as a result of needing to compensate for the loss I felt when I came to earth.

OM AMOGASIDDHI AH

Amogasiddhi, release the All-Accomplishing Wisdom to give me awareness that if I deal with that self and overcome it, then I can overcome the envy of anyone else.

OM AMOGASIDDHI AH

Amogasiddhi, release the All-Accomplishing Wisdom to give me awareness that I am part of the mandala and therefore I have a unique gift to bring forth in the Aquarian Age.

OM AMOGASIDDHI AH

Amogasiddhi, release the All-Accomplishing Wisdom to give me awareness that what I really came to earth to accomplish was not the goal that may be defined in any of the separate selves that spring from my primal self. These are all false goals that will not lead me to feel that I have fulfilled my reason for coming to earth.

OM AMOGASIDDHI AH

Amogasiddhi, release the All-Accomplishing Wisdom to give me awareness that will help me look at my motivation and realize it was not necessarily the highest motivation I had when I came to earth.

OM AMOGASIDDHI AH

Amogasiddhi, release the All-Accomplishing Wisdom to give me awareness that the omega reason for me coming to earth was my growth in self-awareness.

OM AMOGASIDDHI AH

Amogasiddhi, release the All-Accomplishing Wisdom to give me awareness that the alpha reason was to be an open door for the I AM Presence whereby I can bring something into the physical octave that is absolutely unique to me.

OM AMOGASIDDHI AH

Amogasiddhi, release the All-Accomplishing Wisdom to give me awareness that the all-accomplishment for me is to bring forth my unique gift. There is absolutely no reason for me to have envy of another person who is expressing his or her unique gift.

OM AMOGASIDDHI AH

Amogasiddhi, release the All-Accomplishing Wisdom to give me awareness that I have the potential to bring a gift to this planet that is absolutely unique to me.

OM AMOGASIDDHI AH

Amogasiddhi, release the All-Accomplishing Wisdom to give me awareness that in uniqueness there can be no comparisons and when there are no comparisons, there can be no envy.

OM AMOGASIDDHI AH

Amogasiddhi, release the All-Accomplishing Wisdom to give me awareness that what Jesus did was not more important or better than what I could bring forth. Our gifts are equally important.

OM AMOGASIDDHI AH

Amogasiddhi, release the All-Accomplishing Wisdom to give me awareness that God does not discriminate and apply a value judgment to co-creators who are expressions of the One Mind.

OM AMOGASIDDHI AH

Amogasiddhi, release the All-Accomplishing Wisdom to give me awareness that one I AM Presence is not better than another I AM Presence. There is no value judgment that can be applied to I AM Presences. Each is unique.

OM AMOGASIDDHI AH

Amogasiddhi, release the All-Accomplishing Wisdom to give me awareness that the only question to apply to myself is: "How open of a door am I to my I AM Presence?"

OM AMOGASIDDHI AH

Amogasiddhi, release the All-Accomplishing Wisdom to give me awareness that if I see that another person is more of an open door, then instead of going into envy, I say: "But then, I need to look at the separate selves that I have that are preventing me from being the open door.

OM AMOGASIDDHI AH

Amogasiddhi, release the All-Accomplishing Wisdom to give me awareness that when I get rid of those selves, then I can have the all-accomplishment of being the fully open door for my I AM Presence. This is how I have the ultimate sense of accomplishment on earth.

OM AMOGASIDDHI AH

Amogasiddhi, release the All-Accomplishing Wisdom to give me awareness that all of these lesser goals defined by these separate selves are unreal goals. They will not give me the ultimate sense of accomplishment, the ultimate sense of fulfillment, the ultimate sense of being at peace with being on earth.

OM AMOGASIDDHI AH

Amogasiddhi, release the All-Accomplishing Wisdom to give me awareness that I can indeed accomplish all things on earth, not all things that my separate selves want, or that other people want, or that the fallen beings project that *I* should want.

OM AMOGASIDDHI AH

Amogasiddhi, release the All-Accomplishing Wisdom to give me awareness that I can accomplish all things that my I AM Presence wants to accomplish through me and that I, as the Conscious You, want to accomplish.

OM AMOGASIDDHI AH

Amogasiddhi, release the All-Accomplishing Wisdom to give me awareness that I am a formless being and I am not identified with these separate selves—I let them die.

OM AMOGASIDDHI AH

Amogasiddhi, release the All-Accomplishing Wisdom to give me awareness that the Conscious You, when it becomes an open door for the I AM Presence, does not become a robot, a puppet on a string.

OM AMOGASIDDHI AH

Amogasiddhi, release the All-Accomplishing Wisdom to give me awareness that as the Conscious You, I make choices concerning what I want to accomplish, what I want to experience, what I want to enjoy.

OM AMOGASIDDHI AH

Amogasiddhi, release the All-Accomplishing Wisdom to give me awareness that I am not making these choices through an identification with a separate self. I am making a free choice as to what I, as a formless being, want to experience in form, what I want to accomplish in form, what I want to enjoy while I am still in a physical body.

OM AMOGASIDDHI AH

Amogasiddhi, release the All-Accomplishing Wisdom to give me awareness that these are free choices and they are legitimate desires.

OM AMOGASIDDHI AH

Amogasiddhi, release the All-Accomplishing Wisdom to give me awareness that there is nothing wrong with the Conscious You having a desire to experience some aspect of life on earth, to accomplish something on earth, to enjoy something on earth while I am still in embodiment.

OM AMOGASIDDHI AH

Amogasiddhi, release the All-Accomplishing Wisdom to give me awareness that it is a free choice I am making, not a choice I am compelled to make by a separate self through which I can never feel that sense of accomplishment, enjoyment and a sense of peace with being here.

OM AMOGASIDDHI AH

Sealing

In the name of the Divine Mother, I call to Mother Mary for the sealing of myself and all people in my circle of influence in the creative flow of the Divine Mother, the River of Life. I call for the multiplication of my calls by all representatives of the Divine Mother, so that we form the perfect figure-eight flow of "As Above, so below." Thus, I accept that this is fully manifest, because the mouth of the Lord, the Divine Mother that I AM, has spoken it. Amen.

21 | THE WILL OF YOUR I AM PRESENCE IS YOUR WILL

I AM indeed the Buddha Vajrasattva. The poison for which I provide the antidote is non-will and non-being. Then, what is that? Well, we have given you some very profound teachings on free will. Quite frankly, we have given you teachings on free will that are beyond what has ever been released on this planet. This is not said to elevate the teaching but to give you an appreciation for the fact that there is much here for you to ponder because the only way to overcome non-will and non-being is to have a deeper understanding of free will than what most people on earth have.

Free will is both limited and free

What I wish to give you is a certain perspective on this. What we have said is that the Creator created self-aware extensions of itself as co-creators and gave them *free* will. Free will. Now, most people on earth, when they hear the concept or the words "free will," they think that there are always some restrictions to your will, that there are restrictions to the options you have, the options you could potentially choose. As we have said before, that is correct in the sense that when you start out as a co-creator, you are projecting through your current sense of self onto the Ma-ter light and the Ma-ter light out-pictures that.

Your current sense of self limits your free will in the sense that your current sense of self limits what you can see, what you can envision, what you can imagine. There are limitations on free will in the sense that the choices you can see will be limited by the vision, the perspective, of your current sense of self. There are no limitations in the sense that you are free to explore whatever you can do as a co-creator in an unascended sphere.

That means you are free to raise your sense of self, to expand your sense of self, to the highest degree possible in an unascended sphere so you can ascend. Then, of course, you can continue to exercise your will in the ascended realm. Actually, your will becomes more free, although free in a different way than what you can currently envision when you are in embodiment.

You also have the option, with your free will, to go the other way and restrict your sense of self, even going into duality and creating a separate self and then exploring the full range of what you can possibly envision and do through that separate self. Now, there are those who will say: "But I don't have complete freedom to do whatever I want to do through a separate self because of karma, or because of other restrictions, or other people, or the way the Ma-ter light works. In other words, my previous choices limit my current choices and that is not truly free will."

Well, as we have said before, the simple reality is that if you make a choice and the choice has no consequence, you have not actually made a choice. When you make a choice to project through your current sense of self, if the Ma-ter light did not send anything back to you, did not outpicture what you are projecting onto it, you would in effect not have made a choice. As we have also said, what you currently experience in the matter world is the result of what you have projected through your current sense of self.

You have the option to expand that sense of self. Not only what you get back in the physical circumstances will change (at least gradually), but your *experience* of those physical changes will change immediately when you change your sense of self. Even though you experience consequences of your choices, you still have the free will to transcend your sense of self or to limit your sense of self, to *transcend* or *descend*.

The definition of non-will

However, there is a special case that I would like to explain to you. Let me, as an example, begin with the fallen beings. You have in the fourth sphere certain fallen beings who use their co-creative abilities, including the light they receive from their I AM Presences, to start creating not in a creative way but in a controlling manner. They manage to create for themselves certain planets where they can create these sophisticated civilizations with a very controlled environment and culture. It is a very hierarchical structure where one, two or maybe a few fallen beings have absolute power over the potentially billions of people embodying on that planet.

What happens to these beings is that they begin to think that they can do anything they want and escape the consequences because the people are, so to speak, following them and in many cases they bear the burden of the consequences of the leaders. The leaders can sit in an ivory tower, like you saw the kings and the emperors of old, and the people do all the work and they absorb all the problems. The leaders can build the illusion that free will means that you can do anything you want and escape the consequences.

Now, this can lead to a special state of mind where these beings become centered on themselves. Even though they have not yet fallen, they still become so centered on themselves that they now adopt an attitude, a belief that: "If I have truly free will, if I – as only me, as a separate being – if I have truly free will, then the entire universe should bend to my will." This is the ultimate, we might say, outplaying of free will. It is also the ultimate illusion of free will and it is, in fact, a denial of the freedom of will and therefore it is the definition of non-will.

These beings in the fourth sphere had the illusion, based on their experience on their own planet, that because the planet to a large degree conformed to their will, then the entire universe should do the same. They did not realize, of course, that the rest of their sphere was ascending and was reaching the ascension point. They did not realize their illusion until they were confronted with the illusion by the ascended masters. Suddenly, they had this awakening and they decided that if the entire universe would not respond to their will as an individual being, then they do not truly have free will. Therefore, the Creator has lied to them, it is a scam, they have not really received free will.

The illusion of non-will

Now, you can see, of course, that this illusion can only arise in a being who is completely focused on itself, has no respect, no kinship, no sense of oneness, no compassion for all other beings. They are essentially acting as if, here is a planet with billions of people and all of those billions of people should submit themselves to the will of one individual.

Beyond that, they also say that all of the billions of other planets in their sphere, with countless billions of other beings, they should also conform to their will. More than that, the ascended realm that has ascended and become permanent should conform to the will of this one individual. The Creator should conform to the will of that one individual. We can say, of course, that this is the extreme outplaying of free will. You can put yourself in such a state of separation, such a state of being focused on yourself, that you believe the entire universe, the entire spiritual realm and the Creator, should conform to your will.

This, of course, means you essentially believe that all other beings, including ascended masters and the Creator, should suspend their free will in order to give you the illusion that your will is completely free. This is, of course, a complete misunderstanding that is only possible when you are in that state of separation based on duality.

When these beings are confronted with the ascended masters, some of them actually realize this is an illusion. Some of them come to see this and they are therefore given help and they can ascend with the rest of their sphere. Those who will not see this illusion, but deny this illusion, they fall and now they are in an entirely different situation.

Before, they still received light from their I AM Presences. They were qualifying that light with duality and they were using it, not only to build that sense of being a separate individual that is more important than all others, but also to build whatever ability they had to control other beings and to even control matter. Now, they take embodiment in the next sphere that is created. It is denser than the previous one. Suddenly, the abilities they had for controlling matter are not quite as strong as what they had before.

At the same time they do not have the light from their I AM Presences so they cannot override the density of matter as they could in their first sphere. They now experience that they cannot maintain the sense that: "I am the only one that matters and the universe should conform to my choices." The reason they cannot maintain this is that they experience that they cannot quite gain the same power in the sphere they fall into as in the one that was their first sphere.

The origin of non-being

Some of these fallen beings become very angry at this and they go into a state of mind of deciding that they are going to use all the power they have to prove the Creator wrong, to prove that the Creator was wrong for giving free will, or just in any way possible to prove the Creator wrong. This, of course, puts them in a more severe struggle that makes their lives even more difficult, that makes their state of mind more and more tense. This means, as we have explained the law, that they create more and more opposition to themselves. This is often out-pictured in the sense that there can still be certain planets in the sphere they fall into where these fallen beings will gravitate. What happened in the previous sphere was that either there was already one controlling being on a specific planet or there were only a few and they were able to agree with each other on sharing power.

In the sphere that they fall into, this is no longer the case. There are always at least two fallen beings on a planet and they cannot agree with each other. This means that the fallen beings now form the opposition to each other and they enter this power struggle between themselves that makes their life even more intense, even more burdensome. They have to work harder and harder to build the sense that they are in control.

Now, there are some fallen beings who throw themselves into this power struggle, use all of their energy and attention on defeating their opponent or proving God wrong or whatever the case may be. There are others who, at least after some time, become tired of this power struggle. Because they will not give up the illusion that the universe should conform to their will, they decide that since the universe obviously will not conform to their will, they do not want to be here. They do not want to engage in life in this universe.

That is when they then create and go into the state of non-being. They do not want to be, they do not want to be conscious, they do not want to be aware. You could say it is one poison with two sides or you could say it is two poisons. You have this throughout the spheres where fallen beings have fallen, you have created this very powerful momentum of non-will and non-being.

The enigma of non-will

The momentum of non-will does not necessarily mean that you have *no* will. There are some people, not usually fallen beings but there are people on earth, for example, who have been affected by the poison of non-will to the point where they have no will. You can say that this is the case for those who follow the fallen beings. They go into a state of non-will, surrendering their will to following the will of the fallen beings.

The fallen beings do not go into a state of having no will. They have that misunderstood will where they are seeking to force the universe to conform to their will. This is non-will in the sense that it denies the entire purpose of free will, namely that when you project something onto the Ma-ter light, the Ma-ter light outpictures what you project. This gives you the potential to expand your sense of self and therefore raise the way you exercise your free will.

You are essentially making your will more free when you expand your sense of self. When you contract your sense of self, you are making your will less free even though you may have a false sense of having power because other people submit their will to yours—but it is just an illusion. Your will, will be more and more limited because when you limit the sense of self, you limit what you can see.

Now, you may say this is a paradox because some fallen beings actually have a greater understanding of how the universe works than many people on earth. Yes they do, because they have acquired this understanding over so many lifetimes in several spheres. What you have to recognize is that this is not the highest understanding of the universe. It is an understanding acquired through very long experience through a separate self.

They do not actually *understand* how the universe works, they *do* understand how matter works. Therefore, they have learned through experience how to manipulate matter from the fallen state of consciousness and without receiving light from the spiritual realm but by stealing light from other beings. In this sense, they have a certain knowledge, they have a certain mastery. They might be very knowledgeable in an intellectual sense but this is not true knowledge. This is not the knowledge that comes from an expanded sense of self. We could say there is knowledge, there is wisdom, there is intellectual knowledge, there is direct experience, intuitive experience, mystical experience of a higher state of consciousness.

Avatars and non-will

We now have a situation on earth where avatars descend and encounter the fallen beings. Now, what is the situation for an avatar who has evolved on a natural planet? Well, as an avatar you do not have a sense that you are a separate being. You do have a sense that you are an individual being and some avatars have experienced that they have raised themselves above the average in their environment and they have become more capable than other beings on their natural planet.

They have acquired some mastery, some sense that they can make matter conform to their will. This does not mean that the avatar has developed the idea that the entire universe should conform to its will because it knows it is part of a larger whole. You do not see any conflict on a natural planet between you exercising your will and other beings around you exercising their individual will. On a natural planet there is not that conflict. Now, what comes in is that the avatar decides, for a variety of reasons (not an enlightened consciousness) to descend to earth.

You come down here as an avatar and you have, before you come, a sense that you want to create a positive change on earth. You have a high degree of confidence that you will be able to do this because you are used to, on a natural planet, that when you really apply yourself, you can manifest whatever you can envision. Now, you are envisioning, not necessarily that you want to come down here and remove all evil on earth but most avatars are focused on a specific issue. They decide to come down here to remove that particular kind of suffering and they have a fairly high degree of confidence that they can accomplish this. Not necessarily alone because sometimes avatars decide to descend in groups.

You come with this sense of confidence that you can achieve your goal. Now, you come down here, you experience, first: the fallen beings and how they attack you and seek to destroy you, and second: that humankind at large and the original inhabitants of the earth are not nearly as responsive as you thought they would be. Suddenly, for the first time in the lifespan of an avatar, you begin to doubt that you can accomplish your goal, that you can actually manifest your will.

This can also be a shock and part of the birth trauma where you cannot understand why suddenly matter does not conform to your will. You have not fully realized how dense matter is on earth, compared to what it is on a natural planet. You also do not understand why people do not respond to your will or your attempts to help them, even though you are clearly showing them a way out of suffering.

Suddenly, you begin to doubt: "Can I actually carry out my goal for coming here and if I cannot, then it must have been a mistake for me to come here. I must have made a mistake by deciding to come here." This can be a hard thing to deal with for an avatar because on a natural planet you never actually doubted your ability to accomplish what you could envision and you never felt that you had made a wrong choice. You never felt that you should not have made that decision.

Now, you are beginning to doubt that you should have made the decision to come to earth. You feel that this was a wrong choice and this is partly because you are now in this denser realm where duality is so prevalent. Therefore, you now start to wonder: "What is actually the point of exercising will on a planet where your will is as unfree as it is on earth?" When you encounter the opposition from the fallen beings and how they want to destroy you, they tell you that you have no right to be here, you have no right to challenge them. When you encounter the non-responsiveness of the beings on earth, then you can (and not all avatars do this but many do this) open your mind to this poison of non-will that the fallen beings have created and brought to this planet.

Suddenly, you begin to feel: "What is the point of me exercising my will on this planet? Maybe I shouldn't challenge the fallen ones. Maybe, just in order to survive, I shouldn't challenge the fallen beings so they don't kill and torture me in every embodiment. Maybe I have no right to try and make the people on earth escape their suffering if they don't want to." Now, instead of doing what we have encouraged you to do, of re-examining your motives for coming here, realizing they were based on a certain illusion, you now decide: "I don't want to do anything on this planet. I don't want to exercise my will on this planet."

There are also some avatars, as is even described in the book about *My Lives,* who go to the opposite extreme and they make their will very, very strong and very, very determined. They will prove the fallen beings wrong or they will fight the fallen beings, they will oppose the fallen beings or they will do something to really make the people on earth see that there is a way out of suffering

There are the two polarities. Some give up their will, some go into adopting, actually, that active non-will of the fallen beings. Others adopt a passive non-will. What does this lead to?

Avatars and non-being

Well, it leads to a very turbulent period, as is also described in the book where the protagonist fought the fallen beings for a million years. However long it takes for an individual avatar, there will come a point where you have fought for so long that you are simply worn out by it. You are tired of it, you have had enough of it. Or you have been in a passive state of mind for so long that you begin to feel that life on earth is just more and more pointless. If you are fighting, you feel that the fighting is more and more pointless but this also very quickly leads you into feeling that life on earth is just pointless.

That is when you can, then, become open to that poison of non-being where you also become susceptible to creating a self that feels life is not worth living. Maybe you feel life on earth is not worth living but you do not see a way out. Or you feel, in general, life is not worth living, it is not worth it to be conscious, to be self-aware. Then, you can begin to deny self-awareness and you can begin to feel that God should not have given you self-awareness because it only causes you suffering. This can lead to all kinds of blaming God, or why has God not changed his mind about free will and all of these considerations. The essence here is that, as with everything else we have told you, this is not *you* feeling this, this is a separate self.

Once the separate self is created, it is constantly projecting at you that life is not worth living or that it is not worth fighting. What do many avatars do? Well, some of them then go into a phase where they seek to actually numb their consciousness. They go into all kinds of addictions that make them less and less conscious. Others seek to withdraw from the world, for example as the monks and nuns of various religious traditions. Or even as many spiritual people today who want to withdraw from an active life, do not want to engage in an active life or who are living a somewhat active life but never really engaging, always sitting between two chairs, trying to do the minimum to maintain a living but not really engaging in any aspect of life.

The way out through the diamond will

The way out of this is, of course, to use the teachings we have given on why you came to earth as an avatar, recognize that your motivation for coming was based on an illusion, deal with the primal self so you are free of that primal self. Then, you can begin to see that the only reason you felt that life was not worth living, or that it was not worth fighting, or that you could not exercise your will on this planet was that there were things you had not understood.

Now, you can begin to understand these things. You can begin to examine your reasons for coming here. Therefore, you can also see that there is no validity to this consciousness, this poison of non-will and non-being. It is, as all poisons, based on an illusion. Then, if you are willing to apply yourself to me, you can absorb the antidote to the poison of non-will, which has been called the Diamond Will.

This is, of course, to signify that this will is immovable by anything on earth. As you know, the diamond is the hardest substance currently known to man and therefore nothing else can damage it. The Diamond Will cannot be in any way affected by the non-will, the non-being or even the anti-will, the very aggressive will of the fallen beings.

When you tune in to this antidote and allow it to come into your being, it will consume whatever remnants you have of the non-will and the non-being. This means that you can now begin to attain a much higher sense of peace. We have given you the teachings and the tools that actually will allow you to come to the point where you can make peace with the way that earth currently functions. You can realize the purpose of it, the out-playing of free will, the fact that this is not a natural planet. All of these teachings we have given you, can help you come to the point where you realize that the purpose, the *real, higher* purpose for you coming to earth, was to grow in awareness to the point where you could actually ascend from earth.

Then, you can lock in to the fact that at the level of your I AM Presence, there is a will to go into the unascended sphere and to ascend from that sphere. This is also a diamond will in the sense that it is higher than anything on earth, meaning nothing the Conscious You has experienced on earth has changed the will of the I AM Presence.

When you begin to reconnect to the I AM Presence and realize that, as the Conscious You, you are an extension of the I AM Presence, you are not in any way separated from it or in opposition to it, then you realize that the will of the Presence is also *your* will. You have a will to expand your consciousness. You have a will to ascend. That is when you can begin to see that regardless of how conditions are on earth, these conditions – regardless of how they are – form the perfect opportunity for you to ascend. My beloved, you can ascend from a natural planet but because you have not had the wide range of experiences that you can have on an unnatural planet, you do not ascend with the same awareness.

A higher ascension from unnatural planets

The ascension is still essentially the same process. You start with a point-like sense of identity, you build certain selves. Even on a natural planet you build selves, though they are not quite the same as the separate selves on earth. In order to ascend from a natural planet you have to come to see them as selves, see that you only use them as vehicles for your co-creative efforts and you have to let them go, you have to let them die. You did not have those selves with you when you descended to the natural planet, therefore you cannot ascend from a natural planet with those selves.

It is the same process as you are going through on earth. You have to come to see that there are certain selves you have in your four lower bodies and you need to let them die. Because you have a broader range of selves in your four lower bodies on earth, you actually ascend with a higher level of awareness. There are more positive experiences in your causal body and as a result of that, your I AM Presence has a higher sense of awareness after you ascend from an unnatural planet than from a natural planet.

That is when you can, then, really make peace with being here and say: "Regardless of what I thought before I came here, this planet is a great opportunity for me to ascend." Then, you can come to the point where you no longer look back and say: "Oh, I made a mistake for coming here" or "It was a mistake of being in this illusion that brought me here." You just look at it and say: "Well, that was where I was at in consciousness at the time and I made the best choice I could make, given the self I had at the time." You can then let go of any sense of regret. You can just be at peace with the fact that this is the path to the ascension that you chose and it is perfectly acceptable according to any standard in the spiritual realm.

Therefore, you can come to the point where you say: "The rest of this lifetime is the perfect, the ideal, opportunity for me to ascend, to look at my reactions, to look at the selves I have left, to let them die. To also be the open door for the I AM Presence to express itself, to come to the point where I, as the Conscious You, am free of all these lower selves and now I have a free will to experience and express myself on this planet." That is when you can come to the point, as we have said, of shifting your focus away from producing a result on earth but actually embracing and enjoying the process of being on earth, the process of expressing yourself on earth and the process of ascending from earth.

Even this, we have more to say on, but this I will leave for Gautama. Therefore, I have given you the gift I want to give you and I am grateful for your receiving it. With this I bid you: Go in the absolute peace of the Diamond Will.

22 | INVOKING THE DIAMOND WILL

In the name I AM THAT I AM, Jesus Christ, I call to all representatives of the Divine Mother, especially Vajrasattva, to help me tune in to your Diamond Will and overcome the poisons, including…

[Make personal calls.]

Vajrasattva, release the Diamond Will to give me awareness that the only way to overcome non-will and non-being is to have a deeper understanding of free will than what most people have.

    OM VAJRASATTVA HUM

Vajrasattva, release the Diamond Will to give me awareness that when I start out as a co-creator, I am projecting through my current sense of self onto the Ma-ter light and the Ma-ter light out-pictures that.

    OM VAJRASATTVA HUM

Vajrasattva, release the Diamond Will to give me awareness that my current sense of self limits my free will, in the sense that it limits what I can see, what I can envision, what I can imagine, what I can accept as possible.

OM VAJRASATTVA HUM

Vajrasattva, release the Diamond Will to give me awareness that there are limitations on free will in the sense that the options I can see will be limited by the vision of my current sense of self.

OM VAJRASATTVA HUM

Vajrasattva, release the Diamond Will to give me awareness that there are no limitations in the sense that I am free to explore whatever I can do as a co-creator in an unascended sphere.

OM VAJRASATTVA HUM

Vajrasattva, release the Diamond Will to give me awareness that I am free to raise my sense of self to the highest degree possible in an unascended sphere so I can ascend.

OM VAJRASATTVA HUM

Vajrasattva, release the Diamond Will to give me awareness that I also have the option to go the other way and restrict my sense of self, even going into duality and creating a separate self and then exploring the full range of what I can envision and do through that separate self.

OM VAJRASATTVA HUM

Vajrasattva, release the Diamond Will to give me awareness that if I make a choice and the choice has no consequence, I have not actually made a choice.

OM VAJRASATTVA HUM

Vajrasattva, release the Diamond Will to give me awareness that when I make a choice to project through my current sense of self, if the Ma-ter light did not send anything back to me, I would in effect not have made a choice.

OM VAJRASATTVA HUM

22 | Invoking the Diamond Will

Vajrasattva, release the Diamond Will to give me awareness that what I experience in the matter world is the result of what I have projected through my current sense of self.

OM VAJRASATTVA HUM

Vajrasattva, release the Diamond Will to give me awareness that when I expand my sense of self, my physical circumstances will change over time.

OM VAJRASATTVA HUM

Vajrasattva, release the Diamond Will to give me awareness that when I expand my sense of self, my *experience* of my physical circumstances will change immediately.

OM VAJRASATTVA HUM

Vajrasattva, release the Diamond Will to give me awareness that even though I experience the consequences of my choices, I still have the free will to transcend my sense of self or to limit my sense of self, to *transcend* or *descend*.

OM VAJRASATTVA HUM

Vajrasattva, release the Diamond Will to give me awareness that some beings have built the illusion that free will means that you can do anything you want and escape the consequences.

OM VAJRASATTVA HUM

Vajrasattva, release the Diamond Will to give me awareness that this can lead to a special state of mind where beings become centered on themselves.

OM VAJRASATTVA HUM

Vajrasattva, release the Diamond Will to give me awareness that some beings can adopt an attitude that: "If I have truly free will, then the entire universe should bend to my will."

OM VAJRASATTVA HUM

Vajrasattva, release the Diamond Will to give me awareness that this is the ultimate outplaying of free will. It is also the ultimate illusion of free will and it is a denial of the freedom of will and therefore it is the definition of non-will.

OM VAJRASATTVA HUM

Vajrasattva, release the Diamond Will to give me awareness that this illusion can only arise in a being who is completely focused on itself, has no sense of oneness, no compassion for all other beings.

OM VAJRASATTVA HUM

Vajrasattva, release the Diamond Will to give me awareness that the extreme outplaying of free will is to put yourself in such a state of separation that you believe the entire universe, the entire spiritual realm and the Creator, should conform to your will.

OM VAJRASATTVA HUM

Vajrasattva, release the Diamond Will to give me awareness that this means you essentially believe that all other beings, including ascended masters and the Creator, should suspend their free will in order to give you the illusion that your will is completely free.

OM VAJRASATTVA HUM

Vajrasattva, release the Diamond Will to give me awareness that this is a complete misunderstanding that is only possible when you are in that state of separation based on duality.

OM VAJRASATTVA HUM

Vajrasattva, release the Diamond Will to give me awareness that some fallen beings became very angry and went into a state of mind of deciding that they are going to use all the power they have to prove that the Creator was wrong for giving free will.

OM VAJRASATTVA HUM

Vajrasattva, release the Diamond Will to give me awareness that this means they create more and more opposition to themselves. They are creating a more and more intense struggle.

OM VAJRASATTVA HUM

Vajrasattva, release the Diamond Will to give me awareness that some fallen beings become tired of this struggle and decide that since the universe obviously will not conform to their will, they do not want to be here. They do not want to engage in life in this universe.

OM VAJRASATTVA HUM

Vajrasattva, release the Diamond Will to give me awareness that this is when they create and go into the state of non-being. They do not want to be, they do not want to be conscious, they do not want to be aware.

OM VAJRASATTVA HUM

Vajrasattva, release the Diamond Will to give me awareness that the momentum of non-will does not necessarily mean that you have *no* will.

OM VAJRASATTVA HUM

Vajrasattva, release the Diamond Will to give me awareness that there are people on earth who have been affected by the poison of non-will to the point where they have no will.

OM VAJRASATTVA HUM

Vajrasattva, release the Diamond Will to give me awareness that those who follow the fallen beings go into a state of non-will, surrendering their will to following the will of the fallen beings.

OM VAJRASATTVA HUM

Vajrasattva, release the Diamond Will to give me awareness that the fallen beings do not go into a state of having *no* will. They have a misunderstood will where they are seeking to force the universe to conform to their will.

OM VAJRASATTVA HUM

Vajrasattva, release the Diamond Will to give me awareness that this is non-will in the sense that it denies the entire purpose of free will, namely that projecting onto the Ma-ter light gives you the potential to expand your sense of self.

OM VAJRASATTVA HUM

Vajrasattva, release the Diamond Will to give me awareness that I am making my will more free when I expand my sense of self. When I contract my sense of self, I am making my will less free.

OM VAJRASATTVA HUM

Vajrasattva, release the Diamond Will to give me awareness that there is knowledge, there is wisdom, there is intellectual knowledge, there is direct experience, intuitive experience, mystical experience of a higher state of consciousness.

OM VAJRASATTVA HUM

Vajrasattva, release the Diamond Will to give me awareness that as an avatar I do not have a sense that I am a *separate* being. I do have a sense that I am an *individual* being.

OM VAJRASATTVA HUM

Vajrasattva, release the Diamond Will to give me awareness that some avatars have experienced that they have raised themselves above the average in their environment, and they have become more capable than other beings on their natural planet.

OM VAJRASATTVA HUM

22 | Invoking the Diamond Will

Vajrasattva, release the Diamond Will to give me awareness that an avatar has acquired some mastery, some sense that it can make matter conform to its will.

OM VAJRASATTVA HUM

Vajrasattva, release the Diamond Will to give me awareness that this does not mean that an avatar has developed the idea that the entire universe should conform to its will.

OM VAJRASATTVA HUM

Vajrasattva, release the Diamond Will to give me awareness that on a natural planet there is no conflict between me exercising my will and other beings around me exercising their individual will.

OM VAJRASATTVA HUM

Vajrasattva, release the Diamond Will to give me awareness that when an avatar descends to earth, it wants to create a positive change.

OM VAJRASATTVA HUM

Vajrasattva, release the Diamond Will to give me awareness that an avatar comes here with this sense of confidence that it can achieve its goal.

OM VAJRASATTVA HUM

Vajrasattva, release the Diamond Will to give me awareness that the avatar then experiences the fallen beings, who attack it, and humankind who ignore it.

OM VAJRASATTVA HUM

Vajrasattva, release the Diamond Will to give me awareness that an avatar then begins to doubt that it can accomplish its goal, that it can manifest its will.

OM VAJRASATTVA HUM

Vajrasattva, release the Diamond Will to give me awareness that this can also be a shock and part of the birth trauma where I cannot understand why suddenly matter does not conform to my will.

OM VAJRASATTVA HUM

Vajrasattva, release the Diamond Will to give me awareness to see if I began to doubt: "Can I actually carry out my goal for coming here and if I cannot, then it must have been a mistake for me to come here. I must have made a mistake by deciding to come here."

OM VAJRASATTVA HUM

Vajrasattva, release the Diamond Will to give me awareness to see if I started to wonder: "What is actually the point of exercising will on a planet where my will is as unfree as it is on earth?"

OM VAJRASATTVA HUM

Vajrasattva, release the Diamond Will to give me awareness to see if this opened my mind to the poison of non-will that the fallen beings have created and brought to this planet.

OM VAJRASATTVA HUM

Vajrasattva, release the Diamond Will to give me awareness to see if I began to feel: "What is the point of me exercising my will on this planet? Maybe I shouldn't challenge the fallen ones. Maybe, just in order to survive, I shouldn't challenge the fallen beings so they don't kill and torture me in every embodiment. Maybe I have no right to try and make the people on earth escape their suffering if they don't want to."

OM VAJRASATTVA HUM

Vajrasattva, release the Diamond Will to give me awareness to see if I ever decided: "I don't want to do anything on this planet. I don't want to exercise my will on this planet."

OM VAJRASATTVA HUM

Vajrasattva, release the Diamond Will to give me awareness to see if I went to the opposite extreme and made my will very strong and very determined.

OM VAJRASATTVA HUM

Vajrasattva, release the Diamond Will to give me awareness to see if I decided I wanted to prove the fallen beings wrong or wanted to fight the fallen beings.

OM VAJRASATTVA HUM

Vajrasattva, release the Diamond Will to give me awareness to see if there came a point where I had fought for so long that I was worn out by it. I was tired of it, I had had enough of it.

OM VAJRASATTVA HUM

Vajrasattva, release the Diamond Will to give me awareness to see if I had been in a passive state of mind for so long that I began to feel that life on earth is just more and more pointless.

OM VAJRASATTVA HUM

Vajrasattva, release the Diamond Will to give me awareness that if I am fighting, I feel that the fighting is more and more pointless but this also very quickly leads me into feeling that life on earth is just pointless.

OM VAJRASATTVA HUM

Vajrasattva, release the Diamond Will to give me awareness to see if I became open to the poison of non-being where I became susceptible to creating a self that feels life is not worth living.

OM VAJRASATTVA HUM

Vajrasattva, release the Diamond Will to give me awareness to see if I felt life on earth is not worth living but I did not see a way out.

OM VAJRASATTVA HUM

Vajrasattva, release the Diamond Will to give me awareness to see if I felt life in general is not worth living, it is not worth it to be conscious, to be self-aware.

OM VAJRASATTVA HUM

Vajrasattva, release the Diamond Will to give me awareness to see if I began to deny self-awareness and to feel that God should not have given me self-awareness because it only causes me suffering.

OM VAJRASATTVA HUM

Vajrasattva, release the Diamond Will to give me awareness to see if I ever went into blaming God or wanting God to change his mind about free will.

OM VAJRASATTVA HUM

Vajrasattva, release the Diamond Will to give me awareness that this is not *me* feeling this, this is a separate self.

OM VAJRASATTVA HUM

Vajrasattva, release the Diamond Will to give me awareness that once the separate self is created, it is constantly projecting at me that life is not worth living or that it is not worth fighting.

OM VAJRASATTVA HUM

Vajrasattva, release the Diamond Will to give me awareness to see if I have gone into a phase of seeking to numb my consciousness through addictions that make me less and less conscious.

OM VAJRASATTVA HUM

Vajrasattva, release the Diamond Will to give me awareness to see if I attempted to withdraw from the world, for example as the monks and nuns of religious traditions.

OM VAJRASATTVA HUM

Vajrasattva, release the Diamond Will to give me awareness to see if I have a feeling that I want to withdraw from an active life, I do not want to engage in an active life.

OM VAJRASATTVA HUM

Vajrasattva, release the Diamond Will to give me awareness to see if I am living a somewhat active life but never really engaging, always sitting between two chairs, trying to do the minimum to maintain a living but not really engaging in any aspect of life.

OM VAJRASATTVA HUM

Vajrasattva, release the Diamond Will to give me awareness that my motivation for coming to earth was based on an illusion. Help me overcome the primal self.

OM VAJRASATTVA HUM

Vajrasattva, release the Diamond Will to give me awareness that the only reason I felt that life was not worth living, or that it was not worth fighting, or that I could not exercise my will on this planet was that there were things I had not understood.

OM VAJRASATTVA HUM

Vajrasattva, release the Diamond Will to give me awareness that will help me examine my reasons for coming here.

OM VAJRASATTVA HUM

Vajrasattva, release the Diamond Will to give me awareness that will help me see that there is no validity to this consciousness, this poison of non-will and non-being. It is, as all poisons, based on an illusion.

OM VAJRASATTVA HUM

Vajrasattva, release the Diamond Will to give me awareness of how I can fully absorb the antidote to the poison of non-will and acquire the Diamond Will.

OM VAJRASATTVA HUM

Vajrasattva, release the Diamond Will to give me awareness that this will is immovable by anything on earth. The Diamond Will cannot be in any way affected by the non-will, the non-being or even the anti-will, the very aggressive will of the fallen beings.

OM VAJRASATTVA HUM

Vajrasattva, release the Diamond Will to give me awareness that will help me tune in to this antidote and allow it to come into my being and consume whatever remnants I have of the non-will and the non-being.

OM VAJRASATTVA HUM

Vajrasattva, release the Diamond Will to give me awareness that will help me attain a much higher sense of peace.

OM VAJRASATTVA HUM

Vajrasattva, release the Diamond Will to give me awareness that will help me come to the point where I can make peace with the way that earth currently functions.

OM VAJRASATTVA HUM

Vajrasattva, release the Diamond Will to give me awareness that the purpose of earth is the outplaying of free will.

OM VAJRASATTVA HUM

Vajrasattva, release the Diamond Will to give me awareness that the purpose, the *real, higher* purpose for me coming to earth, was to grow in awareness to the point where I could ascend from earth.

OM VAJRASATTVA HUM

Vajrasattva, release the Diamond Will to give me awareness that will help me lock in to the fact that at the level of my I AM Presence, there is a will to go into the unascended sphere and to ascend from that sphere.

OM VAJRASATTVA HUM

Vajrasattva, release the Diamond Will to give me awareness that this is also a diamond will in the sense that it is higher than anything on earth, meaning nothing the Conscious You has experienced on earth has changed the will of the I AM Presence.

OM VAJRASATTVA HUM

Vajrasattva, release the Diamond Will to give me awareness that will help me reconnect to my I AM Presence and realize that, as the Conscious You, I am an extension of my I AM Presence. I am not in any way separated from it or in opposition to it.

OM VAJRASATTVA HUM

Vajrasattva, release the Diamond Will to give me awareness that the will of my Presence is also *my* will. I have a will to expand my consciousness. I have a will to ascend.

OM VAJRASATTVA HUM

Vajrasattva, release the Diamond Will to give me awareness that regardless of how conditions are on earth, these conditions form the perfect opportunity for me to ascend.

OM VAJRASATTVA HUM

Vajrasattva, release the Diamond Will to give me awareness that because I had not had the wide range of experiences that I can have on an unnatural planet, I did not ascend from a natural planet.

OM VAJRASATTVA HUM

Vajrasattva, release the Diamond Will to give me awareness that there are certain selves I have in my four lower bodies and I need to let them die.

OM VAJRASATTVA HUM

Vajrasattva, release the Diamond Will to give me awareness that because I have a broader range of selves in my four lower bodies on earth, I actually ascend with a higher level of awareness.

OM VAJRASATTVA HUM

Vajrasattva, release the Diamond Will to give me awareness that there are many positive experiences in my causal body. As a result of that, my I AM Presence has a higher sense of awareness after I ascend from an unnatural planet than from a natural planet.

OM VAJRASATTVA HUM

Vajrasattva, release the Diamond Will to give me awareness that will help me really make peace with being here and say: "Regardless of what I thought before I came here, this planet is a great opportunity for me to ascend."

OM VAJRASATTVA HUM

Vajrasattva, release the Diamond Will to give me awareness that will help me come to the point where I no longer look back and think it was a mistake to come here.

OM VAJRASATTVA HUM

Vajrasattva, release the Diamond Will to give me awareness that will help me say: "Well, that was where I was at in consciousness at the time and I made the best choice I could make, given the self I had at the time."

OM VAJRASATTVA HUM

Vajrasattva, release the Diamond Will to give me awareness that will help me let go of any sense of regret and be at peace with the fact that this is the path to the ascension that I chose, and it is perfectly acceptable according to any standard in the spiritual realm.

OM VAJRASATTVA HUM

Vajrasattva, release the Diamond Will to give me awareness that will help me say: "The rest of this lifetime is the perfect, the ideal, opportunity for me to ascend, to look at my reactions, to look at the selves I have left, to let them die."

OM VAJRASATTVA HUM

Vajrasattva, release the Diamond Will to give me awareness that will help me say: "The rest of this lifetime is the perfect opportunity to be the open door for my I AM Presence to express itself, to come to the point where I, as the Conscious You, am free of all these lower selves and now I have a free will to experience and express myself on this planet.

OM VAJRASATTVA HUM

Vajrasattva, release the Diamond Will to give me awareness that will help me shift my focus away from producing a result on earth but actually embracing and enjoying the process of being on earth, the process of expressing myself on earth and the process of ascending from earth.

OM VAJRASATTVA HUM

Sealing

In the name of the Divine Mother, I call to Mother Mary for the sealing of myself and all people in my circle of influence in the creative flow of the Divine Mother, the River of Life. I call for the multiplication of my calls by all representatives of the Divine Mother, so that we form the perfect figure-eight flow of "As Above, so below." Thus, I accept that this is fully manifest, because the mouth of the Lord, the Divine Mother that I AM, has spoken it. Amen.

23 | BEING THE CHRIST IN SAINT GERMAIN'S GOLDEN AGE

I AM the Ascended Master Saint Germain. I wish to discourse with you on what it means to be the Living Christ and the Living Buddha in action in the Aquarian Age. What did it mean to be the Living Christ in action in the Piscean Age? It meant to attune yourself to the Ascended Master Jesus Christ and come into some form of oneness with him so you could receive something from him, either for your personal life or for the help of others and society.

What it takes to bring forth a new idea

Now, you may look at what has been brought forth of change in the Piscean Age and you may see that all of the people who were able to bring forth some positive contribution in any area of life and society, have been able to have some attunement with the planetary Christ, with Jesus, during that age. This, of course, does not mean that all ideas that were brought forth in the last 2,000 years came exclusively from Jesus but they came through him as the hierarch of the Piscean Age. We can therefore say that if you look at many of the people who have brought forth new ideas in some areas, they had some attunement with Jesus, they were therefore open to receiving some idea.

Now, if you look at some of these people, you can see that many of them were not even religious or spiritual. Many of them may have had various unresolved psychology, various idiosyncrasies, even various beliefs that were certainly not in accordance or in alignment with ascended master teachings. Still, they had some attunement so that, through the clouds of all of this outer stuff in their minds, there was an opening where some idea could descend into their minds—as of course it will be in Aquarius. It is not so that in order to attune to the Ascended Master Saint Germain, people have to know that I exist, believe in ascended master teachings, follow ascended master teachings, practice ascended master teachings. They do not need to have resolved all of their psychology. The reason for this is very simple. Bringing forth a new idea on earth has an alpha and an omega aspect. The alpha aspect is that it comes from the ascended realm and therefore the people must be able to attune to the ascended realm. The omega aspect is that in order to receive an idea and implement it, people must have some kind of expertise in a particular field. If I want to bring forth a new idea in the field of education, I need someone who has some knowledge, some expertise, some experience in that field. Of course, I also need a person who is able to tune in to me, at least for a brief moment, and therefore receive that idea.

You have many, many people who have a genuine desire to see an improvement in a particular area of life. These people have the experience in their daily lives, they have studied and they engage their minds in the process of wanting to bring forth this new idea, this improvement. Now, in some cases they may have an imperfect understanding of their field or the improvement that needs to be brought forth but they have the genuine desire.

What you will see, even if you study some of the scientists that have brought forth new ideas in the field of science, is that sometimes they just get overwhelmed. It becomes too intense for them and they decide to take a break, to withdraw from their normal daily engagement with the issue. As they withdraw and let go, suddenly there is an opening where what they call a "flash of inspiration" strikes and now they see the issue from a new perspective. They see some new idea and then they are able to move forward.

Inspiration beyond the physical brain

Even the most materialistic scientists will recognize that they need a certain amount of inspiration. They are not particularly willing to speculate on where that inspiration comes from, but it does not take much speculation to see that it does not come from the physical brain. If the physical brain had been able to produce the idea, then certainly, in the period where the scientist was very intensively engaging his physical brain in trying to figure out the problem, then the physical brain should have brought forth the solution.

What brings forth the solution is that the scientist steps back, disengages the outer mind and now there is an opening for inspiration to come from a higher realm. This is, therefore, the process that in the Aquarian Age will become more and more known, more and more common, we might say, in the sense that people begin to understand and acknowledge that intuition is actually the key.

Intuition can often only be unlocked when you have gone through that outer engagement with an issue, of really seeking to understand it, really desiring an improvement and then you have the foundation. You have, in a sense (as the idea we gave during the Piscean Age of the chalice, the Holy Grail) the chalice that is raised up so that the elixir of Spirit can be poured into it. If there is no chalice, then you cannot pour anything into it, as it would just be wasted. There is that alpha and omega action: The omega is raising up the chalice of the mind and the alpha is to then open yourself up, using your intuitive faculties rather than the outer mind and opening yourself to an idea from above.

In a sense, this is what it means to be the Christ in action in the Aquarian Age. You attune to me because even though there may be other masters (and there certainly will be other masters that will be bringing forth ideas), they will come through the office that I am. Of course, if you are an ascended master student and you know you have an affinity with a particular master, you should focus on that master and not necessarily on me. This is not to say that you should exclusively focus on me but it is to say that they do come through the office that I am the leader of.

The result of the masters' efforts

I now wish to shift gears a little bit, and I wish to look back at previous ascended master organizations that we have sponsored, as Master MORE did the other day. I wish to have you consider the question: Given that I stepped forward publicly during the 1930s and sponsored the I AM Movement and we have sponsored other organizations since then, what has been the result of these efforts? How many ascended master students have actually come to a point where they were able to express their Christhood, able to receive new ideas from the ascended masters and bring them out into some area of society? Well, it is not that I wish here to discuss numbers. What I wish to point out to you is that there certainly has not been as many as we had hoped for. I wish to have a discussion about why that is so.

What I want to point out to you is that we have, over the last couple of years, given you more insight into how we look at the issue of what we are doing in seeking to work with unascended humankind. We have talked about the difficulties we face, such as Jesus saying we are like the used car-salesmen using "bait-and-switch." We have to appeal to people's current level of consciousness to get them to even study the teachings. Then, when they come in, we can hopefully give them a higher teaching that will actually give them growth rather than appealing to their egos and making them feel superior to others.

What we had to do in previous ages – the problem we faced there – was that the collective consciousness was very, very dense. In order to engage our students (to even awaken them to the path, to get them to engage in the path), we had to instil in them a certain sense of enthusiasm, a certain desire to do something. Some of the students used to describe it by saying they were "on fire," they were "fired up." We had to do this to simply create a momentum that would allow people to break free of the collective consciousness, the mass consciousness. However, the inevitable downside of this was that many of the students became so on fire with changing the world for Saint Germain that they became very unbalanced. We have said before that many students have had a correct view of *what* needs to change but an incorrect or incomplete view of *how* this could be accomplished.

Students becoming unbalanced

We have seen many of these students who were awakened to the existence of Saint Germain and my desire to bring forth a golden age. They became so on fire with going out, changing the entire world with the wave of their hand and approaching people in this very unbalanced way so that they would either push people away from them or they would incur some kind of negative reaction from people.

What we saw in many students is that they went out with this very unbalanced seller's approach as you also see in some of the born-again Christians and other groups. They have suddenly been converted to some belief system and are now going out, thinking they have to convert the whole world. They run into this opposition from the mass consciousness and a negative reaction from other people so they go from this artificial high to a low. Some of them often went so low that they became discouraged, maybe even left the teachings or in other ways decided to withdraw. This is, of course, a reaction that we did not desire to see in our students, but at the time there was really no way to avoid it in some students.

Others took a more balanced, a more long-term approach, seeking to balance their karma or however they saw making progress on the spiritual path. Unfortunately, many of those, then, became or remained passive and did not really feel that they could do anything in society. Many of them reasoned that the contribution they could make to society was to give the decrees. Of course, it was valuable that they gave the decrees but this caused some people to actually postpone or abort their Christhood because they had a greater potential than giving decrees. You can look back at these movements and see how they often spent hours and hours and hours giving decrees. Although this had a positive effect, it also in some cases had the effect that people actually postponed their Christhood. They did not express their Christhood, and in order to avoid a negative reaction, they reasoned in their minds that: "It is enough that I give the violet flame, I don't have to go out and engage in society."

On the other hand, there were those who were so eager to go out and convert others that they went into the unbalanced reaction. To avoid this being too serious, I would like to inject a little bit of humour here. In the United States there is an organization called Weight Watchers and there is a joke going around about Weight Watchers that at their meetings, all of the participants hold hands and sing because that is the only way to make sure nobody is eating! You might create a similar joke about ascended master students: Why do they have to give so many hours of decrees? Because it keeps them from going out there and getting into trouble! This is partly why we had to have the students of past organizations give so many hours of decrees. It was the only way to stop some people from going out there and acting on this very unbalanced reaction that they had built up with their zeal, their being so on fire for changing the world for Saint Germain.

They immediately thought that changing the world for Saint Germain or saving the world meant convincing everybody else to come into an ascended master teaching, their particular organization. I want to make it very clear, even though we have said it before, that in the Aquarian Age we are not in any way looking at all people coming to acknowledge the existence of ascended masters. We are certainly not looking for all people coming to acknowledge a specific ascended master teaching or organization, including the teaching we are giving through this messenger.

Not a goal to convert everyone

It may be that, as we move further into the Aquarian Age, there will be a general recognition of the existence of ascended masters and a general openness to ascended master teachings. I say it "may be" because it is impossible to predict the time span. When will that happen? It will happen at some point but *when* will it happen? For the foreseeable future, certainly for the remainder of your lifetimes, you need to make very clear in your minds that expressing your Christhood does not mean you have to go out and try to convert everybody to follow this particular teaching or to accept the existence of ascended masters or our teachings.

Being the Living Christ in the Aquarian Age means, first of, all as I said, tuning in to me and receiving some idea that you can implement in your own life so that you can help the people around you in your personal circle of influence or perhaps it can have some beneficial effect on society. It is not a matter of going on this crusade to convert people to a particular belief system.

It was actually one of the tests of Pisces to overcome that state of consciousness. Of course, you can see how many people, including many ascended master students, failed it. What we need in the Aquarian Age is, first of all, students who have worked on their personal psychology, who have used the teachings (especially on the birth trauma and on all of these selves you have created, from the primal self and others) so that you have resolved that primal self and some of these other selves. Meaning, you are as the alpha approach, free to tune in to your I AM Presence and to the ascended masters because these selves are no longer blocking your attunement.

On the other hand, as the omega, you are free to go out and bring to other people what you have received from us but you can do so in a completely balanced manner. In other words, you are not doing this based on your birth trauma and your primal self. You are not doing it to compensate for anything, to gain recognition, to gain validation or any of these matters that can spring from these separate selves that were created in reaction to you coming here and feeling rejected.

When you look back at ascended master students in the past, why did they not, why could they not, express their Christhood? Well, because they had not resolved their primal selves. Why did we not give the teachings back then? Because these teachings, for a variety of reasons, could not be given during the Piscean Age and through an organization that was created specifically for the purpose that Master MORE described. The planet, the collective consciousness, ascended master students simply were not ready to receive these teachings.

Work on your separate selves

You can see that we have waited fifteen years through this messenger to give these teachings. We have very carefully built up to where you have the understanding where you can accept and apply the teachings. Let me make one very, very clear, very direct statement: Any person who has studied the teachings given through this messenger, I very strongly advise you to make use of these latest teachings on the avatars, on the birth trauma, on the primal self and other selves and how to overcome them.

Do not assume that you have already done this. If you have not worked with these teachings, do not assume that you do not need to work with them. If you are serious about fulfilling your Divine plan and serving the ascended masters, then use these teachings. Work through them so you can overcome that primal self and the other selves so that your service is not colored by, or even *driven* by, these selves and the birth trauma. You will not fulfill the highest potential of your Divine plan until you are free of all of this conglomerate. I wish to give you, again based on previous ascended master organizations, some teachings on this.

How do you recognize if you have a primal self, if you have not yet resolved it? We have, of course, given many teachings on this but I wish to give one more. What we have seen in many of our students is that you have come into an ascended master teaching with a clear sense that you are here on earth to do something, you feel compelled to do something. Now, we have told you that many of you (most of you) have come to the earth as avatars and you wanted to do something on earth so you came in with this desire to do something. We have also told you that the view you had before you descended was not the highest so you actually came in with a certain compulsion to do something.

Then, after your initial birth trauma, some of you have built this other self that has given you a new compulsion, or given a new twist to your original compulsion, so that you are now reacting to a certain condition on earth, feeling you have to do something about that condition. What I simply wish to point out to you is this: If you feel this compulsion, this drive to do something (where you feel you *have* to), then you know this comes from the primal self and other selves. You know there is something you have not resolved.

Taking life on earth personally

Now, the other thing that comes in is that (as other masters, especially Master MORE have explained) when you received your birth trauma, everything on earth, your life on earth, became very personal and you started to take everything personally. What exactly does that mean? Well, the essence of this is that you became self-conscious, you became *very* self-conscious.

It is almost as if there is a part of you that is always watching yourself, analyzing, evaluating, judging how you are doing but you are not doing this based on self-observation—you are doing this based on observing how other people react to you. Many of you will be able to recognize this in yourselves. There is a part of you that is always watching you and evaluating and judging. There is a part of you because after your birth trauma, you created a separate self that is doing this.

Now, we have said that the Conscious You has the ability to be self-aware but what I am talking about is not self-awareness—it is what we might call self-consciousness because you are self-conscious. You are very, very conscious of how other people react to you. What has happened here is that you came to earth, you received the birth trauma and now you felt that you had been put down or ignored. You created a self that wants to compensate for this, that wants to undo the problem, undo the wrong, that you felt happened.

There is a self that drives you to get attention. Part of your drive to do something on earth comes from this desire to get attention, to do something important that other people will recognize and acknowledge. You have a self that desires approval from others and this self is driving you to do something. Maybe it has been driving you throughout your life to always be the funny person who could crack a joke, maybe to be the smart person who always knew what other people did not know. There is a myriad of these selves but it is basically that you desire to get recognition and validation from other people so you do something to get that.

On the other hand, you have the self-conscious self that is constantly evaluating how other people react to you. When they do not react in a completely approving way, then you feel bad about yourself in various ways. You might feel embarrassed, you might feel rejected, you might feel you are no good, you might feel you made a mistake. Whatever it may be, there is a feeling attached to this.

You are in this push-pull and your life is revolving around this. On the one hand, you are seeking approval and on the other hand seeking to avoid a negative reaction. Do you see that the one self is driving you to get other people to react to you in order to get their approval but the other self is afraid of any negative reaction? You are constantly in this state where you are taking a risk. It is a high-risk business because you are driven to get people's attention but if they do not react with approval, then you go into the other self and the negative reaction. Your entire life can be driven by this. This has happened to many people, of course, but we have seen many ascended master students be in this pattern.

In fact, this messenger was in this pattern for the first part of his life, constantly driven this way. For some of you it goes back to childhood but, of course, for all of you it goes back several lifetimes. Many of you experienced, for example, that when you were small children, you figured out very quickly that you could make the adults laugh. You felt good about yourself when you made the adults laugh. You have continued to this day wanting to make people laugh but if they do not, then you feel bad. Again, there is this push-pull.

Some of you have realized as children that you were smarter than other children so you could come up with some ideas that others could not come up with. You have continued to this day seeking to impress people by coming up with these ideas, and some you have gone into using ascended master teachings for this. Then, when they do not agree with you, you go into a negative reaction.

What I wish to see for you is that you come to the point where you have resolved this entire conglomerate of the primal self and these other selves. This entire push-pull, this entire intense battle that is going on in your mind falls away from you. You are not trapped, on the one hand, seeking something that is impossible and, on the other hand, putting yourself down or feeling bad when you do not achieve the impossible. You see that it is impossible, it is unnecessary, it is completely unreal.

When you come to see that, when you separate yourself from these selves, you can look at them and just let them go. You do not need to solve the problem that the self projects at you. You do not need to attain the condition, you do not need to change the entire world in order to make yourself feel better. You just need to let the self die. That is what we desire to see for you.

You are not the Christ through a separate self

That is how you can begin to be the Living Christ in the Aquarian Age. You can begin to, instead of being driven by these outer selves, be directed from within, from me. You see, my beloved, what is the main problem that I see in ascended master students and why they have not been able to have the impact on the world that they could have had? It is precisely because they have had these selves, these ideas in their outer minds. They come into an ascended master teaching, they pick up something that they think validates the approach to life they have taken through one of these separate selves. Now, they actually believe that the way to be the Christ on earth is to act through that separate self.

Some have created a separate self that makes you feel you have to challenge everybody. Other people are in a state of illusion, they do not want to get out of it—you have to challenge them (they think). Now, you come into an ascended master teaching that may have given you this sense of enthusiasm that you have to go out there and awaken people. Suddenly, your self that is based on this desire to challenge people thinks you are being the Christ by challenging people.

Many ascended master students have felt that they themselves have experienced in a dictation where something we said with a very strong, firm voice suddenly awakened them. It made them see something that they could not see before. It has sometimes been necessary for us to speak with a very powerful voice in order to penetrate the density of the mass consciousness and of people's consciousness. Now, these people have a desire to produce that same experience in other people. They think they have to go out there and blue-ray these people and talk to them in a very firm, strong voice in order to awaken them. But what does this come from? It comes from the self that felt rejected when you received your birth trauma and that has ever since then been looking for a way to do something that other people could not ignore or deny. It is an unbalanced reaction. It will not achieve the results and you will never feel at peace, you will never feel good. You will never feel you have accomplished what you came to accomplish, as long as you are acting through these selves.

Again, as other masters have said at this conference, we have given you the teachings, we have given you the tools. Please my beloved, make use of them because when you do, and when you overcome that primal self, you will feel as this messenger felt. He has said that in forty years of striving on the spiritual path, using all kinds of teachings and practices, using all kinds of psychological tools and therapies, nothing has given him the breakthrough that these teachings on the primal self have given him. The same can happen for you and has happened for some of you who have done this. My beloved, you know how Jesus gave you a variety of ideas and said that you did not all have to pay attention to all of them. You had to pick the one that appealed to you, but I am hoping that this one idea can appeal to all of you because all of you can benefit from it.

Now, I can assure you that many of you, and many of the people who will be attracted to the teachings in the future, do have a potential to do something valuable and important in society. In order to fulfill what we in Holland called the highest potential of your Divine plan, you simply have to overcome that primal self and the other selves so that you are not seeking to make a contribution to society while being colored by this. Then, you will not achieve your highest potential and, my beloved, we desire you to achieve your highest potential, the highest potential that you chose. You chose this because you knew it could be done, given that you would find this teaching and you would receive it. Naturally, I look to you, all of you, to make some kind of contribution to the Aquarian Age.

Idolatry of the messenger

Now, you know we have talked about the idolatry of Jesus that people have had during the Piscean Age. We have talked about this for 70-80 years in ascended master organizations. Jesus was meant to be an example on the path to Christhood but many, many ascended master students have still not freed themselves from this idolatrous image, portrayed and projected out there by the fallen beings through the Catholic church and other Christian churches. They still thought that Jesus was way up there and that there was no way that they could do what Jesus did. We have attempted to dispel this and certainly the book *My Lives* is an important step to help people dispel the idolatry of Jesus.

We also want to make sure that those of you who are open to the teachings given through this messenger do not build some kind of idolatry of this messenger. If you look back at his life, you will see that he was born in a normal family, had a normal upbringing. *We* have never claimed, and *he* has never claimed, that there was anything special about him, that he was somehow more advanced when he came to earth or that he has gone through some kind of process in past lives that makes him more advanced today. I know that in previous dispensations, claims have been made that being a messenger is very, very difficult and you have to be trained for millions of years. We have never made that claim about this messenger because we have not wanted to build up any kind of idolatry around him. You know that he found an ascended master teaching, he applied that teaching, he made an effort to resolve his psychology and he gradually walked the path until he came to a point where he was now open to be able to do something, to have a more direct relationship with the ascended masters. Before he started the *Ask Real Jesus* website, he had the experience he has described, a feeling that he let go of his human ambitions and then he felt the Presence of Jesus.

At that moment, he was, in a sense, in the same situation as Jesus was in at the wedding of Cana. He had before him a fork in the road and he could go this way or that way. He could have said: "Oh, I can't possibly do this" or he could do what he did and say: "I am willing to do this even though I recognize I am not perfect, I have not fully resolved my psychology, I haven't fully manifested Christhood." This means that when he started the Ask Real Jesus website, he was by no means fully in the Christ-consciousness. He was certainly at a considerably lower level of consciousness than he is today.

You do not have to be perfect

The question here is this: Do you have to be perfect to do something for the ascended masters? The answer is "No." We look to all of you to not build some kind of idolatry of the messenger that says: "Oh, I couldn't possibly do what the messenger has done." Now, you may look at what this messenger has done in terms of receiving teachings, more teachings, more teachings, more teachings, more teachings and more teachings until it is quite frankly overwhelming to most of you. You may say: "But I could never bring forth that much teaching, I could never do what this messenger has done." You are perfectly correct, my beloved, you cannot do what this messenger has done. What you *can* do is what this messenger is not able to do because all of you are unique individuals. You have a unique I AM Presence, you have a unique history on earth, you have a unique experience in this lifetime and therefore *you* can do what this messenger cannot do.

There is something you can do that is your gift that nobody else can bring out. As we have said before, there is no comparison in uniqueness. Look at this messenger as an inspiration, if it inspires you, but do not build the idolatry that you cannot do anything special compared to what this messenger has done. There is no reason to compare yourself to anyone. The focus is: Resolve your psychology, tune in to your I AM Presence, be the open door for expressing your unique individuality. Make the choices you are perfectly allowed to make as the Conscious You in embodiment: what you desire to express, what you desire to experience, what you desire to enjoy on earth.

Each and every one of you has the potential to reach a certain group of people that nobody else can reach. This messenger can reach a certain mandala, we might say, of people. There are many other people on earth whom he cannot reach. Many of you can reach those people. You each have a certain mandala of people that you can reach, that you can help bring up higher.

Therefore, I simply say to you: Be *inspired* by the messenger but do not be *discouraged* by the messenger. Use him as an inspiration to say: "I see here is a person who has found his unique calling, his unique gift. Let me look at how he did this and see what applies to me, how I can learn from this." Then, you focus on bringing forth your gift, your contribution.

My beloved, for some of you, you have a special area of expertise in the world and you have the potential to bring forth some ideas in that area of expertise. Even if in your Divine plan your potential is to bring forth one idea, then focus on that and be at peace that this is your contribution. Make sure that it is the highest idea that you have the potential to bring forth according to your Divine plan.

Recognize also, my beloved, that what you can see in this messenger is that, yes, when you come into embodiment you have a Divine plan, it has a low potential, it has a high potential. Of course, you want to make sure that you manifest the highest potential, but this messenger manifested the highest potential of his Divine plan some time ago. What he has been able to bring forth since is beyond that potential. Many of you also can go beyond even the highest potential that you defined in your Divine plan because you defined your Divine plan from the vision you had at the time. Now, that you have raised your consciousness, or at least have the potential to raise your consciousness by overcoming the primal self, you can go higher than that. Of course, we are always happy to see our students transcend themselves. It is not that we are looking for particular results but we are looking for students to transcend themselves.

My beloved, when a student has reached the highest potential of his or her Divine plan, we do not want that student to stop for the rest of that lifetime. We, of course, want the student to continue to transcend him- or herself and that is what some of you, indeed, have the potential to do. With all the teachings we have given you, you have the potential to avoid some of the pitfalls that we have seen in previous dispensations where ascended master students would go into the mind-set we have described.

Finding a balanced approach

You have the potential to have a more balanced approach where you can actually begin to have an impact. You can go out there and express yourselves like Jesus encouraged you to do, making use of the Internet. It is not, again, a matter of that you always have to talk about ascended masters or ascended master teachings. You are completely free to take some of our ideas and express them in a neutral context where you do not say that they come from ascended masters. In other words, the problem we have seen in the past is that people thought that the most important point is to bring people into accepting this ascended master teaching. No, my beloved, the most important point is to get people to accept certain ideas that will bring society or individuals forward.

Do not put this barrier in front of these people that they first have to jump over the hurdle and come into the fold before they can receive the idea. Feel free to give them the ideas and let the ideas themselves do the work in these people's minds. You are not doing it to produce a result because, my beloved, when you get rid of the primal self and these other selves, you are not approaching people in order to *create* a feeling in yourself or in order to *avoid* a feeling in yourself. You can be the *open* door, which means you are free to give people that idea and you are free to set them free to receive it. Many, many times, my beloved, an idea goes into a person's mind, they might even reject it at the conscious level but it goes into their mind, it starts an alchemical process and it takes time before it surfaces to the conscious mind. Sometimes, it can take years, and suddenly people have a shift and now they accept the idea without really knowing why.

Be content to give the idea and let the idea do its work. This is, in essence, what happened to you when you found an ascended master teaching. There was some idea that pulled you into the teaching but there were other ideas that took a long time to germinate and to come to the point that you are now at. You are ready to deal with this primal self and overcome it and thereby overcome what has historically been the greatest obstacle for avatars having the impact on earth that they could potentially have.

With this, I want to express my deep gratitude for this conference, those who have arranged it, those who have come. All of you have been part of the omega aspect where you interact with us during the conference, and you become the broadcasting stations for radiating this into the mass consciousness.

You might see that there is a figure-eight flow between us Above and you here at the conference. There is the vertical figure-eight flow and there is a horizontal figure-eight flow between you who are here and the people in the world, the mass consciousness. This is what we desire to establish on a permanent basis. It is, of course, there to some degree but we desire that horizontal figure-eight flow to become much stronger. This can only happen when you individually establish a figure-eight flow with us and this can only happen when you remove the barriers (again) as you have the teaching to do.

My beloved, my deep gratitude. As the Hierarch of the Aquarian Age, I dare say, I carry in that the gratitude of all ascended masters, especially those who have been able to speak at this conference and, of course, Gautama who will speak later. With this, I seal you in the love that I AM, truly the love that can make matter sing. The matter in your four lower bodies has been singing during this conference, and I hope you will keep it singing for a long time, in fact for the indefinite time, for the rest of the time you are here—and beyond.

24 | INVOKING CHRISTHOOD IN SAINT GERMAIN'S GOLDEN AGE

In the name I AM THAT I AM, Jesus Christ, I call to all representatives of the Divine Mother, especially Saint Germain, to help me overcome all conditions in the four levels of my mind that prevent me from tuning in to you and receiving an idea that can help manifest your Golden Age, including…

[Make personal calls.]

Part 1

1. Saint Germain, give me the awareness that being the Living Christ in action in the Piscean Age meant to attune myself to the Ascended Master Jesus Christ and come into oneness with him, so I could receive something from him, either for my personal life or for the help of others and society.

> O Saint Germain, you do inspire,
> my vision raised forever higher,

with you I form a figure-eight,
your Golden Age I co-create.

O Saint Germain, what love you bring,
it truly makes all matter sing,
your violet flame does all restore,
with you we are becoming more.

2. Saint Germain, give me the awareness that all of the people who were able to bring forth some positive contribution in any area of life and society, have been able to have some attunement with the planetary Christ, with Jesus, during the Piscean age.

O Saint Germain, what Freedom Flame,
released when we recite your name,
acceleration is your gift,
our planet it will surely lift.

O Saint Germain, what love you bring,
it truly makes all matter sing,
your violet flame does all restore,
with you we are becoming more.

3. Saint Germain, give me the awareness that bringing forth a new idea on earth has an alpha and an omega aspect. The alpha aspect is that it comes from the ascended realm and therefore I must be able to attune to you.

O Saint Germain, in love we claim,
our right to bring your violet flame,
from you Above, to us below,
it is an all-transforming flow.

O Saint Germain, what love you bring,
it truly makes all matter sing,
your violet flame does all restore,
with you we are becoming more.

4. Saint Germain, give me the awareness that the omega aspect is that in order to receive an idea and implement it, I must have some kind of expertise in a particular field.

> O Saint Germain, I love you so,
> my aura filled with violet glow,
> my chakras filled with violet fire,
> I am your cosmic amplifier.

> **O Saint Germain, what love you bring,**
> **it truly makes all matter sing,**
> **your violet flame does all restore,**
> **with you we are becoming more.**

5. Saint Germain, give me the awareness that in order to receive an idea, I must first focus my mind on the issue and then step back to create an opening for the idea to descend to the conscious mind.

> O Saint Germain, I am now free,
> your violet flame is therapy,
> transform all hang-ups in my mind,
> as inner peace I surely find.

> **O Saint Germain, what love you bring,**
> **it truly makes all matter sing,**
> **your violet flame does all restore,**
> **with you we are becoming more.**

6. Saint Germain, give me the awareness that intuition can be unlocked when I have gone through that outer engagement with an issue, of really seeking to understand it, really desiring an improvement, thereby setting the foundation.

> O Saint Germain, my body pure,
> your violet flame for all is cure,
> consume the cause of all disease,
> and therefore I am all at ease.

> O Saint Germain, what love you bring,
> it truly makes all matter sing,
> your violet flame does all restore,
> with you we are becoming more.

7. Saint Germain, give me the awareness that my mind needs to become a chalice that is raised up so that the elixir of Spirit can be poured into it. If there is no chalice, then you cannot pour anything into it, as it would be wasted.

> O Saint Germain, I'm karma-free,
> the past no longer burdens me,
> a brand new opportunity,
> I am in Christic unity.

> O Saint Germain, what love you bring,
> it truly makes all matter sing,
> your violet flame does all restore,
> with you we are becoming more.

8. Saint Germain, give me the awareness that will help me use my intuitive faculties rather than the outer mind and opening myself to an idea from above.

> O Saint Germain, we are now one,
> I am for you a violet sun,
> as we transform this planet earth,
> your Golden Age is given birth.

> O Saint Germain, what love you bring,
> it truly makes all matter sing,
> your violet flame does all restore,
> with you we are becoming more.

9. Saint Germain, give me the awareness that being the Christ in action in the Aquarian Age means that I attune to you or another ascended master with whom I have an affinity.

O Saint Germain, the earth is free,
from burden of duality,
in oneness we bring what is best,
your Golden Age is manifest.

**O Saint Germain, what love you bring,
it truly makes all matter sing,
your violet flame does all restore,
with you we are becoming more.**

Part 2

1. Saint Germain, give me the awareness to see if I have become so on fire with changing the world for Saint Germain that I have become unbalanced. Help me see if I have a correct view of *what* needs to change but an incomplete view of *how* this could be accomplished.

O Saint Germain, you do inspire,
my vision raised forever higher,
with you I form a figure-eight,
your Golden Age I co-create.

**O Saint Germain, what love you bring,
it truly makes all matter sing,
your violet flame does all restore,
with you we are becoming more.**

2. Saint Germain, give me the awareness of how to take a balanced long-term approach without becoming passive and feeling I can do nothing in society.

O Saint Germain, what Freedom Flame,
released when we recite your name,
acceleration is your gift,
our planet it will surely lift.

**O Saint Germain, what love you bring,
it truly makes all matter sing,
your violet flame does all restore,
with you we are becoming more.**

3. Saint Germain, give me the awareness to see if I have become so focused on giving decrees and invocations that it has postponed my Christhood because I have a greater potential than giving decrees.

O Saint Germain, in love we claim,
our right to bring your violet flame,
from you Above, to us below,
it is an all-transforming flow.

**O Saint Germain, what love you bring,
it truly makes all matter sing,
your violet flame does all restore,
with you we are becoming more.**

4. Saint Germain, give me the awareness that changing the world for Saint Germain or saving the world does not mean convincing everybody else to come into an ascended master teaching.

O Saint Germain, I love you so,
my aura filled with violet glow,
my chakras filled with violet fire,
I am your cosmic amplifier.

**O Saint Germain, what love you bring,
it truly makes all matter sing,
your violet flame does all restore,
with you we are becoming more.**

5. Saint Germain, give me the awareness that in the Aquarian Age all people do not need to acknowledge the existence of ascended masters or a specific ascended master teaching or organization.

O Saint Germain, I am now free,
your violet flame is therapy,

transform all hang-ups in my mind,
as inner peace I surely find.

**O Saint Germain, what love you bring,
it truly makes all matter sing,
your violet flame does all restore,
with you we are becoming more.**

6. Saint Germain, give me the awareness that expressing my Christhood does not mean I have to go out and try to convert everybody to follow this particular teaching or to accept the existence of ascended masters or the teachings.

O Saint Germain, my body pure,
your violet flame for all is cure,
consume the cause of all disease,
and therefore I am all at ease.

**O Saint Germain, what love you bring,
it truly makes all matter sing,
your violet flame does all restore,
with you we are becoming more.**

7. Saint Germain, give me the awareness that being the Living Christ in the Aquarian Age means tuning in to you and receiving some idea that I can implement in my own life, so that I can help the people around me or have some beneficial effect on society.

O Saint Germain, I'm karma-free,
the past no longer burdens me,
a brand new opportunity,
I am in Christic unity.

**O Saint Germain, what love you bring,
it truly makes all matter sing,
your violet flame does all restore,
with you we are becoming more.**

8. Saint Germain, give me the awareness that in the Aquarian Age, you need me to resolve the primal self and be free to tune in to my I AM Presence and to the ascended masters because these selves are no longer blocking my attunement.

> O Saint Germain, we are now one,
> I am for you a violet sun,
> as we transform this planet earth,
> your Golden Age is given birth.
>
> **O Saint Germain, what love you bring,**
> **it truly makes all matter sing,**
> **your violet flame does all restore,**
> **with you we are becoming more.**

9. Saint Germain, give me the awareness that you also need me to be free to go out and bring to other people what I have received from you, but I can do so in a completely balanced manner. I am not doing this based on my birth trauma and my primal self.

> O Saint Germain, the earth is free,
> from burden of duality,
> in oneness we bring what is best,
> your Golden Age is manifest.
>
> **O Saint Germain, what love you bring,**
> **it truly makes all matter sing,**
> **your violet flame does all restore,**
> **with you we are becoming more.**

Part 3

1. Saint Germain, I am willing to make use of the teachings on the avatars, on the birth trauma, on the primal self and other selves and how to overcome them. I will not assume that I have already done this.

O Saint Germain, you do inspire,
my vision raised forever higher,
with you I form a figure-eight,
your Golden Age I co-create.

**O Saint Germain, what love you bring,
it truly makes all matter sing,
your violet flame does all restore,
with you we are becoming more.**

2. Saint Germain, give me the awareness to see if I have an outer self that is reacting to a certain condition on earth, giving me a compulsion to do something about that condition.

O Saint Germain, what Freedom Flame,
released when we recite your name,
acceleration is your gift,
our planet it will surely lift.

**O Saint Germain, what love you bring,
it truly makes all matter sing,
your violet flame does all restore,
with you we are becoming more.**

3. Saint Germain, give me the awareness that if I feel such a compulsion, this drive to do something, then this comes from the primal self and other selves. There is something I have not resolved.

O Saint Germain, in love we claim,
our right to bring your violet flame,
from you Above, to us below,
it is an all-transforming flow.

**O Saint Germain, what love you bring,
it truly makes all matter sing,
your violet flame does all restore,
with you we are becoming more.**

4. Saint Germain, give me the awareness that when I received my birth trauma, everything became very personal. The essence of this is that I became self-conscious, as if there is a part of me that is always watching myself, analyzing, evaluating, judging.

> O Saint Germain, I love you so,
> my aura filled with violet glow,
> my chakras filled with violet fire,
> I am your cosmic amplifier.

> **O Saint Germain, what love you bring,**
> **it truly makes all matter sing,**
> **your violet flame does all restore,**
> **with you we are becoming more.**

5. Saint Germain, give me the awareness to see if I am doing this based on self-observation or based on observing how other people react to me. Help me see if I am very conscious of how other people react to me.

> O Saint Germain, I am now free,
> your violet flame is therapy,
> transform all hang-ups in my mind,
> as inner peace I surely find.

> **O Saint Germain, what love you bring,**
> **it truly makes all matter sing,**
> **your violet flame does all restore,**
> **with you we are becoming more.**

6. Saint Germain, give me the awareness that when I received the birth trauma and felt that I had been put down or ignored, I created a self that wants to compensate for this, that wants to undo the problem, undo the wrong that I felt happened.

> O Saint Germain, my body pure,
> your violet flame for all is cure,
> consume the cause of all disease,
> and therefore I am all at ease.

> O Saint Germain, what love you bring,
> it truly makes all matter sing,
> your violet flame does all restore,
> with you we are becoming more.

7. Saint Germain, give me the awareness that I have a self that desires approval from others and this self is driving me to do something. On the other hand, I have the self-conscious self that is constantly evaluating how other people react to me.

> O Saint Germain, I'm karma-free,
> the past no longer burdens me,
> a brand new opportunity,
> I am in Christic unity.

> O Saint Germain, what love you bring,
> it truly makes all matter sing,
> your violet flame does all restore,
> with you we are becoming more.

8. Saint Germain, give me the awareness to see if I am in this push-pull and my life is revolving around seeking approval and also seeking to avoid a negative reaction. One self is driving me to get other people to react to me in order to get their approval, but the other self is afraid of any negative reaction.

> O Saint Germain, we are now one,
> I am for you a violet sun,
> as we transform this planet earth,
> your Golden Age is given birth.

> O Saint Germain, what love you bring,
> it truly makes all matter sing,
> your violet flame does all restore,
> with you we are becoming more.

9. Saint Germain, give me the awareness to see if I am constantly in this state where I am taking a risk, where I am driven to get people's attention but if they do not react with approval, then I go into the other self and the negative reaction. Help me see if my life is driven by this.

> O Saint Germain, the earth is free,
> from burden of duality,
> in oneness we bring what is best,
> your Golden Age is manifest.
>
> **O Saint Germain, what love you bring,**
> **it truly makes all matter sing,**
> **your violet flame does all restore,**
> **with you we are becoming more.**

Part 4

1. Saint Germain, give me the awareness that will help me come to the point where I have resolved this entire conglomerate of the primal self and these other selves, overcoming this entire push-pull, this intense battle that is going on in my mind.

> O Saint Germain, you do inspire,
> my vision raised forever higher,
> with you I form a figure-eight,
> your Golden Age I co-create.
>
> **O Saint Germain, what love you bring,**
> **it truly makes all matter sing,**
> **your violet flame does all restore,**
> **with you we are becoming more.**

2. Saint Germain, give me the awareness that will help me stop being trapped, on the one hand seeking something that is impossible, and on the other hand putting myself down or feeling bad when I do not achieve the impossible. Help me see that it *is* impossible, it *is* unnecessary, it *is* completely unreal.

O Saint Germain, what Freedom Flame,
released when we recite your name,
acceleration is your gift,
our planet it will surely lift.

**O Saint Germain, what love you bring,
it truly makes all matter sing,
your violet flame does all restore,
with you we are becoming more.**

3. Saint Germain, help me separate myself from these selves, look at them and just let them go. Help me see that I do not need to solve the problem that the self projects at me. I do not need to attain the condition, I do not need to change the entire world in order to make myself feel better. I just need to let the self die.

O Saint Germain, in love we claim,
our right to bring your violet flame,
from you Above, to us below,
it is an all-transforming flow.

**O Saint Germain, what love you bring,
it truly makes all matter sing,
your violet flame does all restore,
with you we are becoming more.**

4. Saint Germain, give me the awareness to see if I have used an ascended master teaching to validate the approach to life I have taken through one of my separate selves, therefore thinking the way to be the Christ on earth is to act through that separate self.

O Saint Germain, I love you so,
my aura filled with violet glow,
my chakras filled with violet fire,
I am your cosmic amplifier.

> **O Saint Germain, what love you bring,**
> **it truly makes all matter sing,**
> **your violet flame does all restore,**
> **with you we are becoming more.**

5. Saint Germain, give me the awareness to see if I have created a separate self that makes me feel I have to challenge everybody, thinking that being the Christ means challenging people.

> O Saint Germain, I am now free,
> your violet flame is therapy,
> transform all hang-ups in my mind,
> as inner peace I surely find.

> **O Saint Germain, what love you bring,**
> **it truly makes all matter sing,**
> **your violet flame does all restore,**
> **with you we are becoming more.**

6. Saint Germain, give me the awareness to see if I have a self that thinks I have to talk to people in a very firm, strong voice in order to awaken them. Help me see that this comes from my birth trauma and the desire to do something that other people could not ignore or deny.

> O Saint Germain, my body pure,
> your violet flame for all is cure,
> consume the cause of all disease,
> and therefore I am all at ease.

> **O Saint Germain, what love you bring,**
> **it truly makes all matter sing,**
> **your violet flame does all restore,**
> **with you we are becoming more.**

7. Saint Germain, give me the awareness that I will never achieve results, I will never feel at peace, I will never feel good, I will never feel I have accomplished what I came to accomplish, as long as I am acting through these selves.

O Saint Germain, I'm karma-free,
the past no longer burdens me,
a brand new opportunity,
I am in Christic unity.

**O Saint Germain, what love you bring,
it truly makes all matter sing,
your violet flame does all restore,
with you we are becoming more.**

8. Saint Germain, give me the awareness that I do not have to be perfect in order to do something for the ascended masters. Help me see that I have a unique I AM Presence, I have a unique history on earth, I have a unique experience in this lifetime and therefore I can do what no one else can do.

O Saint Germain, we are now one,
I am for you a violet sun,
as we transform this planet earth,
your Golden Age is given birth.

**O Saint Germain, what love you bring,
it truly makes all matter sing,
your violet flame does all restore,
with you we are becoming more.**

9. Saint Germain, give me the awareness that there is something I can do that is my gift that nobody else can bring out. There is no comparison in uniqueness and I do not need to compare myself to anyone.

O Saint Germain, the earth is free,
from burden of duality,
in oneness we bring what is best,
your Golden Age is manifest.

**O Saint Germain, what love you bring,
it truly makes all matter sing,
your violet flame does all restore,
with you we are becoming more.**

Part 5

1. Saint Germain, give me the awareness that I have the potential to reach a certain group of people that nobody else can reach. I have a certain mandala of people that I can reach, that I can help bring up higher.

> O Saint Germain, you do inspire,
> my vision raised forever higher,
> with you I form a figure-eight,
> your Golden Age I co-create.
>
> **O Saint Germain, what love you bring,**
> **it truly makes all matter sing,**
> **your violet flame does all restore,**
> **with you we are becoming more.**

2. Saint Germain, give me the awareness to see if I have a special area of expertise in the world and I have the potential to bring forth some ideas in that area. Help me bring forth the highest idea that I have the potential to bring forth according to my Divine plan.

> O Saint Germain, what Freedom Flame,
> released when we recite your name,
> acceleration is your gift,
> our planet it will surely lift.
>
> **O Saint Germain, what love you bring,**
> **it truly makes all matter sing,**
> **your violet flame does all restore,**
> **with you we are becoming more.**

3. Saint Germain, give me the awareness to see if I can go beyond even the highest potential that I defined in my Divine plan. Help me continue to transcend myself and go beyond the vision I had when I formulated my Divine plan.

> O Saint Germain, in love we claim,
> our right to bring your violet flame,

from you Above, to us below,
it is an all-transforming flow.

O Saint Germain, what love you bring,
it truly makes all matter sing,
your violet flame does all restore,
with you we are becoming more.

4. Saint Germain, give me the awareness that the most important point is not to bring people into accepting an ascended master teaching. The most important point is to get people to accept certain ideas that will bring society or individuals forward.

O Saint Germain, I love you so,
my aura filled with violet glow,
my chakras filled with violet fire,
I am your cosmic amplifier.

O Saint Germain, what love you bring,
it truly makes all matter sing,
your violet flame does all restore,
with you we are becoming more.

5. Saint Germain, give me the awareness that will help me be free to give people the ideas, and let the ideas themselves do the work in these people's minds.

O Saint Germain, I am now free,
your violet flame is therapy,
transform all hang-ups in my mind,
as inner peace I surely find.

O Saint Germain, what love you bring,
it truly makes all matter sing,
your violet flame does all restore,
with you we are becoming more.

6. Saint Germain, give me the awareness that will set me free so I am not approaching people in order to *create* a feeling in myself or in order to *avoid* a feeling in myself. I am the *open* door, which means I am free to give people an idea and I set them free to receive it.

> O Saint Germain, my body pure,
> your violet flame for all is cure,
> consume the cause of all disease,
> and therefore I am all at ease.
>
> **O Saint Germain, what love you bring,**
> **it truly makes all matter sing,**
> **your violet flame does all restore,**
> **with you we are becoming more.**

7. Saint Germain, give me the awareness that it often takes time for people to integrate and accept an idea. Help me overcome all compulsion about getting other people to accept what I tell them.

> O Saint Germain, I'm karma-free,
> the past no longer burdens me,
> a brand new opportunity,
> I am in Christic unity.
>
> **O Saint Germain, what love you bring,**
> **it truly makes all matter sing,**
> **your violet flame does all restore,**
> **with you we are becoming more.**

8. Saint Germain, give me the awareness of how to deal with this primal self and overcome it, thereby overcoming what has historically been the greatest obstacle for avatars having the impact on earth that they could have.

> O Saint Germain, we are now one,
> I am for you a violet sun,
> as we transform this planet earth,
> your Golden Age is given birth.

**O Saint Germain, what love you bring,
it truly makes all matter sing,
your violet flame does all restore,
with you we are becoming more.**

9. Saint Germain, give me the awareness of how to establish a permanent vertical figure-eight flow between myself and you, so I can be the open door for you bringing forth any and all ideas that you want to bring forth through me for the rest of this lifetime.

O Saint Germain, the earth is free,
from burden of duality,
in oneness we bring what is best,
your Golden Age is manifest.

**O Saint Germain, what love you bring,
it truly makes all matter sing,
your violet flame does all restore,
with you we are becoming more.**

Sealing

In the name of the Divine Mother, I call to Mother Mary for the sealing of myself and all people in my circle of influence in the creative flow of the Divine Mother, the River of Life. I call for the multiplication of my calls by all representatives of the Divine Mother, so that we form the perfect figure-eight flow of "As Above, so below." Thus, I accept that this is fully manifest, because the mouth of the Lord, the Divine Mother that I AM, has spoken it. Amen.

25 | BEING READY FOR THE TEACHING

The Buddha, I AM. Gautama is the name I have used when working with the evolutions of earth. Some of the other masters have given you the perspective of looking back to previous ascended master dispensations and seeing what the results have been. I would like to broaden the perspective, going back to when I was in physical embodiment and I gave teachings at the physical level 2,500 years ago.

Idolatry of the Buddha

It is said that after following a certain path, the ascetic path, and coming to realize its limitations, I discovered the eight-fold path, or the path of the Buddha, and I attained nirvana, I became enlightened. Many, many Buddhists, even to this day so many centuries later, they look at this with a form of idolatry. Either I was the only being to ever attain enlightenment, or I was the highest being or I attained some ultimate, absolute state of enlightenment.

In other words, they think that the state of enlightenment that I attained 2,500 years ago was some absolute, highest possible state that could never be surpassed. However, when you consider the reality we have given you about the 144 levels of consciousness, then you can ask yourself the question: When I attained enlightenment 2,500 years ago, I did so by reaching the 144th level of consciousness. Was the 144th level of consciousness 2,500 years ago the same as the 144th level of consciousness today? Now, if the answer was: "Yes, it was the same," what would the consequence be? Well, the consequence would be that the planet had made no progress at all in 2,500 years. The consequence of that would have been that the teachings I gave 2,500 years ago had failed to raise the consciousness of the planet and therefore had failed their purpose. The reality is that the 144th level today is considerably higher than it was 2,500 years ago, 2,000 years ago when Jesus attained that level, even a 100 or so years ago when Master MORE and Kuthumi attained that level and so forth and so on.

How consciousness is raised

What is it, then, that raises that level of consciousness? Well, it is, first of all, as the omega aspect, that the collective consciousness is raised. That happens when a critical mass of individuals raise their consciousness and pull up on the bottom 80% or 90% and therefore the bottom level is raised. There can come times where there is a shift in the collective awareness and people decide that a certain manifestation is no longer acceptable to them. As a result of that, the bottom level of consciousness is raised up and beings who are at that level of consciousness will not be allowed to take physical embodiment.

However what raises the highest level? Well, someone has to reach the 144th level of their time and then go higher before they ascend. In a sense, that is what I did 2,500 years ago, even though I entered nirvana at what was the 144th level at that time. When I came back to teach in my teaching mission, I did not come back in an absolute state of consciousness. I was still growing and evolving and transcending myself for the years I was teaching. I raised the 144th level to a higher plateau. Jesus, of course, did the same, other masters have done the same and that is how that is raised. Some of you have the potential to be part of this process of attaining the 144th level before you are ready to leave embodiment, therefore still going higher while you are in embodiment and therefore helping to raise that level up.

You see that the entire concept that a teaching could be absolute, that a certain state of consciousness could be absolute, is a complete illusion, it is Maya, it is, of course, a projection of the fallen beings. They cannot transcend themselves and therefore they do not want anyone else to transcend themselves. They have come up with a lot of clever schemes for making people think that it is not possible. They want you to think that I attained an ultimate, absolute state of consciousness, that I was an exception, that no one can go higher. They want you to think that Jesus also reached the level that no one else can follow.

For the past 2,500 years there are actually a relatively small number of individuals who have used the teachings of Buddhism to also reach the 144th level and then go beyond. Some of those are known to people in the Buddhic tradition, others are not known because they did not have a public mission. Certainly, when I look back, Buddhism has produced a contribution to the forward progression of the collective consciousness and raising the levels of consciousness.

A teaching is for a level of consciousness

Now, where this goes is that when you realize that the consciousness is higher today than it was 2,500 years ago (that the scale of the 144 levels has shifted upwards), you can also see that the teaching that was given so long ago was actually given for a lower level of consciousness than is the average today. This partly points, of course, to the need for progressive revelation. It also points to the realization that any teaching at any time can only be given for the level of consciousness that is there. It does not necessarily mean that the teaching is given for the average level of consciousness or for the lowest level of consciousness, for certain teachings are given for people in the top 10%.

Nevertheless, you always need to recognize that when a specific teaching is given, it is very much given based on the level of consciousness on the planet at the time. If the teaching is successful, the consciousness will shift. What should, then, ideally happen? Well, what should ideally happen is that some people have taken that teaching, used the teaching to reach the 144th level of consciousness. They then become instruments for either bringing forth a new teaching, bringing forth a new aspect of the old teaching, a new interpretation of the old teaching. Therefore, they can now bring forth a teaching for the new level of consciousness that has been reached as a result of the old teaching. This means, of course, that progressive revelation ideally should never stop. This means also that it is, in a sense, a sad thing (if we want to use that word) when the followers of one teaching become dogmatic, become closed to anything new and therefore become the instruments of actually aborting the efficiency of that teaching. They are not allowing the transcendence of the teaching.

When I gave my teachings 2,500 years ago, you will see (if you read some of the scriptures) that they contain a certain story or anecdote. Then, the exact same anecdote in the exact same words is repeated three times. Well, this was, in a sense, necessary because of the density of the consciousness at the time and also because there was no written records given. It was all an oral tradition and instead of people being able to read the text several times, they could now hear it three times and therefore have a better grasp of it. This brings up a topic I want to touch upon, and it is the topic of repetition.

Do the masters repeat themselves?

Do we of the ascended masters ever repeat ourselves in our dictations? Some would immediately say: "Yes, you often talk about the same topic, you often give a teaching that is almost the same as what you have given before."

Well, my beloved, *do* we repeat ourselves? Or do we always give a teaching based on the consciousness at the time and the consciousness of the recipients—the intended recipients. When you look at the earth, you see that there is a constant movement in this very, very complex matrix of the collective consciousness, but also the individual consciousness of all of those people who are above a certain level of consciousness—the 48th level. Those who are below often do not move or they move with the mass consciousness because they are overpowered by the mass consciousness.

As you go above the 48th level, you begin to reclaim your individuality and that means you are constantly moving. If you could look at a visual representation of the earth at the level of consciousness, you would see a very complex pattern of energy waves, of images. To give you an illustration of this (and mark you, it is an *illustration,* not entirely literal and accurate), we could say that the collective consciousness on earth looks like a very intricate pattern of vibrating energy waves that form certain images. As people can have images in their minds, there can be images in the collective mind. It is a little bit like these photographs you have seen where from a distance there seems to be one image, but when you go closer,

25 | Being ready for the teaching

you will see that the image is made up of smaller images, individual photographs. This can also be compared to the concept of a hologram, only all of the small images that make up the whole are not the same because different groups of people and different individuals have different images, at least slightly different images, in their minds. It is a very, very complex picture. Now, if you could see this, you would see that it is never standing still, it is always moving. In other words, it is a process. There can be ups, there can be downs, but there is never still-stand.

There is never, ever, a point where you could take a snapshot of the collective consciousness and two hours later you take another snapshot and they are the same. You could take a snapshot with the shortest time interval or shutter speed that your camera can produce, say a 5000th of a second. You could take another snapshot right after and they would not be the same. That is how quickly everything shifts. When we give one dictation, it is given based on this very complex equation that exists in the collective consciousness of the whole, but more specifically in the collective consciousness of the group of people for which we are giving the teaching.

Now, if the people who are hearing the teaching, reading the teaching, if they do what is the highest potential for the teaching, they use the teaching to shift their consciousness. This means that once they have allowed that shifting to occur, the equation both of the collective and of the group consciousness and of the individual has shifted. Well, we of course have technology today that allows you to record a dictation and put it in writing. You could read a dictation for the first time, you could absorb it to the best of your ability as you can with the current level of consciousness. You could have a shifting experience and now the equation of your consciousness has shifted. Then, you can go back, read the dictation a second time, and even though the words would be exactly the same, your experience of reading them would not be the same because you shifted the first time. Meaning, you can now absorb something the second time that you could not absorb the first time.

I am not saying that the first time you read a dictation, you need to get everything out of that dictation that you can. I am only saying that you have to allow the dictation to shift your consciousness, to have some shifting experience. If you have done this, then you can read the same dictation again (whether five minutes later or five months later) and you will not have the exact same experience. Meaning, you can shift your consciousness a second time, grasp more of the dictation and that means that the third time you now have a different experience and so on. This can, for many of you, go on for quite some time. This means that if you come to a point where you are reading a dictation and you are not sensing a shift, there can be two reasons for this. One can be that you have gotten all from that dictation that you can get right now and you therefore need to study something else in order to shift your consciousness again. It can also be that you have closed your mind because you feel you already know what the dictation is trying to say.

Now, we take a situation where you are not hearing the same dictation again but you are hearing us give another dictation live that talks about some of the same concepts. The question is again: Did you shift your consciousness when you heard the first dictation where we talked about this topic? If you did, then you can hear the second dictation and you will get something out of it that you did not get out of the first. Therefore, you will not really feel that we are repeating ourselves.

The complexity of dictations

You recognize here that during this conference, those of you who have truly been willing to open yourself to the messages we have been giving, to the energies we have been releasing, you have shifted your consciousness tremendously. This means that if you now go back and hear Kuan Yin's first dictation, you will get more out of it than you did when you heard it live. That is because that dictation started the shifting process that has led you to your current state.

Now again, we never actually repeat ourselves even if we use very similar words and talk about the same concepts. In some cases, it is because we are actually addressing a slightly different audience. You could say that some of the things we have said during this conference are said because we are now in a specific geographical location and we are addressing the people who live in this area of the broader Asian area and giving some teachings for them also.

Our teachings are not restricted to a geographical location. There are elements of the dictations we have given at this conference that are adapted to this. There are also some that are adapted to the fact that even in this relatively short time span since the teachings on the primal self were given in Estonia, there has been a shift, not only in the collective but also in the consciousness of the student body. Those who have taken those dictations and used them, have been instrumental in producing this shift.

25 | Being ready for the teaching

What we give now is based on the very complex equation that is here now. *You,* of course, do not experience this because it would be too overwhelming for you. *We* do experience it when we plan to give a dictation. That is why I am simply telling you so you know where we are coming from, why we sometimes talk about the same concepts but we talk about them from a different angle. It is almost as if you could say that even though the words are similar, the matrix, the geometry in the higher realms (the emotional, mental and identity realms) can be very different. This means that from our perspective, we clearly see the differences and we also see that sometimes the words are primarily chalices for releasing these geometric matrices in the three higher bodies.

Misusing a spiritual teaching

Now, we take this teaching and we look back at the 2,500 years since I gave the teachings in the Dhammapada and the teachings on the eight-fold path. What has been accomplished is, of course, the shifting of consciousness but it has not been to the degree that was the highest potential—and why not? Well, the primary reason for this is that there has always been a certain group of students who have had a tendency to use the teaching based on the linear, analytical mind. They have wanted to analyze the teaching, to put it in some kind of linear context or time line. They have done what other masters have talked about at this conference: They have used them to validate or reinforce the separate selves they created as a result of their birth trauma.

Avatars always have a desire to understand, which is a perfectly healthy and legitimate desire. What you need to recognize is that this desire can be colored or even aborted by these separate selves. Some have a need for control so they want to believe that they have now found an absolute teaching that explains the workings of the universe, be it the Buddha's teachings, Christianity, Islam, Communism, materialism or whatever you have.

They will, then, use the previous teaching to build this sense that this is the absolute. The linear, analytical mind, of course, loves this. Therefore, they will not only abort their own progress but when (we might say) a priesthood of such students emerges in a particular religion, they can actually abort the progress of the entire movement by preventing the transcendence of the teaching. This is what you have seen in many religions and that is why you saw me challenge the Brahmins of the Hindu religion. You saw Jesus challenge the Scribes and the Pharisees of the Jewish religion.

What I am aiming at here is to show those of you who are ascended master students that this is merely a tendency of some of these separate selves that either want to put everything in a context that is absolute, or they want security, or they want some kind of sense of being important or sense of having attained something. Whatever the outer self needs, it can use the linear mind. The result of this is that beginning 2,500 years ago (of course even going beyond to the Hindu religion and all the way up through ascended master organizations), we have seen that a certain percentage of students are in this mindset where they are open to the teaching but they are approaching the teaching through that outer, analytical mind, the very linear mind and, of course, colored by their selves. The linear mind is very sensitive to repetition because the linear mind, of course, is linear because it has a time line. It is always comparing the now to the past and in some cases projecting into the future.

When the linear mind encounters a spiritual teaching, it draws out of it what it can draw out of it. This is primarily an outer, intellectual, logical, rational understanding. It uses that to analyze the teaching, break it down into components and say: "Okay, this component goes in this file-folder in my database, that component goes in that file-folder." Now, when the student hears another teaching that talks about similar concepts, the linear mind will say: "Oh, I don't need to file that concept away because I already have it in my database, that's a repetition." It ignores the concept, it does not pick up the nuances that it was said in a different way. The linear mind cannot pick up anything new from hearing it again.

That is why you have these students in all ascended master organizations and in all other religions and mystical philosophies we have released (even the ones, of course, that we have not released but that have been produced by the fallen beings and the false hierarchy). We have seen students go into this state of mind where they allow themselves to come to a certain point where they feel: "Now, I have a basic grasp of the teaching." From that moment on, their growth basically stops. Or if something new comes up that they do not have in their database, then they file it away. There comes a point where the student feels: "I now understand the overall matrix of the teaching." From that moment, they think that everything else that comes is just details that have to fit into that overall matrix.

Beginner's mind

However, my beloved, whenever you allow yourself to create this matrix in your mind (that now you have grasped the basics of the teaching), what you are grasping is based on your current level of consciousness. It is not – *it is not* – the highest possible understanding and experience. What really makes the difference between those students who come into a teaching, reach a certain plateau and then stall and those students who continue to grow, is that the latter are not so attached to having an overall grasp of the teaching. They are willing to actually approach the teaching with what Jesus called the childlike mind or what the Buddhists talk about: Beginner's mind, the mind that sees everything anew.

Once in a while, you allow yourself to set aside what you thought was the basic grasp or the ultimate grasp of the teaching. You allow yourself to go into a neutral state of mind and read or hear the teaching anew. Then, you will receive something even from a teaching you have read before that you could not receive previously. That is when the teaching, even though you may have read it many times, can again produce a shift. In other words, is the repetition (that some students perceive) in the mind of the ascended masters or is it in the mind of the student?

I submit to you that the answer to that question really does not matter. Because the important point is that *your* progress or lack of progress is not in the mind of the ascended masters—it is in *your* mind. What does this mean? This means that, as other masters have hinted at, when you overcome the primal self and these separate selves that spring from it, you can really transcend the linear, analytical mind. You no longer have a need to have everything under control, to have a basic grasp of the universe. You can then approach the teaching with a greater degree of freedom than you had before because you are not colored by these separate selves.

The separate selves fear a new teaching

Basically, all of you will see that at certain points on your path, you have received a new teaching that suddenly stirred up something in you, that provoked something in you. For example, back in the time when Jesus gave his discourses on the ego, there were some students that were provoked by this. There were even some students that went into a certain fear of reading the next ego discourse because their egos feared that they could expose that aspect of the ego.

You will always have this certain tendency that the separate self that you have (and that feels it has you under control and your path under control) fears a new teaching that might be disturbing to its sense of being in control. If you identify this in yourself, you can just use the tools we have given to step back and realize this is just a separate self that is feeling this. It is not *you* because you cannot be threatened by anything that can help you transcend yourself. The Conscious You, when it is conscious of its true nature, cannot be threatened by any teaching.

From results to process

What you can come to, when you get over this primal self and the other selves, is that you now have the potential to make a shift. Other masters have set the foundation, have talked about this and there is not so much for me to say other than point you to the fact that the shift is a shift away from being focused on results to being focused on process. We have given you the teachings that you started out (most of you) as avatars on natural planets. You started out with a limited sense of identity. You have expanded it by experimenting with your co-creative abilities. Many of you have built this great momentum on envisioning a certain situation or form in the physical realm and then manifesting that form.

You have actually built this great momentum on making matter conform to the images and matrices in your mind. You have worked on obtaining mastery of mind over matter. When you looked down at the earth and saw the suffering you thought: "I want to go down there and manifest a certain positive result that sets people free from suffering." Other masters have said that your original motivation for coming here was not the highest possible. In order to really be free to ascend, you need to re-examine your motivation based on the higher consciousness you now have. Therefore, you let go of that previous motivation and the beliefs behind it. What is the primary belief that you need to let go of as an avatar in order to ascend? Well, it is that you need to shift from being focused on results to being focused on process.

We have told you that there is continued growth in the ascended realm and you can grow all the way to the Creator consciousness. We have told you that nobody on earth will reach an ultimate state of enlightenment from which no growth is possible. Ask yourself: "What is it that our Creator has created? Is it a result, a fixed Result, or is it an ever, forever ongoing process?" The answer, of course, is that the Creator is not focused on creating a result but focused on the process. The Creator has created a universe to facilitate the process. "The process of what?," you might ask. The process of self-transcendence, which we have called the River of Life.

The linear mind will ask: "Well, but self-transcendence implies movement from one stage to the next. If I extend that all the way forward, there must come some ultimate point of transcendence where I reach an ultimate level and there is no more transcendence. If I project all the way back, there must have come a point where there also was no transcendence but transcendence started for the first time." That, my beloved, is the main limitation of the linear mind. The River of Life has no beginning and no ending. The linear mind will never fathom this. The separate selves you have created on earth will never fathom this. The Conscious You can fathom it. It cannot *understand* it, you cannot *understand* that there is no beginning and no end but you can *experience*, you can experience the flow and the continuity of the flow.

How avatars can block their ascension

The shift that you have the potential to make by using these teachings and tools is a shift from being focused on results to being focused on process. Why is this so important? Because, my beloved, what have we said about the ascension? You come to a point where you are standing in front of the gate that leads to the ascended realm. If you walk through, you are ascended, but in order to walk through, you have to look back at earth and see if there is anything that pulls you back.

What if you descended to earth as an avatar with the vision that there was a certain result you wanted to accomplish but you have not yet accomplished it? Well, then how can you ascend? The simple answer is: You cannot! This means you can come to a point where in all other ways you have qualified for your ascension. In this particular way you have not qualified because you have not surrendered, you have not given up, you have not lost your attachment to this result produced on earth.

This also means that you are allowing your ascension to depend on the choices of other people on earth who are in a much lower consciousness than yourself. Obviously, the reason you have not produced the results here on earth is that other people have not been willing to change. This means that now, as an avatar, you could potentially go into the fallen consciousness and go out and seek to force people to change, but that, of course, would not allow you to ascend.

You could also go into a state where you do not know what to do. You are sort of in a vacuum, you are in suspended animation, as they say. You can actually sit there for some time (even for several embodiments) not knowing how to solve the enigma that there is something on earth you cannot leave unfinished.

Do you see, here, the central question for an avatar? You think (or at least you tend to think until you overcome those primal selves) that the only thing that brought you to earth was to alleviate suffering and produce a positive change. You feel that if you cannot produce that change, maybe it was a mistake to come here, maybe it was a waste of time, maybe you cannot leave or whatever. You feel not at peace, unfulfilled. The only way to ascend as an avatar is, not to fulfill your original vision for coming here, but to transcend it, to dissolve it, to give it up, to surrender it, to become non-attached to it, to let the self die and say: "What is that to me? I will follow thee—Jesus, Buddha, Saint Germain, Master MORE," whomever you see as your personal master.

By using these teachings on the primal self, you can come to that point of resolution. The messenger experienced this after having worked for several months with these teachings. There was a shift and suddenly he realized, he *experienced,* he fully accepted: "I don't have to do anything on earth."

This does not mean that you immediately ascend. You can stay in embodiment, you can live an active life. You can even, from an outer perspective, do many things but you are no longer doing them from the coloring of that primal self and other selves that feel that you *have* to do something, you *have* to accomplish something, it *has* to have been worth it for you to come to earth. It *has* been worth it for you because you have shifted your consciousness and that was, as others have said, the greater purpose. When you make peace with this, that is when you have attained at least some degree, if we can talk about degrees, of Buddhahood.

Being the Buddha in action

Now, you can be the Buddha in action on earth but this cannot happen until you have overcome that primal attachment, as we might call it. I wish I could have given that teaching 2,500 years ago but it was not possible because the equation of the matrix in the collective consciousness was not ready. It is ready now. Of course, even though we have put great emphasis on these teachings at this conference and at the previous one, this is not to say that all people are ready for these teachings.

You may look at the body of students who have been studying the teachings given through this messenger and other ascended master teachings and not all of these students are ready for these teachings on the primal self. They have not fully applied the previous teachings because, as other masters have said, we have very carefully built up to being able to release these teachings. You needed to have the teachings on the ego. You needed to have the teachings on duality and the epic mindset. You needed to have the teachings on the 144 levels. You needed to have the concept of shifting up, overcoming internal spirits and separate selves and therefore shifting from one level of consciousness to another.

Dreaming of a higher teaching

Again, there will be students who will use their outer minds to decide: "We need these teachings and we need them now." But they may not be ready to receive the teaching because they have not made sufficient use of the teachings they already have, they have not shifted their consciousness enough. Generally, you can say that what we see (when we look back after 2,500 years and beyond) is that there has always been some students who do not get the basic dynamic I have described here: That you need to take a given teaching and allow it to shift your consciousness.

Only when you have done that, will you be ready for a higher teaching. There has always been a certain group of students who go into this slightly frustrated state of mind because at inner levels they know they have not made the progress they could have made by using the teaching they have. Instead of being willing to look at themselves and realize why they have not made that progress, they think that the reason they have not made progress is that there must be a higher teaching that they have not gotten yet. If only they had that higher teaching, *then* they would be enlightened, then they would make progress. This can be a never-ending spiral.

We have seen some people come to a genuine teaching, embrace the teaching, make some progress, but then come to a plateau where they do not want to go further because they do not want to shift to the inner path and look at themselves. They stagnate and they stand there. Sometimes they become frustrated, they feel like victims, they blame others for the fact that they do not have the teaching. They may even blame the guru for having not gone higher so that is why they cannot go higher. Or they may become critical of the teachings, critical of other people. Or, as other masters have talked about, they may feel that because they have been in the teachings for so long, they must have reached a higher level. Therefore, they are entitled to be judgmental and go and blue-ray those who are newcomers to the teaching.

All of these scenarios can spring up but you see, my beloved, the fact of the matter is this. If you are finding fault with the teacher, the teaching, with other people, with physical conditions, with your astrology, with the fallen beings, with the weather or with this or with that—as long as you are pointing the finger out there, thinking that your progress depends on external conditions, then you have not fully embraced the inner path. If you have not embraced the inner path, you are not ready for the teachings on the primal self—you are not ready for those teachings. Make sure that you have a grasp of what the inner path is about, that you have embraced the inner path, that you are willing to take responsibility for yourself and look at yourself before you take these teachings.

Of course, we give these teachings because there is, indeed, a large number of the people, who have been following these teachings and applying these teachings for a while, who are ready. Therefore, we are very joyful, we are very, very grateful that you have raised yourselves up to the point where you can receive these teachings and also be the instruments for spreading these impulses into the collective consciousness.

When the student is ready, the teacher appears—meaning that if the student is not ready, the teacher cannot appear. What is the highest joy of the ascended teacher? To be able to appear and give a teaching. What is the greatest gratitude we have? It is when the students have made themselves ready, allowing us to appear with a new teaching. For this, my beloved, you have our gratitude. For this conference, you have our gratitude. All of you, from those who arranged it to those who participated, you have our gratitude. In that Flame of Gratitude, a Buddhic gratitude, I seal you and I seal this conference in the love of my heart.

26 | INVOKING READINESS FOR THE TEACHING

In the name I AM THAT I AM, Jesus Christ, I call to all representatives of the Divine Mother, especially Gautama Buddha, to help me overcome the illusions that prevent me from being truly open to the teachings, including…

[Make personal calls.]

Part 1

1. Gautama, give me the awareness to see if I have the potential to be part of the process of attaining the 144th level before I am ready to leave embodiment, therefore still going higher while I am in embodiment and helping to raise that level.

> Gautama, show my mental state
> that does give rise to love and hate,
> your exposé I do endure,
> so my perception will be pure.

> Gautama, Flame of Cosmic Peace,
> unruly thoughts do hereby cease,
> we radiate from you and me
> the peace to still Samsara's Sea.

2. Gautama, give me the awareness that when a specific teaching is given, it is given based on the level of consciousness on the planet at the time. If the teaching is successful, the consciousness will shift.

> Gautama, in your Flame of Peace,
> the struggling self I now release,
> the Buddha Nature I now see,
> it is the core of you and me.

> Gautama, Flame of Cosmic Peace,
> unruly thoughts do hereby cease,
> we radiate from you and me
> the peace to still Samsara's Sea.

3. Gautama, give me the awareness to see if I have the potential to use a given teaching to reach the 144th level of consciousness and then become an instrument for either bringing forth a new teaching or a new interpretation of the old teaching. Therefore, I can bring forth a teaching for the new level of consciousness that has been reached as a result of the old teaching.

> Gautama, I am one with thee,
> Mara's demons do now flee,
> your Presence like a soothing balm,
> my mind and senses ever calm.

> Gautama, Flame of Cosmic Peace,
> unruly thoughts do hereby cease,
> we radiate from you and me
> the peace to still Samsara's Sea.

4. Gautama, give me the awareness that progressive revelation ideally should never stop because the collective consciousness is constantly shifting.

26 | Invoking readiness for the teaching

Gautama, I now take the vow,
to live in the eternal now,
with you I do transcend all time,
to live in present so sublime.

**Gautama, Flame of Cosmic Peace,
unruly thoughts do hereby cease,
we radiate from you and me
the peace to still Samsara's Sea.**

5. Gautama, give me the awareness of how to open myself to the messages you are giving, to the energies you are releasing, so I can shift my consciousness to the maximum degree.

Gautama, I have no desire,
to nothing earthly I aspire,
in non-attachment I now rest,
passing Mara's subtle test.

**Gautama, Flame of Cosmic Peace,
unruly thoughts do hereby cease,
we radiate from you and me
the peace to still Samsara's Sea.**

6. Gautama, give me the awareness of how to overcome the tendency to use a teaching based on the linear, analytical mind. Help me overcome the tendency to analyze the teaching, to put it in some kind of linear context or time line.

Gautama, I melt into you,
my mind is one, no longer two,
immersed in your resplendent glow,
Nirvana is all that I know.

**Gautama, Flame of Cosmic Peace,
unruly thoughts do hereby cease,
we radiate from you and me
the peace to still Samsara's Sea.**

7. Gautama, give me the awareness of how to avoid using a teaching to validate or reinforce the separate selves I created as a result of my birth trauma.

> Gautama, in your timeless space,
> I am immersed in Cosmic Grace,
> I know the God beyond all form,
> to world I will no more conform.

> **Gautama, Flame of Cosmic Peace,**
> **unruly thoughts do hereby cease,**
> **we radiate from you and me**
> **the peace to still Samsara's Sea.**

8. Gautama, give me the awareness that the desire to understand can be colored or even aborted by my separate selves. Some selves have a need for control so they want me to believe that I have now found an absolute teaching.

> Gautama, I am now awake,
> I clearly see what is at stake,
> and thus I claim my sacred right
> to be on earth the Buddhic Light.

> **Gautama, Flame of Cosmic Peace,**
> **unruly thoughts do hereby cease,**
> **we radiate from you and me**
> **the peace to still Samsara's Sea.**

9. Gautama, give me the awareness that the linear, analytical mind loves the sense that a teaching is absolute. Therefore, if a priesthood of such students emerges in a particular religion, they can abort the progress of the entire movement by preventing the transcendence of the teaching.

> Gautama, with your thunderbolt,
> we give the earth a mighty jolt,
> I know that some will understand,
> and join the Buddha's timeless band.

**Gautama, Flame of Cosmic Peace,
unruly thoughts do hereby cease,
we radiate from you and me
the peace to still Samsara's Sea.**

Part 2

1. Gautama, give me the awareness that this is merely a tendency of some of these separate selves that either want to put everything in a context that is absolute, or they want security, or they want a sense of being important or having attained something.

> Gautama, show my mental state
> that does give rise to love and hate,
> your exposé I do endure,
> so my perception will be pure.

**Gautama, Flame of Cosmic Peace,
unruly thoughts do hereby cease,
we radiate from you and me
the peace to still Samsara's Sea.**

2. Gautama, give me the awareness that will help me rise above the tendency to approach the teaching through the outer, analytical mind, the very linear mind colored by my outer selves.

> Gautama, in your Flame of Peace,
> the struggling self I now release,
> the Buddha Nature I now see,
> it is the core of you and me.

**Gautama, Flame of Cosmic Peace,
unruly thoughts do hereby cease,
we radiate from you and me
the peace to still Samsara's Sea.**

3. Gautama, give me the awareness of how to avoid going into the state of mind where I allow myself to feel I understand the overall matrix of the teaching, and everything else is just details that have to fit into that overall matrix.

> Gautama, I am one with thee,
> Mara's demons do now flee,
> your Presence like a soothing balm,
> my mind and senses ever calm.
>
> **Gautama, Flame of Cosmic Peace,**
> **unruly thoughts do hereby cease,**
> **we radiate from you and me**
> **the peace to still Samsara's Sea.**

4. Gautama, give me the awareness that when I allow myself to create this matrix in my mind, what I am grasping is based on my current level of consciousness. It is not the highest possible understanding and experience.

> Gautama, I now take the vow,
> to live in the eternal now,
> with you I do transcend all time,
> to live in present so sublime.
>
> **Gautama, Flame of Cosmic Peace,**
> **unruly thoughts do hereby cease,**
> **we radiate from you and me**
> **the peace to still Samsara's Sea.**

5. Gautama, give me the awareness of how to overcome any attachment to having an overall grasp of the teaching. I am willing to approach the teaching with the childlike mind, the beginner's mind, the mind that sees everything anew.

> Gautama, I have no desire,
> to nothing earthly I aspire,
> in non-attachment I now rest,
> passing Mara's subtle test.

> Gautama, Flame of Cosmic Peace,
> unruly thoughts do hereby cease,
> we radiate from you and me
> the peace to still Samsara's Sea.

6. Gautama, I will allow myself to set aside what I thought was the basic grasp or the ultimate grasp of the teaching. I will allow myself to go into a neutral state of mind and read or hear the teaching anew.

> Gautama, I melt into you,
> my mind is one, no longer two,
> immersed in your resplendent glow,
> Nirvana is all that I know.

> **Gautama, Flame of Cosmic Peace,**
> **unruly thoughts do hereby cease,**
> **we radiate from you and me**
> **the peace to still Samsara's Sea.**

7. Gautama, I will be open to receive something even from a teaching I have read before that I could not receive previously. I will be open to going through a shift, even from a teaching I have read before.

> Gautama, in your timeless space,
> I am immersed in Cosmic Grace,
> I know the God beyond all form,
> to world I will no more conform.

> **Gautama, Flame of Cosmic Peace,**
> **unruly thoughts do hereby cease,**
> **we radiate from you and me**
> **the peace to still Samsara's Sea.**

8. Gautama, give me the awareness that my progress or lack of progress is not in the mind of the ascended masters—it is in *my* mind.

> Gautama, I am now awake,
> I clearly see what is at stake,

and thus I claim my sacred right
to be on earth the Buddhic Light.

**Gautama, Flame of Cosmic Peace,
unruly thoughts do hereby cease,
we radiate from you and me
the peace to still Samsara's Sea.**

9. Gautama, give me the awareness that when I overcome the primal self and these separate selves that spring from it, I can transcend the linear, analytical mind. I no longer have a need to have everything under control, to have a basic grasp of the universe. I can approach the teaching with a greater degree of freedom because I am not colored by these separate selves.

Gautama, with your thunderbolt,
we give the earth a mighty jolt,
I know that some will understand,
and join the Buddha's timeless band.

**Gautama, Flame of Cosmic Peace,
unruly thoughts do hereby cease,
we radiate from you and me
the peace to still Samsara's Sea.**

Part 3

1. Gautama, give me the awareness that the separate self, that feels it has me and my path under control, fears a new teaching that might be disturbing to its sense of being in control.

Gautama, show my mental state
that does give rise to love and hate,
your exposé I do endure,
so my perception will be pure.

> Gautama, Flame of Cosmic Peace,
> unruly thoughts do hereby cease,
> we radiate from you and me
> the peace to still Samsara's Sea.

2. Gautama, help me step back and realize it is just a separate self that is feeling this. It is not *me* because I cannot be threatened by anything that can help me transcend myself. The Conscious You, when it is conscious of its true nature, cannot be threatened by any teaching.

> Gautama, in your Flame of Peace,
> the struggling self I now release,
> the Buddha Nature I now see,
> it is the core of you and me.

> Gautama, Flame of Cosmic Peace,
> unruly thoughts do hereby cease,
> we radiate from you and me
> the peace to still Samsara's Sea.

3. Gautama, help me make a shift away from being focused on results to being focused on process.

> Gautama, I am one with thee,
> Mara's demons do now flee,
> your Presence like a soothing balm,
> my mind and senses ever calm.

> Gautama, Flame of Cosmic Peace,
> unruly thoughts do hereby cease,
> we radiate from you and me
> the peace to still Samsara's Sea.

4. Gautama, help me see if, as an avatar, I have built this momentum on envisioning a certain situation or form in the physical realm and then manifesting that form. Help me see if I have built this momentum on making matter conform to the images and matrices in my mind.

> Gautama, I now take the vow,
> to live in the eternal now,
> with you I do transcend all time,
> to live in present so sublime.
>
> **Gautama, Flame of Cosmic Peace,
> unruly thoughts do hereby cease,
> we radiate from you and me
> the peace to still Samsara's Sea.**

5. Gautama, help me see if I looked at the earth and saw the suffering and thought: "I want to go down there and manifest a certain positive result that sets people free from suffering."

> Gautama, I have no desire,
> to nothing earthly I aspire,
> in non-attachment I now rest,
> passing Mara's subtle test.
>
> **Gautama, Flame of Cosmic Peace,
> unruly thoughts do hereby cease,
> we radiate from you and me
> the peace to still Samsara's Sea.**

6. Gautama, give me the awareness that my original motivation for coming here was not the highest possible. Help me re-examine my motivation based on the higher consciousness I now have.

> Gautama, I melt into you,
> my mind is one, no longer two,
> immersed in your resplendent glow,
> Nirvana is all that I know.
>
> **Gautama, Flame of Cosmic Peace,
> unruly thoughts do hereby cease,
> we radiate from you and me
> the peace to still Samsara's Sea.**

7. Gautama, help me let go of the previous motivation and the beliefs behind it. Help me shift from being focused on results to being focused on process.

> Gautama, in your timeless space,
> I am immersed in Cosmic Grace,
> I know the God beyond all form,
> to world I will no more conform.
>
> **Gautama, Flame of Cosmic Peace,**
> **unruly thoughts do hereby cease,**
> **we radiate from you and me**
> **the peace to still Samsara's Sea.**

8. Gautama, give me the awareness that my Creator has not created a fixed result, but has created a forever ongoing process. The Creator is not focused on creating a result but focused on the process. The Creator has created a universe to facilitate the process of self-transcendence, the River of Life.

> Gautama, I am now awake,
> I clearly see what is at stake,
> and thus I claim my sacred right
> to be on earth the Buddhic Light.
>
> **Gautama, Flame of Cosmic Peace,**
> **unruly thoughts do hereby cease,**
> **we radiate from you and me**
> **the peace to still Samsara's Sea.**

9. Gautama, give me the awareness that the River of Life has no beginning and no ending. The linear mind will never fathom this. The separate selves I have created on earth will never fathom this. The Conscious You can fathom it. It cannot *understand* it. I cannot *understand* that there is no beginning and no end but I can *experience,* I can experience the flow and the continuity of the flow.

> Gautama, with your thunderbolt,
> we give the earth a mighty jolt,

I know that some will understand,
and join the Buddha's timeless band.

**Gautama, Flame of Cosmic Peace,
unruly thoughts do hereby cease,
we radiate from you and me
the peace to still Samsara's Sea.**

Part 4

1. Gautama, give me the awareness that if I descended to earth as an avatar with the vision that there was a certain result I wanted to accomplish but I have not yet accomplished it, then I cannot ascend.

Gautama, show my mental state
that does give rise to love and hate,
your exposé I do endure,
so my perception will be pure.

**Gautama, Flame of Cosmic Peace,
unruly thoughts do hereby cease,
we radiate from you and me
the peace to still Samsara's Sea.**

2. Gautama, help me surrender, give up, lose my attachment to this result produced on earth.

Gautama, in your Flame of Peace,
the struggling self I now release,
the Buddha Nature I now see,
it is the core of you and me.

**Gautama, Flame of Cosmic Peace,
unruly thoughts do hereby cease,
we radiate from you and me
the peace to still Samsara's Sea.**

3. Gautama, give me the awareness that I am allowing my ascension to depend on the choices of other people who are in a much lower state of consciousness than myself.

> Gautama, I am one with thee,
> Mara's demons do now flee,
> your Presence like a soothing balm,
> my mind and senses ever calm.

> **Gautama, Flame of Cosmic Peace,**
> **unruly thoughts do hereby cease,**
> **we radiate from you and me**
> **the peace to still Samsara's Sea.**

4. Gautama, give me the awareness that the reason I have not produced the results here on earth is that other people have not been willing to change. This means I could potentially go into the fallen consciousness and seek to force people to change.

> Gautama, I now take the vow,
> to live in the eternal now,
> with you I do transcend all time,
> to live in present so sublime.

> **Gautama, Flame of Cosmic Peace,**
> **unruly thoughts do hereby cease,**
> **we radiate from you and me**
> **the peace to still Samsara's Sea.**

5. Gautama, give me the awareness that I could also go into a state where I do not know what to do. I am in a vacuum, I am in suspended animation. Help me solve the enigma that there is something on earth I cannot leave unfinished.

> Gautama, I have no desire,
> to nothing earthly I aspire,
> in non-attachment I now rest,
> passing Mara's subtle test.

> Gautama, Flame of Cosmic Peace,
> unruly thoughts do hereby cease,
> we radiate from you and me
> the peace to still Samsara's Sea.

6. Gautama, help me see if I think that the only thing that brought me to earth was to alleviate suffering and produce a positive change. I feel that if I cannot produce that change, it was a mistake to come here, it was a waste of time.

> Gautama, I melt into you,
> my mind is one, no longer two,
> immersed in your resplendent glow,
> Nirvana is all that I know.

> Gautama, Flame of Cosmic Peace,
> unruly thoughts do hereby cease,
> we radiate from you and me
> the peace to still Samsara's Sea.

7. Gautama, give me the awareness that the way to ascend as an avatar is not by fulfilling my original vision for coming here. It is that I transcend it, I dissolve it, I give it up, I surrender it, I become non-attached to it, I let the self die and say: "What is that to me? I will follow thee, Gautama"

> Gautama, in your timeless space,
> I am immersed in Cosmic Grace,
> I know the God beyond all form,
> to world I will no more conform.

> Gautama, Flame of Cosmic Peace,
> unruly thoughts do hereby cease,
> we radiate from you and me
> the peace to still Samsara's Sea.

8. Gautama, give me the awareness that this does not mean that I immediately ascend. I can stay in embodiment and do many things, but I am no longer doing them from the coloring of that primal self and other selves that feel that I *have* to do something, I *have* to accomplish something, it *has* to have been worth it for me to come to earth.

> Gautama, I am now awake,
> I clearly see what is at stake,
> and thus I claim my sacred right
> to be on earth the Buddhic Light.
>
> **Gautama, Flame of Cosmic Peace,**
> **unruly thoughts do hereby cease,**
> **we radiate from you and me**
> **the peace to still Samsara's Sea.**

9. Gautama, give me the awareness that it *has* been worth it for me to come to earth because I have shifted my consciousness and that was the greater purpose. Help me make peace with this and attain some degree of Buddhahood.

> Gautama, with your thunderbolt,
> we give the earth a mighty jolt,
> I know that some will understand,
> and join the Buddha's timeless band.
>
> **Gautama, Flame of Cosmic Peace,**
> **unruly thoughts do hereby cease,**
> **we radiate from you and me**
> **the peace to still Samsara's Sea.**

Part 5

1. Gautama, help me see if I am ready for this teaching or if I need to make better use of the teaching I have and shift my consciousness further.

Gautama, show my mental state
that does give rise to love and hate,
your exposé I do endure,
so my perception will be pure.

**Gautama, Flame of Cosmic Peace,
unruly thoughts do hereby cease,
we radiate from you and me
the peace to still Samsara's Sea.**

2. Gautama, help me see if I am in this frustrated state of mind because at inner levels I know I have not made the progress I could have made by using the teaching I have.

Gautama, in your Flame of Peace,
the struggling self I now release,
the Buddha Nature I now see,
it is the core of you and me.

**Gautama, Flame of Cosmic Peace,
unruly thoughts do hereby cease,
we radiate from you and me
the peace to still Samsara's Sea.**

3. Gautama, I am willing to look at myself and realize why I have not made that progress. I refuse to think that the reason I have not made progress is that there must be a higher teaching that I have not gotten yet.

Gautama, I am one with thee,
Mara's demons do now flee,
your Presence like a soothing balm,
my mind and senses ever calm.

**Gautama, Flame of Cosmic Peace,
unruly thoughts do hereby cease,
we radiate from you and me
the peace to still Samsara's Sea.**

4. Gautama, help me see if I have used the teaching to reach a plateau where I do not want to go further because I do not want to shift to the inner path and look at myself. Help me see if I have stagnated and become frustrated, feeling like a victim or blaming others for the fact that I do not have the teaching.

> Gautama, I now take the vow,
> to live in the eternal now,
> with you I do transcend all time,
> to live in present so sublime.
>
> **Gautama, Flame of Cosmic Peace,**
> **unruly thoughts do hereby cease,**
> **we radiate from you and me**
> **the peace to still Samsara's Sea.**

5. Gautama, help me see if I blame the guru for not having gone higher and that is why I cannot go higher. Help me see if I have become critical of the teachings, critical of other people.

> Gautama, I have no desire,
> to nothing earthly I aspire,
> in non-attachment I now rest,
> passing Mara's subtle test.
>
> **Gautama, Flame of Cosmic Peace,**
> **unruly thoughts do hereby cease,**
> **we radiate from you and me**
> **the peace to still Samsara's Sea.**

6. Gautama, help me see if I feel that because I have been in the teachings for so long, I must have reached a higher level. Therefore, I am entitled to be judgmental and go and blue-ray those who are newcomers to the teaching.

> Gautama, I melt into you,
> my mind is one, no longer two,
> immersed in your resplendent glow,
> Nirvana is all that I know.

> Gautama, Flame of Cosmic Peace,
> unruly thoughts do hereby cease,
> we radiate from you and me
> the peace to still Samsara's Sea.

7. Gautama, help me see if I am finding fault with the teacher, the teaching, with other people, with physical conditions, with my astrology, with the fallen beings, with the weather or with this or with that. Help me see that as long as I am pointing the finger out there, thinking that my progress depends on external conditions, then I have not fully embraced the inner path.

> Gautama, in your timeless space,
> I am immersed in Cosmic Grace,
> I know the God beyond all form,
> to world I will no more conform.

> **Gautama, Flame of Cosmic Peace,**
> **unruly thoughts do hereby cease,**
> **we radiate from you and me**
> **the peace to still Samsara's Sea.**

8. Gautama, give me the awareness that if I have not embraced the inner path, I am not ready for the teachings on the primal self. Help me grasp what the inner path is about and embrace the inner path. I am willing to take responsibility for myself and look at myself.

> Gautama, I am now awake,
> I clearly see what is at stake,
> and thus I claim my sacred right
> to be on earth the Buddhic Light.

> **Gautama, Flame of Cosmic Peace,**
> **unruly thoughts do hereby cease,**
> **we radiate from you and me**
> **the peace to still Samsara's Sea.**

9. Gautama, help me apply the teachings and raise myself to the point where I can receive these teachings and also be the instrument for spreading these impulses into the collective consciousness. Help me feel your joy for being able to give the teaching. Help me feel your gratitude for being allowed to give the teaching.

> Gautama, with your thunderbolt,
> we give the earth a mighty jolt,
> I know that some will understand,
> and join the Buddha's timeless band.
>
> **Gautama, Flame of Cosmic Peace,**
> **unruly thoughts do hereby cease,**
> **we radiate from you and me**
> **the peace to still Samsara's Sea.**

Sealing

In the name of the Divine Mother, I call to Mother Mary for the sealing of myself and all people in my circle of influence in the creative flow of the Divine Mother, the River of Life. I call for the multiplication of my calls by all representatives of the Divine Mother, so that we form the perfect figure-eight flow of "As Above, so below." Thus, I accept that this is fully manifest, because the mouth of the Lord, the Divine Mother that I AM, has spoken it. Amen.

www.ingramcontent.com/pod-product-compliance
Lightning Source LLC
Chambersburg PA
CBHW031721230426
43669CB00007B/203